Meaningful Healthcare
Experience Design

Meaningful Healthcare Experience Design
Improving Care for All Generations

Scott Goodwin

Routledge
Taylor & Francis Group

A PRODUCTIVITY PRESS BOOK

First published 2020
by Routledge
52 Vanderbilt Avenue, New York, NY 10017

and by Routledge
2 Park Square, Milton Park, Abingdon, Oxon, OX14 4RN

Routledge is an imprint of the Taylor & Francis Group, an informa business

Library of Congress Cataloging-in-Publication Data
Names: Goodwin, Scott, author.
Title: Meaningful healthcare experience design : improving care for all generations / Scott Goodwin.
Description: Boca Raton : Routledge, 2020. |
Identifiers: LCCN 2020002593 (print) | LCCN 2020002594 (ebook) |
ISBN 9781498726962 (hardback) | ISBN 9781315120317 (ebook)
Subjects: LCSH: Medical care—Quality control. | Meaning (Psychology) |
Medical personnel and patient.
Classification: LCC RA399.A1 G64 2020 (print) | LCC RA399.A1 (ebook) |
DDC 610.69/6—dc23
LC record available at https://lccn.loc.gov/2020002593
LC ebook record available at https://lccn.loc.gov/2020002594

ISBN: 978-1-4987-2696-2 (hbk)
ISBN: 978-0-367-49491-9 (pbk)
ISBN: 978-1-315-12031-7 (ebk)

Typeset in Garamond
by codeMantra

To God for His mercy, grace and love to me in
my Lord and Savior, Jesus Christ, and
To my wife, BJ, for her love and support through the years.

Contents

SECTION 4 INSIGHTS INTO AMERICAN HEALTHCARE HISTORY

Preface

I lived for 16 years in Peterborough, which is a town of about 6,200 people in the beautiful Monadnock Region in the southwest corner of New Hampshire. Most of those years, I commuted to work in hospitals in the central part of the state. During my last 3 years in New Hampshire, however, I had the privilege to work at Monadnock Community Hospital in Peterborough as an interim director. These were the best years of my professional career, and I will always be grateful for the opportunity to be a part of this special place. It was during this time that the ideas for this book matured. Not only was working at this beautiful small hospital inspirational, but its origin communicates an amazing message of devotion and love. The original structure of the hospital was a summer home built by a man who intended to share it with his beloved wife. Her untimely death at the age of 41 in 1916, after they had spent only one season in the home, so grieved him that he could not return to it. At the request of the town and out of love for the community, he donated the house and property to serve as a hospital. It was converted to a hospital through donations from residents and summer visitors and has served the area since it opened in 1923.

Author

Scott Goodwin, MA, MBA, DA, RN, CPHQ, LSSBB, has worked in healthcare for more than 40 years beginning as a night shift ward clerk in a hospital patient care unit. He has 25 years of experience in senior quality leadership positions in for-profit, religious, community, and critical access hospitals and extensive experience in healthcare quality consulting. He has designed and taught college graduate courses in healthcare quality, Lean, and organizational ethics and has presented at national quality conferences. His doctoral dissertation is titled *Healthcare Organizational Metaphors and the Implications for Leadership.* He owns AWLG Healthcare Consulting, LLC. He is the author of *Transition to 21st Century Healthcare: A Guide for Leaders and Quality Professionals* (CRC Press 2016) and *Mapping the Path to 21st Century Healthcare: The Ten Transitions Workbook* (CRC Press 2016).

Introduction

The goal of this book is to enable the people who deliver healthcare services, the people who receive those services, and the healthcare organizations within which they meet and interact to work together to create meaningful healthcare experiences that are healing and contribute to a sense of well-being.

In healthcare today, people receiving care are more and more defined as customers and consumers. People who deliver healthcare services and healthcare organizations are defined as part of an open marketplace in which success is measured financially. In contrast to this view of healthcare as consumers and competitors striving within a competitive marketplace, this book offers a vision of healthcare as two people interacting within an organizational context to create an experience that is meaningful to them.

This new perspective is inspired by psychologists in the field of Positive psychology and their work over the past 30 years to understand the nature of meaning in life and its importance to the well-being of people. Meaning in life as defined by psychologists consists of three elements: comprehension, purpose, and significance (Martela & Steger, 2016). Based on this tripartite view of meaning in life, this book offers a view of meaning in healthcare as consisting of three elements: beliefs, values, and principles.

An important part of meaning in healthcare for people delivering healthcare is meaning in work. Significance or the sense that work has intrinsic value and is worth doing is the foundation of meaning in work. Significance is expressed and experienced as a sense of a broader purpose in the work beyond the person performing it and as self-realization that the work has value for the person performing it (Martela & Pessi, 2018). By understanding the elements of meaning in healthcare and meaning in work and applying them, organizations are able to create meaningful healthcare experiences for the people receiving care and the people delivering care.

In this book, you will explore (1) the application of the psychological concept of meaning in life and its translation to meaning in healthcare as the basis for the design of meaningful healthcare experiences; (2) the design of meaningful healthcare experiences and the metaphor of value streams representing the influences that shape healthcare experiences; (3) the implementation of meaningful experience design in healthcare improvement programs; (4) mapping and analysis of value streams to improve meaningful healthcare experiences; (5) identifying the organizational structures that support the design of meaningful healthcare experiences; and (6) the historical development of American healthcare and its transitions into the future as offering insights into understanding meaningful experiences.

This book has five sections:

- **Section 1** – Meaningful Healthcare Experiences explores what psychology has learned about meaning in life and its implications for meaning in healthcare and meaning in work. It offers information about healthcare organizations today as the context for the creation of meaningful healthcare experiences, the nature of the people receiving care and the people delivering care, and finally, other factors that shape healthcare experiences.

- **Section 2** – Designing Meaningful Healthcare Experiences offers guidance in applying the concepts developed in the first section to the design of organizational processes and the interactions between people who deliver care and people who receive care in order to create meaningful healthcare experiences.

- **Section 3** – Implementing Meaningful Healthcare Experience Design in Organizations aligns meaning in healthcare with the overall quality improvement work of healthcare organizations and the use of existing organizational structures to support this new approach.

- **Section 4** – Insights into American Healthcare History provides historical context on the development of American healthcare in the nineteenth and twentieth centuries and the implications for healthcare today. By describing specific epochs of American healthcare and the metaphorical transitions that occurred over the past century, this section identifies the forces at work in healthcare in the past to provide a better understanding of the broader influences that shaped healthcare historically and the transitions that are occurring in American healthcare today.

■ **Section 5 –** Reflections on American Healthcare offers two views of important aspects of American healthcare as food for thoughtful reflection on the nature of healthcare in this country. The allegory offers insights into the way in which medicine and healthcare developed in America in the twentieth century. The second fictional account of dying encourages thoughts about the goals of American healthcare and what it takes to achieve them.

Throughout the book, three phrases are used to identify people or the organization that are the focus of the discussions: "people delivering care" refers to anyone working in a healthcare organization; "people receiving care" refers to anyone who is a recipient of healthcare services of any type, clinical or non-clinical; and, finally, "healthcare organization" refers to any type of organization that delivers healthcare services. The specific groups that are included within these phrases are identified at different points in this book when it is important to recognize the distinctions. These generic phrases serve two purposes. The first is to identify everyone who may be involved in meaningful healthcare experiences without trying to name every small group. The second purpose is to be able to include the broad range of healthcare occupations, services, and organizations that are engaged in delivering healthcare services without being required to list them all.

MEANINGFUL HEALTHCARE EXPERIENCES

Chapter 1

Meaning in Life as Meaning in Healthcare

One of the fastest ways to shut down a routine conversation is to ask someone the philosophical question of the ages, "What is the meaning of life?" One of the best questions to start a conversation about healthcare is to ask, "How does a healthcare experience contribute to meaning in your life?"

Meaning in life (not meaning of life) and meaning in healthcare begin with a sense of how each of us experiences and interprets our reality of which healthcare is a part. Sociologists Peter Berger and Thomas Luckmann authored the work *Social Construction of Reality* (1966). They offered the observation that "everyday life presents itself as a reality" (p. 34). We are "wide-awake" when we experience reality, and this state of being awake and able to perceive reality is "taken by you and me to be normal and self-evident" and it "constitutes our natural attitude" (p. 35). In a mysterious way, we encounter the world around us. Moment by moment we experience the world as an "ordered reality" (p. 36), and as long as everything is going smoothly, our "natural attitude is the attitude of common-sense consciousness. The reality of everyday life is taken for granted as reality" (p. 37).

We think of ourselves and the world around us as familiar and something we share with other people in the "normal, self-evident routines of everyday life" (Berger & Luckmann, 1966, p. 37). As they describe it, "As long as the routines of everyday life continue without interruption they are apprehended as unproblematic" (p. 38). When something happens, however, that is not routine and is not part of the familiar rhythm of our lives, our awareness and perception of reality changes. When a situation arises that draws my attention to a part of my reality that suddenly seems odd or there is a problem that I need to address, my attitude changes. I focus my attention and begin to "seek to integrate the problematic sector into what is already nonproblematic" (p. 38). I do this, according to Berger and Luckmann, by using my store of common-sense understanding that is the way I experience my reality every day and that I share with other people.

Based on the way we are oriented toward our everyday existence as described by Berger and Luckmann (1966), healthcare services fall into the problematic aspect. They require that we shift our attitude about our reality from the familiar rhythm of life and routines to an attitude in which we identify a sector of our lives for special attention during that period in which healthcare is a concern. As a way of illustrating this, let's take a routine healthcare procedure such as an intravenous (IV) catheter insertion for the administration of a medication or fluids to address a health issue. Describing the actual insertion helps to replicate the way our attention is focused on the situation during the actual procedure. Here is the insertion of the needle and catheter as described by the steps followed by the nurse performing the insertion:

- Using your non-dominant hand, stretch the skin taught and stabilize the vein 4–5 cm below the insertion site, taking care not to contaminate the point of insertion.
- Holding the over-the-needle catheter between the thumb and the middle finger, with the bevel up at a 15°–20° angle, pierce the skin directly over the vein until a flashback of blood is visible.
- Drop the angle of the catheter a few degrees and advance the catheter with the needle by a few millimeters to ensure that the tip of the catheter has passed into the vein.
- Using the index finger, advance the hub of the catheter fully into the vein, holding the needle steady.
- While stabilizing the needle and catheter with the dominant hand, release the tourniquet with the non-dominant hand (JoVE Science Education Database, 2019).

If you have ever had an IV catheter inserted into you or performed the procedure, reading the brief description of the insertion probably brings back memories of this experience for you.

This frequently repeated procedure is a routine part of healthcare, and it displays so much of what we experience as the reality of healthcare.

It happens in a place that is not a place that most people visit daily and the trip to the location requires planning. It involves two people who are probably strangers and unfamiliar with each other. It requires a process of registration, preparing materials and the room and conversations about the purpose of the procedure, and the way it will occur. The two people involved in the actual procedure come close enough to each other that the warmth of their bodies is discernible. This is an intimate space that is carefully guarded in most situations to prevent the intrusion of strangers. The procedure involves pain and has the potential to result in injury if not performed correctly.

As these two people meet and the procedure is performed, there are three perspectives with this experience. The three perspectives include the person receiving the IV, the person inserting the IV and delivering the care, and the healthcare facility in which it occurs. If we explore these perspectives and how they relate, we begin to develop a sense in which healthcare is a problematic aspect of our existence as identified by Berger and Luckmann (1966) and needs to be viewed as different from our routine. As a non-routine part of our life, the two people interact and seek to discover the meaningfulness of the experience that they are creating so that it can be incorporated into their understanding of reality.

The people involved in the procedures meet in a room. The act of inserting the IV and receiving the solution brings them together to share this experience. Though this is a frequently performed procedure, it still makes them at least slightly anxious. They are focused on this event not as routine or common-sense reality, but as a problem and a way to address a problem. They have arrived at this moment through a series of events, decisions, and actions that resulted in a sharp needle insertion into someone's arm. Where did they come from and how did they get to this point of interacting with each other?

The person receiving the IV medication or solution has arrived at the facility from home or another place by car or ambulance through a series of events that stretch back to an accident or to a visit with a practitioner that led to the need for an IV to be inserted at this time and in this place. Family and others may be aware of the procedure and expressed concerns or support and hope that it would go well. Following instructions from a variety of people in the hospital or emergency department (ED) or clinic, the person signed papers, read signs, traveled down halls, entered rooms, may have changed clothes and perhaps had vital signs taken and used the bathroom. Lying in a bed or a recliner, time was spent looking around the space, waiting and anticipating the procedure, and what would follow afterward. There are possible thoughts of a meal missed and the disruption of the normal routine due to the health concern. Fear, hope, anxiety, and other emotions increase and diminish with the flow of time.

The person inserting the IV arrived at the facility from home or another place by car or bus or other transportation. Routine activities of daily life such as choosing clothing, eating a meal, caring for children or spouse, and other activities preceded the arrival at the facility. Greetings from others in the hall, documenting time of arrival, and following the familiar route through the building and rooms precede the arrival at the place where the work is performed. Routines of obtaining information, setting priorities, searching for supplies, and asking questions of others create the rhythm of the workflow that is performed through well-practiced steps.

As the work ahead begins to take shape, thoughts of what could happen as well as concerns with anything missed in the morning process of arrival run through the mind. The momentum of the day accelerates with possibly putting on protective clothing, gathering supplies, handwashing, and other activities that are part of the work about to begin. Walking into the room, simple introductions are exchanged and the steps that form the procedure enter a familiar pattern of providing information, answering questions, arranging materials, and preparing for the IV insertion.

From different points in their lives, these two people arrived in this room inside this building at this time to accomplish this procedure. The building where they meet is part of an organization that may have come into existence years before. The people in the community took actions to create this building because they felt there was a need for an organization and a space in which a procedure such as an IV insertion could occur. They found enough money to build it and architects to translate their ideas into reality. The building emerged and people came together to work in the building and to give life to the organization. The community recognized the building and the organization as a healthcare facility and sought services within its walls.

As these two people meet in this room, they hold their own understanding of this moment and what they believe is happening and how it makes sense in their lives. The person receiving the IV believes that the room is the appropriate place for this action. The person approaching and preparing to insert the IV is recognized as someone who can perform the procedure and permitted to come into the intimate space of the person receiving the IV. Though the procedure involves some pain, this is accepted as meaningful because the action and the anticipated result are consistent with the goals valued by the person receiving the IV. The overall sense conveyed by the procedure and the actions of the person delivering the care is that the person receiving the IV has significance as a person.

The person preparing to insert the IV believes the actions are consistent with memories and training and the reason for being in the room with the person receiving the IV. Entering the intimate space of the person and causing pain is part of the purpose that brings them together in the room. The result of the insertion and all the preparation that went before to create a functioning IV is a valuable professional goal that the person inserting the IV hopes to accomplish to enable the care of the person to continue. Engaging in this work and performing this action are significant because they are based on the fundamental principles that make work and life meaningful as contributing to the well-being of others.

As they meet in the room and share the experience of the IV insertion, they give expression to the beliefs that are consistent with the plans and goals that were part of the origin and prior history of the organization and building that surround them. The delivery of this healthcare service was envisioned as the purpose of the organization and structure and the goal of providing care to people who need it. Providing the space and materials and people to perform the service accomplishes the goals that were valued as the motivation for the creation of the building and organization. The principles of the people who operate the organization are fulfilled as the organization provides the setting and resources that contribute to the well-being of the people who come there to receive care.

In the interaction of the insertion of an IV within a healthcare organization, the confluence of the perspectives of two people and the organization creates a healthcare experience. This is a microcosm of the overall nature of healthcare and the structure within which healthcare experiences derive their meaning. Understanding the convergence and the alignment of the perspectives involved in these procedures forms the basis for the design of meaningful healthcare experiences.

Meaning in Life

In recent years, psychologists working in the field of Positive psychology have recognized that meaning in our lives is important to our psychological well-being. The application of these views to healthcare provides a valuable perspective for recognizing that healthcare experiences are a part of our lives that are often "interruptions in the continuity" of our lives and therefore viewed as problematic. Our natural response is to seek ways to use our common-sense knowledge of reality to "integrate the problematic sector into what is already unproblematic" (p. 38). By this, we understand that we seek to find meaning in our healthcare experiences that correspond to meaning in our lives.

When talking about meaningful healthcare experiences, the understanding of the word "meaningful" is an important first step. According to psychologists Frank Martela and Michael Steger, the word "meaning" comes from the Old High German word "meinen," translated as "to have in mind" (Martela & Steger, 2016, p. 537). They note that "this already reveals that meaning is tied up with the unique capacity of the human mind for reflective, linguistic thinking" (p. 537). The outcome of reflection is "our mind's capacity to form mental representations about the world and develop connections between these representations" (p. 537). They interpret meaning as "representations of possible relationship among things, events, and relationships." Martela and Steger argue that when we ask what something means, we are trying to locate that something within our web of mental representations. "Meaning is about mentally connecting things. This is true whether we ask about the meaning of a thing or the meaning of our life" (p. 537).

Another way to refer to the "web of mental representations" is as "meaning frameworks" (Martela & Pessi, 2018, p. 2). These frameworks "are built up from the generalizations that we make about our own past experiences" and "they are highly influenced by our society, culture and upbringing from which we acquire our vocabularies, values and making sense of the world" (pp. 2–3). We construct our meaning frameworks and impose them on the world and "they help us to make sense of our current experience, give us direction about what goals and aims to pursue and guide us about what is valuable and what really matters in life and the world" (pp. 2–3).

The generalizations that arise out of our past experiences may be described as beliefs. "A belief is a mental architecture of how we interpret the world" (Alok Jha, 2005). As we experience life in all its many manifestations and react to our experiences, we create memories that ultimately can aggregate into beliefs. These beliefs form the generalizations that become part of our meaning frameworks and shape our emotions (Lawson, 2002).

Kathleen Taylor, a neuroscientist at Oxford University, as cited by Jha (2005), considers "beliefs and memories" as very similar. She describes a process where memories are formed in the brain through networks of neurons that are activated in response to an event. The more times this happens, the stronger the memory it creates. Peter Halligan, a psychologist at Cardiff University, as cited by Jha (2005) says that belief takes the concept of memory a step further. "A belief is a mental architecture of how we interpret the world." Beliefs also provide stability. When a new piece of sensory information comes in, it is assessed against these knowledge units before the brain works out whether it should be incorporated.

Psychologists Login George and Crystal Park (2016a) define "meaning frameworks" as the "web of propositions that we hold about how things are in the world and how things will be" (p. 206). Meaning frameworks are made of the "implicit and explicit propositions abstracted from our experiences" that form "mental representations of expected relationships among people, places, objects and ideas" (p. 207). They "contribute to a sense of meaning in life" according to George and Park, in that "the propositions we hold about the world may contribute to our sense that life makes sense, is directed and motivated by valued goals and matters" (p. 207). They contend that meaning frameworks that are consistent and coherent complement an individual's sense of comprehension. The meaning in life component of purpose is supported by meaning frameworks that "specify worthy high-level goals that are central to one's identity and reflective of one's core values" (p. 207). Finally, a sense of mattering or significance may be complemented by meaning frameworks that "suggest that one's life is of significance, importance and value in world" (p. 207).

Martela and Pessi state that "meaning is descriptive" in that "it tells us about the specific meaning framework" while "meaningfulness is evaluative" and based on how well something fulfills certain values and characteristics (p. 3). Their view is that "meaningfulness is primarily a type of feeling we have" that arises when we think about our something such as our life or our work. The meaningfulness is based on how strong the feeling is present in our recollected experiences. They associate this "subjective interpretation of meaningfulness" with psychological research related to meaning in life as well as meaning in work in that "both are about the experience of meaningfulness" (p. 3).

Meaning in life as an area of focus in Positive psychology traces its origins to work by Victor Frankl, holocaust survivor and psychiatrist, who is widely considered to be a seminal figure in raising the question of meaning as it is experienced in life through his book, *Man's Search for Meaning* (2006). He personally experienced significant tragedy in his life during World War II. He grew up in Austria, and he, his wife, and parents were sent to concentration camps by the Nazis in 1942. His parents and his wife died in the camps, but he survived and used his experiences during the war as the basis for the development of a psychological therapy that he called "logotherapy" to help people understand importance of their search for meaning in their lives.

"Man's search for meaning," according to Frankl, "is the primary motivation in his life…" (Frankl, 2006, p. 99). He refines this view by stating that "What matters…is not the meaning of life in general, but rather the specific meaning of a person's life at a given moment" (p. 108). Frankl emphasized that this meaning is discovered as individuals take responsibility for discovering meaning "in the world" (p. 108).

In 1988, Gary T. Reker and Paul T. P. Wong contributed a chapter in the book *Emergent Theories of Aging* in which they addressed *Aging as an Individual Process: Toward a Theory of Personal Meaning.* They argued that "As the individual passes through time, he or she constructs and reconstructs 'reality'" (p. 2016). Self-construction individualizes the aging process, giving the person the power to accommodate and transcend personal and societal limitations (p. 216). They drew inspiration from Berger and Luckmann (1966) in stating, "Personal meanings constitute reality that is self-evident to both the individual and others who share the same reality of everyday life and with whom one communicates and interacts" (p. 217). Reker and Wong pointed out that "personal meaning" as distinct from "definitional meaning" is concerned with meaning in life. "It is related to such constructs as value, purpose, coherence and belief systems" (p. 220).

In their view of meaning in life, they describe it as a "multidimensional construct with at least three related components: cognitive, motivational and affective" (p. 220). The cognitive component for Reker and Wong "has to do with making sense of one's experiences in life" (p. 220). They view this specifically as the individual's efforts to "construct a belief system, a world view" (p. 220). "In constructing this belief system, the individual is looking to address concerns such as ultimate purpose in life, order and purpose in the universe and the total meaning of life" (p. 220).

The second component is the motivational aspect of personal meaning that "refers to the value system constructed by each individual" (p. 220). Reker and Wong (1988) argued that "Values are essentially guides for living, dictating what goals we pursue and how we live our lives" (p. 220). They trace the origin of values to needs, beliefs, and society. The process of pursuing and attaining goals gives a "sense of purpose and meaning to ones' 'existence'" (p. 220).

Finally, the affective component is the third element of personal meaning. They argue that "the realization of personal meaning is always accompanied by feelings of satisfaction and fulfillment. Whatever is meaningful must also provide satisfaction to the person pursuing it" (p 221).

In summarizing their view of personal meaning within the context of their work in understanding the aging process, they state that "personal meaning is defined as cognizance of order, coherence, and purpose in one's existence, the pursuit and attainment of worthwhile goals, and an accompanying sense of fulfillment" (p. 221). Within the context of the lifespan, Reker and Wong (1988) see personal meaning arising out of the acquisition of shared and private values by young people. People use beliefs they have acquired and constructed to develop personal meaning. Over the span of life, the personal meaning "undergoes transformation as well" and evolves and changes (p. 229).

In 1998, Paul T. P. Wong and Prem S. Fry edited *The Human Quest for Meaning: A Handbook on Psychological Research and Clinical Applications.* In this work, Wong included a chapter on *Implicit theories of meaningful life and the development of the Personal Meaning Profile* (PMP). The studies conducted by Wong approached personal meaning with the goal of having people reveal their "conceptions about an ideally meaningful life" based on the use of his PMP (p. 112). Wong's studies suggested "that there may be a prototypical structure to a meaningful life which provides a relatively objective frame of reference to assess whether an individual's pursuit is meaningful" (p. 131). These studies led him to conclude that "personal meaning plays a major role in maintaining positive mental health and the value in using a survey instrument such as the PMP to create a reliable measure of meaning seeking" (p. 131).

Psychologists Shelly Gable and Jonathan Haidt in their article, *What (and Why) is Positive Psychology?,* in *Review of General Psychology* in 2005 noted that Positive psychology as a discipline found its original expression in a special edition of *American Psychologist* in 2000 (p. 103). Psychologists Martin Seligman, University of Pennsylvania, Department of Psychology, and Mihaly Csikszentmihalyi, Claremont Graduate University, Department of Psychology, editors for the special issue, noted that entering the new millennium was an opportunity to reflect on the state of American life. They commented in the Introduction that "...the United States can continue to increase its material wealth while ignoring the needs of its people and those of the rest of the planet. Such a course is likely to lead to increasing selfishness, to alienation between the more and the less fortunate and eventually to chaos and despair" (p. 5).

Their response to this potential was to call out to the behavioral and social sciences to assume the "enormously important role" of "articulating a vision of the good life that is empirically sound while being understandable and attractive" (p. 5). They anticipated psychology as identifying what actions "lead to well-being, to positive individuals and to thriving communities" (p. 5). "Psychology should be able to help document what kinds of families result in children who flourish, what work settings support the greatest satisfaction among workers, what policies result in the strongest civic engagement, and how people's lives can be most worth living" (p. 5).

Seligman had previously focused attention on the need to develop the positive aspects of psychology in The President's Address to the American Psychological Association in August 1999. He noted in his address that "psychology has moved too far away from its original roots, which were to make the lives of all people more fulfilling and productive and too much toward the important but not all-important area of curing mental illness" (p. 559). His response at the time was to set forth a "presidential initiative...intended to begin building an infrastructure within the discipline...to encourage and foster the growth of the new science and profession of positive psychology" (p. 559). He described the mission as "to utilize quality scientific research and scholarship to reorient our science and practice toward human strength" (p. 561).

In the Introduction of the special edition, Seligman and Csikszentmihalyi (2000) expressed their desire for psychology to take on this monumental task related to Positive psychology and they lamented that "...psychologists have scant knowledge of what makes life worth living" (p. 5). The lack of this work in discovering what enables people to flourish, in their opinion, was due to the preoccupation with repairing the damage and the psychological pathology following World War II.

In the Introduction, the editors argued for a positive orientation to psychology as a missing element that needed to be developed. "The field of positive psychology at the subjective level is about valued subjective experiences: well-being, contentment, and satisfaction (past); hope and optimism (future); and flow and happiness (in the present)" (p. 5). They further defined Positive psychology's opportunity to research the individual traits: "the capacity for love and vocation, courage, interpersonal skill, aesthetic sensibility, perseverance, forgiveness, originality, future mindedness, spirituality, high talent and wisdom" (p. 5). For groups, "civic virtues and the institutions that move individuals toward better citizenship; responsibility, nurturance, altruism, civility, moderation, tolerance and work ethic" (p. 5).

At the end of the Introduction, they offered the hopeful prophesy that "a psychology of positive human functioning will arise that achieves a scientific understanding and effective interventions to build thriving in individuals, families and communities" (p. 13). In 2001, the first *Handbook for Positive Psychology* was published.

Michael F. Steger and Patricia Frazer, psychologists in the Department of Psychology at the University of Minnesota, published a study in 2005 in the *Journal of Counseling Psychology* that sought to explore aspects of meaning in life that related to religion. The goal of the study was to "empirically test recent speculation that meaning in life may be an important mediator between religion and well-being" (p. 580). In 2006, Michael Steger, Patricia Frazier, Shigehiro Oishi, and Matthew Kaler published an article in the *Journal of Counseling Psychology* on "The meaning in life questionnaire: assessing the presence of and search for meaning in life." The article was designed to address the concern that there was not a good measure for meaning in life. "The purpose of the present research was to develop an improved measure of meaning in life" (p. 80).

Based on the three studies reported in the paper, Steger, Frazier, Oishi, and Kaler (2006) reported that "Evidence…demonstrates that…the Meaning in Life Questionnaire appears to represent reliable, structurally sound measures of the presence of meaning and the search for meaning" (p. 89). The questionnaire successfully assessed the presence of meaning separately from the search for meaning. Based on the results, "The studies presented here echo previous findings that feeling one's life is meaningful is important to human functioning" (p. 89).

In 2009, a second edition of the *Handbook for Positive Psychology* was published as the *Oxford Handbook of Positive Psychology*. In the second edition, a chapter by Michael F. Steger (2009), at that time a psychologist in the Department of Psychology at Colorado State University, titled "Meaning in Life" highlighted this area of study within Positive psychology. In his contribution, Steger commented that based on the studies in meaning in life, "it seems prudent to define meaning in life as the extent to which people comprehend, make sense of or see significance in their lives accompanied by the degree to which they perceive themselves to have a purpose, mission or overarching aim in life" (p. 682).

Recent developments in psychology demonstrate further development in the concept of meaning in life in Positive psychology and offer a useful approach to the understanding of meaning and the design of meaningful experiences within the healthcare environment. According to Frank Martela and Michael F. Steger (2016), in their article, "The three meanings of meaning in life: Distinguishing coherence, purpose and significance" which appeared in *The Journal of Positive Psychology*, psychologists believe that there is evidence that "experiencing meaning in life is an important contributor to well-being and health..." (p. 531). They differentiate "meaning in life" in Positive psychology from "meaning of life" or "the meaning of existence" that lies in the field of metaphysics. Their goal in researching meaning in life "...aims to look at the subjective experiences of human beings and asks what makes them experience meaningfulness in their lives" (p. 532).

The view of meaning in life in psychological literature originally "centered on two dimensions: coherence, or one's comprehension and sense made of life, and purpose, or one's core aims and aspirations for life" (p. 531). They argue that more recently, however, psychologists seem to be moving toward understanding "meaning in life as have three facets: one's life having value and significance, having a boarder purpose in life and one's life being coherent and making sense" (p. 533). They make the point that not only are the three elements of coherence, purpose, and significance the basis for understanding meaning in life as a whole, they each "have different psychological roots and fulfill different functions in human life" (p. 532). They contend that "by using these three facets as the foundation for research and understanding, the way is opened to overcome the ambiguity of the past and to move forward" (p. 532).

Martela and Steger (2016) identify the three separate components of meaning in life as "coherence, purpose, and significance," while other researchers use different but similar terms. According to Login George and Crystal Park (2016a), "Meaning in life can be conceptualized multidimensionally as consisting of three subconstructs: comprehension, purpose and mattering" (p. 205). Though the terminology differs slightly, the intent for both seems to be the same. In their article "The multidimensional existential meaning scale: a tripartite approach to measuring meaning in life" that appeared in *The Journal of General Psychology* (2016), they contribute to the ability to analyze meaning in life by creating a survey that differentiates the three subconstructs of coherence, purpose, and mattering in order to provide a more detailed analysis.

Martela and Steger (2016) describe coherence as referring to the ability of people to cognitively recognize patterns in their lives and the need of people to bring these patterns together to create a comprehensible wholeness that makes sense (p. 533). When people can recognize patterns and construct relationships or associations in their environment, this contributes to a sense of meaning in their lives. According to their research, people experience an increase in meaning in their lives through the cognitive recognition of coherence beginning with the moment-to-moment experiences and expanding to a broader awareness of the formation of more elaborate patterns that provide a sense of one's self in world. George and Park (2016a) note that low comprehension is associated with life seeming to be "incoherent, fragmented and unclear" (p. 206).

Drawing inspiration from Victor Frankl, researchers have found evidence that purpose is a component of meaning in life (p. 534). Martela and Steger (2016) note that there are differences among researchers in the precise definition of purpose in life, but there is a growing consensus that it is "essentially about some future-oriented aims and goals that give direction to life" and these "lend significance to one's present actions" (p. 534). Purpose is viewed as separate from the other components of coherence and significance and is not synonymous with the overall meaning in life. George and Park (2016a) expand on this by indicating that people who have a commitment to goals in their lives have a "sense of engagement with life, and they feel pulled and directed toward their goals" (p. 206). Individuals experiencing low purpose have a sense of aimlessness, and nothing in the future seems worthwhile (p. 206).

Finally, significance as a component of meaning in life "has been understood to be about the worthwhileness and value of one's life" (Martela & Steger, 2016, p. 535). It is sometimes referred to as "existential mattering" which can be defined as "the degree to which individuals feel that their existence is of significance and value" (p. 535). Mattering, as it is termed by George and Park (2016a), "conveys the degree to which individuals feel that their existence is of significance, importance and value in the world" (p. 206). "To experience mattering is to feel that the entirety of one's life and actions are consequential" (p. 206). They indicate that people with a low sense of mattering feel that "their existence carries little relevance and their non-existence would make little difference in the world" (p. 206).

The Meaning in Life Questionnaire (MLQ) was developed to gain insight into the presence and the search for meaning in life (Steger, Frazier, Oishi, & Kaler, 2006). It consists of ten statements. Five of the statements relate to the presence of meaning in the individual's life (Questions 1, 4, 5, 6, and 9). Five relate to the search for meaning (Questions 2, 3, 7, 8, and 10). Five specifically refer to purpose (Questions 3, 4, 6, 8, and 9), and four specifically refer to meaning or meaningful (Questions 1, 2, 3, and 8). One statement references to significance (Question 7). The scores for the presence statements and the search statements can be calculated separately and then compared. The questionnaire scores, however, do not differentiate the elements of coherence, purpose, and significance.

The MLQ statements are as follows, and they are responded to by a number ranging from 1 (Absolutely Untrue) to 7 (Absolutely True), and the numbers are aggregated to generate the score. Statement nine is reverse-coded (Steger, 2010).

1. I understand my life's meaning.
2. I am looking for something that makes my life feel meaningful.
3. I am always looking to find my life's purpose.
4. My life has a clear sense of purpose.
5. I have a good sense of what makes my life meaningful.
6. I have discovered a satisfying life purpose.
7. I am always searching for something that makes my life feel significant.
8. I am seeking a purpose or mission for my life.
9. My life has no clear purpose.
10. I am searching for meaning in my life.

According to the MLQ "What Do the Scores Mean?" (Steger, 2010), the aggregate scores are interpreted based on the "presence of meaning in life" and the "search for meaning in life." Scores above twenty-four on Presence and above twenty-four on Search indicate that "You feel your life has a valued meaning and purpose, yet you are still openly exploring that meaning or purpose." For Scores *above* twenty-four on Presence and *below* twenty-four on Search, the following interpretation is offered: "You feel your life has a valued meaning and purpose and you are not actively exploring that meaning or seeking meaning in your life." One might say that you are satisfied that you've grasped what makes your life meaningful, why you're here, and what you want to do with your life. For scores below twenty-four on Presence and above twenty-four on Search, "You probably do not feel your life has a valued meaning and purpose, and you are actively searching for something or someone that will give your life meaning or purpose." For scores *below* twenty-four on Presence and also *below* twenty-four on Search, Steger (2010) offers the following interpretation: "You probably do not feel your life has a valued meaning and purpose and are not actively exploring that meaning or seeking meaning in your life. Overall, you probably don't find the idea of thinking about your life's meaning very interesting or important."

George and Park (2016b) developed their Multidimensional Existential Meaning Scale (MEMS) to provide an assessment of the status of individuals in terms of the tripartite approach to meaning in life. In the article "The multidimensional existential meaning scale: a tripartite approach to measuring meaning in life" that appeared in *The Journal of Positive Psychology* (2016), they emphasized the importance of viewing the three dimensions of meaning in life as distinct from each other and to have a scale "that assesses comprehension, purpose and mattering separately" (p. 3). The results of their study "supported the reliability and validity of the MEMS" and demonstrated that a multidimensional measurement approach can facilitate "the disaggregating of the meaning in life construct and generation of a more nuanced understanding of each of its subconstructs" (p. 11).

The MEMS consists of fifteen statements that are different from those in the MLQ. These statements are specifically aligned with the concepts of comprehension, purpose, and mattering or significance. The scoring is on a seven-point scale with ratings on responses from "very strongly disagree" to "very strongly agree" which is different from the MLQ.

In the MEMS, the following statements assess the comprehension of individuals as a component of meaning in life (George & Park, 2016b).

- My life makes sense.
- I know what my life is about.
- I can make sense of the things that happen in my life.
- I understand my life.
- Looking at my life as a whole, things seem clear to me.

These statements in the MEMS offer insights into the nature of the way people approach comprehension. These statements reflect basic beliefs about life and the way life makes sense. If rated highly, the beliefs of an individual about the way their life makes sense to them are consistent with their experiences of their life and their ability to comprehend what their life is about.

In understanding the nature of purpose in meaning in life, it is helpful to consider the statements in the MEMS that are used to assess this component of meaning in life. The statements are as follows (George & Park, 2016b):

- I have aims in my life that are worth striving for.
- I have certain life goals that compel me to keep going.
- I have overarching goals that guide me in my life.
- I have goals in life that are very important to me.
- My direction in life is motivating to me.

These statements focus on "valued goals" as providing direction and motivation as an aspect of meaning in life. If rated highly, the individual has identified values reflected in specific goals that are important to the meaning in their life. These goals provide guidance as well as motivation to live a life that is meaningful.

Finally, the third component assessed in the MEMS is mattering or significance in the world. The following statements assess this aspect of meaning in life (George & Park, 2016b):

- There is nothing special about my existence (reverse score).
- Even a thousand years from now, it will still matter whether I existed or not.
- Whether my life ever existed matters even in the grand scheme of the universe.
- I am certain that my life is of importance.
- Even considering how big the universe is, I can say that my life matters.

The mattering or significance aspect of meaning in life may seem to be the most challenging as it focuses on the individual within the scope of the world as a whole and the sense of whether their existence matters now and in the future. It is associated with higher principles related to the nature of existence and the world as a whole which can often be related to view of spirituality or religion.

As cited in George and Park (2016b), Park argues that "Mattering is similarly implicated in the literature of religion/spirituality which highlights that a central function of religion/spirituality is to provide a sense of significance by allowing people to transcend the material and ephemeral aspects of existence" (p. 2). According to more recent research the sense of mattering, rather than coherence or purpose, emerged consistently as the strongest in correlation with overall meaning in life (Costin & Vignoles, 2020).

Meaning in Work

Healthcare experiences occur within organizations as the people receiving care interact with the people who deliver care. For those delivering care, the healthcare experience occurs within the context of their work each day. Martela and Pessi (2018) point out that work has come to occupy an important position in the lives of people and "has become one of the key domains from which people derive meaningfulness" (p. 1). Based on a broad review of the literature concerning meaning in work, they identified three meanings of meaningful work (p. 6). Significance or "how much intrinsic value people assign to or are able to find from their work" (p. 6) was one element of meaningful work. Broader purpose or purposefulness associated with work was defined "as a sense that through one's work one is serving something valuable beyond oneself, usually other people" (p. 6). They point out that the "other people" served through work could be one's family (p. 7). The last element they identified as important to meaningful work was "self-realization" (p. 7). "It is about self-connectedness, authenticity and how much we are able to realize and express ourselves in our work" (p. 7). They contend that without a personal sense of connection with the work and the ability to influence the work, "there is the potential for alienation from the work that exceeds even very high compensation" (p. 7).

Martela and Pessi (2018) conclude from their assessment that significance "should be identified as the hallmark of meaningful work" in that it forms the foundation "as the general sense that work has intrinsic value and is worth doing" (p. 8). Broader purpose and self-realization are viewed as elements of significance. Boarder purpose is about the "intrinsic value of work beyond the person" and self-realization is about the "intrinsic value of the work for the person" (p. 8). They argue "for an understanding of meaningful work, where significance is the overall judgment of the worthiness of work, and self-realization and broader purpose are the two key dimensions to two separate types of intrinsic values we look at in making such an overall judgment" (p. 9).

In comparing meaning in work and meaning in life, the contrast is essentially the difference between existence and activity, and they are differentiated based on the nature of the experience. Meaning in work is associated with the activities of working and the sense of meaningfulness that arises from the work and the way in which the work occurs. Meaning in life is about being alive and not simply activities. As Martela and Pessi describe it, "Thus being a part of a community through one's work can probably be important for one's sense of meaning in life, but not what people think about when they assess the meaningfulness of their work" (p. 9).

In summarizing their findings, Martela and Pessi (2018) state that "if we are able to provide people with work where they can realize themselves and where they feel they are serving a broader purpose, we give people the opportunity to truly feel their work is significant and worth doing" (p. 12). They contend that the means for doing this lies with the organizations within which the work occurs. For self-realization, organizations that provide autonomy sufficient to enable employees to actively participate in setting goals and the procedures for achieving the goals will promote a great degree of self-realization and therefore significance for the employee in the work (p. 10). A higher sense of purpose may arise in organizations that enable employees to "feel that their work has a positive impact in the lives of other people" (p. 10). Promoting this sense of a higher purpose may be associated with clear goals and values in the organization and direct contact between the employees and the people they serve (p. 10).

As organizations focus on creating a sense of significance in the work by promoting awareness of a broader purpose and self-realization in the way the work is designed and carried out, these elements become part of the meaning framework that leads to recognition in the employees of the meaningfulness of their work and their work as contributing to meaning in their lives. The realization of significance associated with broader purpose and self-realization in work becomes constituent of the meaning frameworks and complements and supports the individual's sense of comprehension, purpose, and significance as meaning in life. As the sense of significance and meaning in life is enhanced for those delivering care in healthcare organizations, they can engage effectively with those seeking care to create meaningful healthcare experiences.

Meaning in Healthcare

In 1992, James Brian Quinn offered important insights into the way service industries could be successful. He argued that "to optimize flexibility at the customer contact point and to maximize the production efficiencies," companies needed to seek out the "smallest possible core unit at which activity or output can be replicated or repeated" (Quinn, 1992, p. 103). At that point in "knowledge or service-based strategies, the person in contact with the customer – the contact person or point person – become perhaps the most important person in the organization" (Quinn, p. 102). He elaborated on this by stating that "The best performers in this contact role need three things: the personal competence, the organizational empowerment, and the psychological motivation to deliver service in its most effective form during the brief interval they are in contact with clients" (p. 102).

In searching for the point of contact in healthcare that leads to meaningful experiences, Quinn's recommendation seems to direct us to a microcosm of an interaction between a person receiving care, a person delivering care, and the organization within which they meet and interact. This would seem to be the smallest, replicable core unit in healthcare. It is in this space and this configuration that the creation of meaningful experiences may best be understood and visualized. Moving out from this point, what is learned and understood can be applied to scenarios that encompass more people and larger areas in organizations.

When experiences in healthcare are discussed, the focus tends to be on the patient. Interactions with the patient are evaluated from the patient's perspective and the way in which the patient perceives or evaluates what they experience. According to the Agency for Healthcare Research and Quality, "patient experience encompasses the range of interactions that patients have with the health care system, including their care from health plans, and from doctors, nurses, and staff in hospitals, physician practices, and other health care facilities. As an integral component of health care quality, patient experience includes several aspects of health care delivery that patient's value highly when they seek and receive care, such as getting timely appointments, easy access to information, and good communication with health care providers" (https://www.ahrq.gov/cahps/about-cahps/patient-experience/index.html). The Beryl Institute offers a more succinctly expressed but equally broad description of patient experience as "The sum of all interactions, shaped by an organization's culture, that influence patient perceptions across the continuum of care" (https://www.theberylinstitute.org/page/DefiningPX).

In exploring meaning in healthcare, however, it is important to recognize that the meaningfulness of the experience is created through the interactions of the person delivering care and the person receiving care, as they share the experience within the context of the processes created by the organization. All three perspectives contribute to the experience between the two people. If we view each participant in the experience individually, we can use what we have come to understand about meaning in life and meaning in work to look more deeply into the nature of the interaction. In this way, we can begin to understand how healthcare experiences can be designed to be more meaningful and to contribute to meaning in life and meaning in work.

It is also helpful to translate the psychological concepts of comprehension or coherence, purpose, and significance into terms that help to operationalize these concepts in considering the delivery of healthcare and the experiences of people within the context of healthcare organizations.

For comprehension, it is useful to think in terms of what we believe should happen in our ordered reality of everyday life. For example, when I set up a healthcare appointment, I believe that the appointment will occur in a certain way. I believe that the people I encounter will act in a certain way. For purpose, it is useful to think in terms of the values that are important to us. These values may be goals that we are seeking to accomplish or they may be values in terms of what we value in our experiences. For example, I set up a healthcare appointment because I value good health as an important goal in my life. At the same time, I value a practitioner who talks to me in terms I understand so I can participate in my healthcare. Finally, significance can represent the principles that are fundamental to our lives. I want to protect my health because an important principle in my life is my responsibility to support the people who depend on me as a parent or a spouse. By using the terms "beliefs," "values," and "principles" as operational terms for the three components of meaning in life, it makes it a little easier to talk about healthcare experiences from the three perspectives of people receiving care, people delivering care, and the organization.

People receiving care and associated family members bring to the experience of healthcare their beliefs that arise from memories of past experiences and from what they have read and learned that has become part of their meaning frameworks. Out of these meaning frameworks, they are seeking in the experience to satisfy the three elements that form the components of meaning in life. They are looking for comprehension or coherence between their existing beliefs about healthcare and healthcare processes as they engage with the organization and with the people delivering care. As the people receiving care enter into the organization and engage in conversations and meetings, they are seeking to fulfill their purposes that reflect their values and goals related to the healthcare experience. Finally, in their encounters with people delivering care and with the organization's processes, their meaning frameworks associated with their sense of significance and worth are evaluating whether they feel that the interactions support their views of themselves as having significance. As the people receiving care and their meaning frameworks of the three components of meaning in life encounter and react to the organization's processes and to the interactions with the people delivering care, they form the basis for the evaluation concerning the meaningfulness of the healthcare experience and whether they are willing to repeat it in the future.

For the people delivering care, the healthcare experience begins with their own sense of meaning in life based on their meaning frameworks supporting the three components of beliefs, values, and principles, but it includes more. They also bring to the experience their pursuit of meaning in work. Meaning in work includes their sense of the significance of their work as expressed in the self-realization they derive from the work in its affirmation of their meaning in life. The significance of their work also lies in their ability to connect to the idea that through the work they are benefitting others and contributing to a greater good beyond themselves. Within the context of meaning in work, the people delivering care are also engaged in facilitating and interpreting the beliefs, values, and principles that the organization has incorporated into the design of the work to the people receiving care. This creates an additional dimension of the interaction that depends on the ability of the people delivering care to find within their own meaning in life and meaning in work the capacity to fulfill what Quinn describes as "the personal competence, the organizational empowerment, and the psychological motivation to deliver service in its most effective form." As the people delivering care interact with the people receiving care, they are evaluating the meaningfulness of the experience from the perspective of their meaning in life as well as the perspective of their meaning in work.

Finally, the meaningfulness of healthcare experiences is significantly shaped by the beliefs, values, and principles that are incorporated into the design of the processes, the training of the people delivering care, and the communications created to provide specific services to the people receiving care and to ultimately obtain payment from some source for the care delivered. Many organizations have developed extensive mission, vision, and value statements as testimonies to their commitment to the welfare of employees, the community, and to provide products and services that benefit their customers. However, one of the important benefits of the introduction of industrial quality into healthcare was the recognition that healthcare management has very limited insight into the way the design of the processes throughout the organization reflects beliefs, values, and principles that may be considerably different from those espoused publicly. This has become apparent in the current sociotechnical epoch of healthcare in which the introduction of technology often changes processes of care in ways that are counterproductive to the beliefs, values, and principles of the individuals delivering the care. When the people delivering care are integrated into the processes of care as "cogs in the machine" with repetitious activity controlled by others and limited ability to influence the work, the loss of autonomy and influence raises serious ethical issues as well as compromising meaning in life and meaning in work (Mumford, 1996).

Summary

Meaningful healthcare experiences emerge out of encounters between people receiving care and people delivering care as they interact within the context of the processes designed by organizations. As people meet in the processes of healthcare service delivery, they work to incorporate the experiences into their routine lives and into their understanding of meaning in their lives. The tripartite nature of meaning in life is composed of comprehension, purpose, and significance. The meaning frameworks that support these components are shaped by the memories and beliefs of past experiences. Beliefs, values, and principles are terms that will be used in operationalizing the concepts of meaning in life as they are understood and expressed within the context of meaningful healthcare experiences. In addition to meaning in life, the people delivering care are also seeking meaning in work through the significance they find in self-realization and the broader purposes of the work they performed.

The people receiving care and people delivering care evaluate the meaningfulness of their healthcare experience in light of their beliefs, values, and principles as they relate within the context of the organization's design for the processes of care. When the components of meaning in life are supported and affirmed through the interactions between the people and the processes of the organization as healthcare services are delivered, then the healthcare experience is viewed as meaningful to the people involved and they are willing to repeat the experiences in future.

Chapter 2

Meaningful Healthcare Experiences for People Receiving Care

When we talk about meaningful healthcare experiences for people receiving care, we may make the assumption that healthcare can be understood within the context of what Berger and Luckmann (1966) would describe as the "normal, self-evident routines of everyday life" (p. 37). The reality, however, is that healthcare is different from other aspects of life and it tends to fall into the "problematic sector" (p. 38) of our lives. Even when we are going for a checkup in which we have no obvious health issues to address, the experience is outside of the routine of the day in that an appointment is needed. It may require special activities such as diet changes or paperwork. The process of the visit, the possibility that something may be discovered that may change our lives, and, perhaps most significantly, enduring the medical gaze Michel Foucault (1994) described in *The Birth of the Clinic: An Archaeology of Medical Perception* as the practitioner intrudes into our intimate space all contribute to the reasons that healthcare falls into the problematic sector of life. All this and we have not even mentioned the cost.

Given the many aspects of healthcare that make it problematic, it is useful to identify the people receiving care and what we can understand about them. The way we think about ourselves as we receive healthcare services and the way we identify people who receive services from healthcare organizations can give us important insight into the nature of the experience that is created and how to make it meaningful. It's important to remember that our vocabularies, society, and culture all contribute to our meaning frameworks (George & Crystal, 2016, p. 2) and the way we construct and interpret what we encounter in the world.

Whether we describe someone as a patient or a customer or a consumer changes the way we relate to them as these metaphors for a person receiving healthcare designate different expectations and require different responses. As Hugh McLaughlin (2009) of the Salford Center for Social Work Research commented concerning the terms used by social workers, "Before we begin to examine the differing terms used to define the social work relationship, it is important to first consider why this is important. The labels the social work profession has used to describe the social work relationship have included such terms as 'patients', 'clients', 'customers', 'consumers', 'experts by experience' and 'service users'. These different labels are very important, as they all conjure up differing identities identifying differing relationships and differing power dynamics" (McLaughlin, 2009, p. 1102).

In citing the work of a colleague, he argues that the words that are used to describe services and the relationships between people delivering services and those receiving services are metaphors that "operate discursively, constructing both the relationship and attendant identities of the people participating in the relationships, inducing very practical and material outcomes" (p. 1102). The designations we use are "signifiers," and it is important to "deconstruct these meanings" of the labels in order recognize the "the differing nuances and differing assumptions about the nature of the relationship" (p. 1102).

What distinguishes the three roles? Patients are usually viewed as people who are being treated due to an acute sickness and who need relief from symptoms of pain and suffering resulting from injury or illness. Customers are typically defined as people who purchase goods and services. Consumers are people who consume goods and services that they have been acquired through some means. If we consider the characteristics associated with these three terms as they express the roles and experiences of people receiving care, they may offer helpful insights into how experiences differ depending on the roles of the people involved.

When we talk about the people receiving healthcare services, the default has been the term "patient" from the fourteenth century Latin that meant "suffering or sick person under medical treatment (Patient, n.d.)." Significant changes in healthcare and the roles of people seeking healthcare services in the last 20 years have prompted the use of new terms. Today, the designations of "healthcare consumer" and "healthcare customer" are frequently found in many healthcare settings and literature along with "patient." Their usage reflects changes occurring in healthcare.

The patient role emphasizes the relationship between the person receiving care and the person delivering care. This is different from the customer and consumer roles and is an important consideration in understanding healthcare meaningful experiences. The key difference is that a patient is someone under the care of a healthcare professional who has accepted responsibility for the care of that patient. This relationship involves the moral and legal implications of the patient consenting to treatment and the acceptance by the healthcare professional or organization of the responsibility to serve the patient to the best of their ability. This also includes recognized legal and moral implications of failure to act in the best interests of the patient. Traditionally, the status of patients has been viewed as under the care of the professional until the patient or the practitioner states and documents that the relationship has ended and the terms for its discontinuation. It often requires the practitioner to make provisions for the transfer of care to another qualified professional.

The patient relationship with a healthcare professional is the most comprehensive, legally defined and binding relationship between people receiving care and people delivering care. Nurses and others who deliver care to patients in healthcare organizations are trained to assume the responsibility for the welfare of the patients assigned to them in a way that is different from other patients on the floor. They proactively take responsibility to ensure that they receive the care that has been ordered for them by the physicians. They may assist with other patients, but for those who are designated as their patients, the legal and moral implications are significant. Failure to appropriately care for these patients may result in lawsuits initiated by the patient or legal action by their professional board that could result in restriction or relinquishment of the license.

Beyond the legal and moral provisions that pertain to professionals delivering healthcare, the federal government, states, and a number of agencies have laws and regulatory provisions that relate to the rights of patients in a variety of healthcare situations. These pertain to access to care in emergencies; access to information; protection of information; and protection of civil rights, patient rights, and the right to informed consent and the right to refuse treatment. These rights are printed and posted in healthcare facilities and, based on state laws, a copy may be given to patients when entering care and an explanation of their rights provided in a form that can be understood by people with disabilities. The State of New Hampshire, for example, has a state statute that lists twenty-one rights of patients that hospitals and other facilities are required to provide to patients (Patient Bill of Rights, 2019). Medicare and Medicaid patients have specific rights as well pertaining to their care established by the federal government (Your Medicare Rights, n.d.).

The identification as patients is not the only role of people receiving care. In recent years, their role as customers has been increasingly emphasized due to the market dynamics occurring within healthcare. According to Merriam-Webster.com, customers are people who purchase a commodity or service (Customer, 2019). This role defines the person in the process of shopping and purchasing some form of healthcare product or healthcare service which may be for themselves or for someone else. All the typical aspects of the customer relationship that would be expected with any business or service provider are expected by the customer shopping for healthcare. This would include respect for inquiries and responsiveness to requests for information and follow up as with any sales interactions. Customers for healthcare services evaluate potential products and vendors to determine the quality of the service or product provided and make purchase decisions based on comparisons between all sellers in the market.

In the modern healthcare marketplace, the products and services available for purchase have increased significantly. The way purchases are made has changed from physical stores and facilities to online sales and virtual services. They involve a variety of products ranging from traditional medications or treatments to more advanced laboratory services, imaging, surgical services, emergency and urgent care services, and many others. Insurance companies and employers are encouraging healthcare insurance policy holders to act as customers to seek out lower-cost providers. They often offer incentives when people purchase healthcare services for using lower-cost providers. In many respects, the problem facing modern American healthcare in its failure to lower costs has been defaulted to the healthcare customer to find ways to reduce healthcare costs by acting as customers where in the past they would not have assumed this role.

There are legal provisions for customers as well as for patients. For customers, however, the legal protections are focused more on the availability of information concerning the service or product, the safety of the product for ordinary use, and the relationship with the vendor. If the product or service does not meet the expectations of the customer, they have recourse to seek compensation from the vendor under warranties and insurance protections or through legal means.

Women traditionally in America serve as the customers for healthcare products and services because they are more frequent users of healthcare and frequently accompany their children for checkups and other healthcare services. They are often viewed as the healthcare decision-makers for the family in terms of when to seek services and where to go for care. Many healthcare product and service providers focus their attention on women as the most important customers of healthcare in the American markets.

The third role to consider in healthcare is the consumer. This is defined as the person who consumes the product or service. Nancy Tomes, professor of history, wrote a book in 2016 titled *Remaking the American Patient: How Madison Avenue and Modern Medicine Turned Patients into Consumers*. As far back as 2006, in the book *History and Health Policy in the United States*, she was argued in her chapter "Patients or health-care consumers? Why the history of contested terms matters" that "Since the 1980s the use of the term 'health-care consumer' as a synonym for patient...has become commonplace in the United States" (Tomes, 206, p. 84). According to Tomes, it was patient-activists in the 1960s and 1970 rebelling against medical paternalism and the medical-industrial basis of healthcare who initially used the phrase "health-care consumer" (p. 84).

She analyzes the various aspects of patient versus consumer as it relates to roles and rights and contends that they overlap rather than serve as contrasting roles (p. 86). In her 2016 work, Tomes uses the phrase "critical medical consumerism" (Tomes, 2016, p. 5). She notes that consumerism relates to "protecting and informing consumers" as part of a wider movement that promotes "progressively greater consumption of goods as economically beneficial" (p. 8). Tomes believes that medical consumerism is the direct ancestor of the more recent developments in patient engagement and shared-decision making (p. 5).

Within critical medical consumerism, Tomes (2016) covers the broad sense of all aspects of the purchase and consumption of healthcare services. She does not distinguish the customer role from the consumer role. Her book focuses on the historical development of retail pharmacy and physician office experiences from the perspectives of healthcare development in American and the role of healthcare consumers as an active force in the healthcare marketplace. Though I believe that Tomes has captured essential aspects of the customer and consumer roles combined into the "critical medical consumer" designation, I feel there is value in using the three designations of patient, customer, and consumer in exploring the design of meaningful experiences.

If we use the term "consumer" to focus on the individual who actually consumes healthcare products and services, it helps to distinguish the purchasing process and the consumption process since the two may be separated by time and may involve different people. For the consumer of services, the generation of the service and the actual consumption of the service occur simultaneously. This consumption, however, may not occur at the time of purchase. For example, if, as a customer, I shop for an imaging service to perform an MRI as ordered by my physician, I may arrange a date in the future as the date to receive the actual service that I have purchased. The experience that I have in purchasing the service is very different from the experience that I have in consuming the service.

As people receiving healthcare participate in the experience in their various roles as patients, customers, and consumers, they are looking for a meaningful experience within the context of their role when they interact with healthcare organizations and the people delivering care. As a patient, that experience may find its most profound meaning in the relationship and interactions with the professionals responsible for the care of their patients. Within that context, the beliefs, values, and principles of the individual as a patient need to align with those of the professional and with those of the organization within which they meet. If they are aligned, then the patient experience for this person receiving care will be meaningful.

In the same way, the person receiving care in the role of a customer or the role of a consumer is searching for alignment between their beliefs, values, and principles within those roles as they interact with healthcare organizations or with people delivering care. Each role has its own context and its own influences that contribute to the meaningful experience or diminish the experience. It is important that healthcare organizations seek to design meaningful experiences for people receiving care and they recognize the roles involved at each touchpoint and work to understand and incorporate into those interactions the qualities necessary for the creation of a meaningful experience.

Chapter 3

Meaningful Healthcare Experiences for People Delivering Care

During orientation for new staff or at the beginning of a new quality project, I would often ask the people involved to imagine the building (usually a hospital) as an empty shell. The equipment and the signage are gone. There is no furniture in the building. It is only the walls, the halls, the doors, and the windows. The structural features are all that remain. Based on the design, the arrangement of rooms, and other aspects of the structure, the building could be used by different organizations or by private individuals for a variety of purposes.

I would, then, ask, "What makes this building a hospital?" After a few seconds of silence, I would say, "Because you and a number of other people believe that this building is a hospital." You create this hospital whenever you come here and act on that belief by fulfilling the role that you perform whether that is as nurse or physician or therapist or administrative role. Your belief and the belief of the people around you create the hospital. If you were to come in tomorrow and see this building as something different and if you could persuade the other people around you that is building is something other than a hospital, there would be no hospital but something different that you and the others would create.

The point of trying to imagine a building or organization as something different is to demonstrate that what we believe and how we act in response to that belief creates the world in which we live and work. Based on this conccpt, changes in organizations, whether in response to an improvement project or a new policy, begin with changes in what we believe which leads to what we see and how we understand the way things work. We take apart our current belief and work to replace it with a new belief and a new perspective. We must believe in the changes we want to make in order to make those changes and sustain them in the future.

The people working in healthcare and delivering healthcare services today are a different group of people from those who worked in healthcare in the twentieth century and the nature of the work they do today is different. It is still healthcare, but it is healthcare that is permeated by technology and the expectations of a culture infused with the values of the marketplace and the roles of consumers and competitors. It is healthcare in which the majority of people delivering care are female and many in leading roles have training as nurses and physician assistants (PAs).

The practitioners who delivered healthcare in America for most of the twentieth century were physicians who graduated from universities and medical schools and spent years in training. Initially working in homes, they transitioned mostly to offices and hospitals by the middle of the century. They were supported in their work by skilled professional nurses and an ever-expanding cadre of other disciplines emerging as science and technology provided more tools and more knowledge. Due to the high costs of medical education and the long period required to complete training, becoming a doctor as a career was limited for much of the century to men who had families that could support them or who received training and support through the military.

Though the image of the twentieth century physician as described above remains today as an important metaphor for the way people think about healthcare, much has changed in the last 20 years in the way healthcare is delivered. When a person arrives at the emergency department of a local hospital or at an urgent care center, they are as likely to receive care from a nurse practitioner (NP) or a PA as from a physician. With more than 270,000 NPs licensed in the United States in 2019 and their numbers increasing by over 28,000 per year, they are rapidly becoming the primary care providers of choice for many organizations and communities. In many states, NPs are independent practitioners that do not require physician oversight. They can prescribe medications, and many have certifications in their specialties, which range from family and adult care to women's health and pediatrics to psychiatric and mental health. In 2019, 88% of NPs are female (NP Facts, 2019).

According to the Bureau of Labor Statistics, there are 118,000 jobs for PAs in the United States (Physician Assistants, 2019). A 31% increase or 37,000 additional positions for PAs is expected in the next 10 years (2019). PAs serve as extenders who work under the license of their supervising physicians. They are not independent, but they are able to exercise any privileges that are held by the physician with their approval. PAs typically are found in areas such as emergency departments and general and orthopedic surgery where they take care of many tasks performed in the past by the physicians. They also assist in surgery. Of the PAs in the United States, 63% are female (2019).

With an anticipated shortage of 120,000 physicians by the year 2030 according to the Association of American Medical Colleges in a press release, the United States will face a significant shortage of physicians fueled by population growth, an increase in the number of aging Americans, and retirement of practicing doctors (AAMC, 2019). Given the anticipated shortage, NPs and PAs will be especially important in the future in providing care and creating meaningful experiences for many people receiving care.

In the future, women will play a very significant role in American healthcare as physicians, NPs, PAs, and registered nurses and in many other positions. According to the Association of American Medical Colleges, 2017 was the first year that more women enrolled in US medical schools than men (AAMC, 2017). The association reported that women comprised 50.7% of 21,338 enrollees in 2017, compared to 49.8% of 19,254 enrollees in 2016. This data point is particularly noteworthy when you put it in historical context. In 1965, only about one in ten US medical school enrollees was a woman. A hundred years before that, few medical schools admitted women at all (AAMC, 2017). A majority of pharmacist are also women at 56.8% of all pharmacists (DATAUSA: Pharmacists, 2017) and 74% of all physical therapists are women (Bunn, 2018).

Though women are in the majority in many healthcare professions, they are still underrepresented in executive roles. In 2017, it was reported that women held only 26% of hospital CEO positions and 21% of executive positions at Fortune 500 healthcare companies even though they make up 78% of the healthcare workforce (Walker, 2017). The American College of Healthcare Executives' membership totaled 47,523 as of January 1, 2019. Of this number, 55.6% are males and 77.5% are white and 37.8% hold positions are director/department head (26.6%) or managers (11.2%) (Members and Fellow Profile, 2019).

An increase in the number of foreign medical school graduates is another change in people delivering care that influences the meaningfulness of healthcare experiences. According to the American Immigration Council, there are more than 247,000 doctors with medical degrees from foreign countries practicing in the United States, making up slightly more than one-quarter of all doctors (American Immigration Council, 2018). This is an increase of more than 31,000 international medical graduates (IMGs) compared to 2004. The AMA Physicians' Professional Data (AMA-PPD) file indicates that 215,928 IMGs were active physicians in the United States in 2004, constituting 23.7% of the total physician workforce (Akl et al., 2007). Most foreign-trained doctors are not US citizens – meaning that the majority are foreign-born and they represent an important source of physicians in the future especially in underserved areas in America and in the disciplines of internal medicine and primary care (American Immigration Council, 2018).

The importance of the demographic changes that are occurring in the people who deliver healthcare should not be underestimated in terms of understanding meaningful healthcare experience. The people delivering care are involved in the development of the beliefs, values, and principles that shape and influence the interactions with the people receiving care individually and in the design of the organizational processes within which the healthcare experience occurs. In the past, the people delivering healthcare understood healthcare and its delivery as shaped by a tradition of white, male physicians who were trained in private practice. This was a group that had throughout the twentieth century "resisted innovation in the organization and financing and provision of medical care" (Rosen, 1983, p. 13). This resistance should be understood "as a consequence of a process extending over a period of roughly a century during which the medical profession has fought to maintain a medical market which would safeguard the basic structure of private practice" (Rosen, p. 14).

In the future, at the individual level, the delivery of care from the physician to the technician will mostly consist of a female delivering the care and working to create a meaningful experience for the person receiving care without the tradition that was manifested so strongly in the physicians of the past. This change will also shape the portion of meaningful experience that involves the beliefs, values, and principles of the organization. Though senior management in healthcare continues to be shaped by a male administrative perspective, this is changing as females initially trained in clinical professions and work begin to occupy higher-level positions in healthcare organizations. An important aspect of the structure supporting meaningful experience design within healthcare requires full representation by women in the organizational process designs and in the expression of beliefs, values, and principles that shape the context for the interaction between the people delivering care and the people receiving care.

Chapter 4

Proxemics, Emotions, Power, and Generations in Meaningful Healthcare Experiences

Healthcare is often presented as a routine part of our lives, but it is often anything but routine for the people receiving it. There are several factors that are inherent to healthcare that contribute to its problematic nature, but these are rarely addressed as part of the design of processes in healthcare organizations or in healthcare experiences because for the people who deliver care they routine. When a person receiving care interacts with people delivering care, there are at least four factors that may work against these interactions producing meaningful experiences. These factors are proxemics, emotions, power, and generations. Proxemics involves the physical closeness of people delivering care to the person receiving care. Emotions are often the way in which people receiving care express the meaningfulness of the experience, and these can play a significant role in healthcare experiences. Power is subtle and inherent in the organizations and professions that deliver healthcare, but it may also be experienced as a means for shaping healthcare experiences. Finally, generations are cohorts of people identified by age who share common experiences and people delivering care and people receiving care may be of different generations, and this may shape their healthcare experiences. Identifying these factors and understanding how they are present in healthcare experiences provides important context to understand how they relate to meaning in healthcare.

Proxemics and Meaningful Experience Design

Though most of us like to think that our actions and reactions to things are something that we decide, but in terms of proxemics, we revert back to some very basic instincts concerning the presence of someone, their closeness, and the sense of comfort we have based on their identity and distance from use. When people approach, we monitor their movements and evaluate them without directly facing them. If they come close enough, we turn to face them. If they are a stranger, their presence within a certain distance, depending on cultural norms and other factors, can make us very uncomfortable.

One of the most important characteristics of healthcare that makes it unique is the way in which the people delivering care who are complete strangers are permitted by people receiving care to touch them in the most intimate ways and intrude into their physical existence in unique way to deliver services. The goal of this section is to recognize that the physical closeness that healthcare requires may not be acknowledged as significant when in fact it is one of the reasons that the interactions between people delivering care and people receiving care are not routine. Developing a sense of the importance of closeness in healthcare can provide insights into creating meaningful healthcare experiences.

Edward T. Hall, an anthropologist, in his 1966 book, *The Hidden Dimension*, addressed the importance of physical closeness. "The central theme of this book is social and personal space and man's perception of it" (Hall, 1966, p. 1). "Proxemics" is the term that Hall created to describe "the interrelated observations and theories of man's use of space as a specialized elaboration of culture" (p. 1). He states that a person's sense of space is closely related to the sense of self and in an intimate transaction with the environment (p. 63). "No matter what happens in the world of human beings, it happens in a spatial setting and the design of that setting has a deep and persisting influence on the people in that setting" (p. xi). Hall points out that people have visual, tactile or touch, kinesthetic or movement, thermal or temperature aspects as they relate physically. He found that depending on the culture, there was great significance attached to the closeness of people, particularly strangers. His work on spatial relations between people uncovered what was always present in human communities but which was not actually analyzed as a factor that shaped the experiences of people as they related to each other.

Literature searches do not produce references concerning research or studies of proxemics in healthcare settings, but differences between cultures that may include awareness of spatial distance are commonly included in nursing and training for other health professionals. Hall offers important insights in the way that individuals are predisposed to interpret their environment. He indicates that "people from different cultures not only speak different languages, but what is possibly more important, inhabit different sensory worlds" (p. 2). This means for Hall that "The relationship between man and the cultural dimension is one in which both man and his environment participate in molding each other" (p. 2). He concludes with the caveat that we "need to broaden our view of the human situation" (p. 2).

Hall (1966) describes proxemic manifestations as infracultural, pre-cultural, and micro-cultural. Infracultural is behavioral and biologic and may relate to generational differences in the use of space or changes individuals make in response to crowding (p. 101). Pre-cultural is physiological and may relate to such things as the ability to see or hear (p. 101). Finally, micro-cultural is where proxemics observations are made in response to space in an environment.

Micro-culture is expressed in fixed feature, semifixed feature, and informal. Hall describes the fixed-feature space as reflecting the innate territoriality that people maintain for life activities as seen in arrangements in buildings or arrangement of rooms in a house for specific activities (p. 103). Semifixed features may be the arrangement of a kitchen or the furniture in the house. Finally, the informal space is the category that includes "the distances maintained in encounters with others" (p. 111). It is interesting to note that Hall considers informal distances to be "for the most part outside of our awareness" (p. 111).

Hall describes the "distances of man" as falling into four distances that he terms "intimate, personal, social and public (each with its close and far phase)" (p. 114) and our responses to interactions with people within these distances mark "the simplest form of situational personality" (p. 115). He encourages the perception of people as "surrounded by a series of expanding and contracting fields, which provide information of many kinds" because this helps to understand the interactions between people (p. 115). This is illustrated, for example, in the distinction between intimate and non-intimate space. Hall states that the presence or absence of the sensation of warmth from the body of another person marks the line between these two distances (p. 115).

Intimate distances occur when the presence of the other person is very close. Intimate distance, close phase, is sensed when the actual physical contact occurs or there is high probability of contact (p. 117). Intimate distance, far phase, is a distance of 6–18 inches when hands touch but other parts of the body are not in contact (p. 117). Hall notes that the use of intimate distance in public is not usually considered appropriate and people have special techniques for managing intimate spatial relation on crowded subways or other confined spaces by becoming immobile and maintaining muscle tension. He describes the way in elevators "the hands are kept at the side or used to steady the body by grasping the railing. The eyes are fixed on infinity and are not brought to bear on anyone for more than a passing glance" (p. 118). These reactions to closeness should be indications that are taken into consideration when entering intimate distance in a care setting.

For people delivering care and people receiving care in a healthcare organization, the far phase of the intimate distance in which hands can touch the other person is a common distance in which the work occurs. Part of the way in which Hall's work is valuable in healthcare is in recognizing the importance of this intimate space. For people delivering care, coping strategies have already been developed that enable them to enter intimate spaces with other people on a routine basis. For the person receiving care, this may not be the case. Having a stranger enter the intimate space may produce a stress response and discomfort in the person receiving care that the person delivering care may not experience.

Personal distance is the "small protective bubble that an organism maintains between itself and others," according to Hall. The personal space, close phase, is 18–30 inch in distance and is defined as a space within which one person can hold or grasp another (p. 119). Hall points out that a husband and wife will enter close personal space with impunity, but a spouse sharing personal space with someone else, "may not go well" (p. 119). The personal space, far phase, is 30–48 inch and can be referred to as "arm's length" (p. 120).

Social distance, close phase, is 48–84 inch and is the distance that is most often used for routine impersonal business. It is a common distance for people who work together or when attending a casual social gathering. Standing and looking down at someone who is seated within the social distance close phase may be viewed as intimidating. The far phase of social distance is 7–12 ft and is most frequently used for more formal interactions. Desks in offices are often designed to keep visitors at far phase social distance. It is this distance that permits people in the same area to continue working without appearing rude (p. 123).

Public distance is the final distance identified by Hall (1966). The close phase is 12–25 ft, and this is considered the distance that someone who is aware of a threat could take evasive action. It is also a distance in which formal speech would be expected (p. 123). The far phase of 25 ft or more is automatically set around important public figures (p. 124).

Hall points out that there is a tendency to see human spatial requirements in terms of "the actual amount of air displaced by the body" (p. 128). It is more accurate, he contends, to recognize that a person's personality extends into the distance zones described as intimate, personal, social, and public and that his territoriality is a part of human consciousness and shapes human experiences.

Given the importance of spatial distances in most situations, it would seem reasonable for this to be a consideration in understanding the meaning in healthcare. If people delivering care enter the intimate space of people receiving care abruptly or without gaining approval or acceptance, this would reflect a serious disregard for the beliefs and values of the person receiving care and would undermine the meaningfulness of the experience for them. Recognizing the importance of spatial distances in the interactions between people delivering healthcare and people receiving healthcare and developing strategies that facilitate coping with repeated entry into intimate and personal distances offers benefits in creating healthcare experiences that are meaningful.

Emotions and Meaningful Experience Design

Healthcare brings people together at moments in life when emotions are profoundly touched. The painful struggles of moms giving birth and the crying of babies being born are heard not far from rooms where elderly people quietly pass during the night as the family watches at the bedside. In these and many other experiences, it is not surprising that emotions are expressed. The question, however, is what do the emotions inherent in healthcare experiences mean? Are emotions physiological reactions to forms of stress or do they originate from deep within the memories and beliefs of the people involved and represent responses that reveal those beliefs?

From the perspective of meaningful experiences in healthcare, emotions offer insights into the beliefs of the people involved. Candy Lawson (2002), a clinical psychologist, points to the limbic system in the human brain as the "mediator" between thought and feelings. It is involved in the memories that form beliefs and that in turn give rise to emotions and reaction to current events. The origin of emotions is largely a result of beliefs that are attributions of our memories as "we try to explain our own behavior and that of others" (Lawson, 2002).

Nico H. Frijda, Anthony S. R. Manstead, and Sacha Bem, in "The influence of emotions on beliefs" in *Emotions and Beliefs: How Feelings Influence Thoughts* (2000), state that "Beliefs thus are regarded as one of the major determinants of emotion…" (p. 1). At the same time, "Beliefs fueled by emotions stimulate people to action or allow them to approve of the actions of others…" (p. 1). The relationship between the two is complementary. "Although beliefs may guide our actions, they are not sufficient to initiate action. No matter how rational your thoughts about helping the needy, you need an emotional impulse before you actually volunteer to help. Emotions are prime candidates for turning a thinking being into an actor" (p. 3).

Mary Lamia, a clinical psychologist, notes that "even the simplest beliefs have emotional memory at their core" (Lamia, 2012). She describes the process by which this develops as beginning with "visceral responses regarded as feelings" and these in turn "are transformed into thoughts and the formation of beliefs" that we use to make sense of current and future events (Lamia, 2012). Our present beliefs, according to Lamia, "are governed by past experiences that are linked to unconscious emotional memories" (2012).

It is important to recognize that the interplay of emotions, feelings, and beliefs underlie much of modern advertising and marketing and the efforts by businesses to evoke strong emotions and feelings in people in relation to objects and services. This view of emotions as the basis for action is an important area of consideration for businesses and organizations who use experiences as a way of reaching their customers and increasing sales. Scott Magids, Alan Zorfas, and Daniel Leemon (2015a), in their article "The new science of customer emotions: a better way to drive growth and profitability" in the *Harvard Business Review*, argued that organizations and businesses can "rigorously measure and strategically target the feelings that drive customers' behavior" through the use of "emotional motivators" (p. 4). According to their research, the importance of emotions was well known to businesses, but no one had identified a way to make this awareness a part of the operations of their business. Over 8 years "working with experts and surveying anthropological and social science research," they came up with a list 300 "emotional motivators" (p. 4). These are emotions or desires that drive customer behavior. The goal is to align customer emotions with brands or products in a way that motivates them to be "fully connected" to them (p. 5).

In describing these motivators, they refer to them as "desires that inspire customers" and they include inspiring customers who may desire "to stand out from the crowd" or "to have confidence in the future" or "to enjoy a sense of well-being" (p. 4). By leveraging these motivators, companies attempt to create emotional connections between their customers and products, services and the brand. The stronger these connections, the more likely these customers are to be loyal and to want to buy more of the products the company sells. They developed a "customer emotional connection pathway" to transition customers from "being disconnected" to being "fully connected" (p. 5). They content that by investing resources to strengthen the customer experience around the desires or emotional motivators that drive purchase behavior, companies can achieve their highest return on investment and fully connect with their customers (p. 5).

In another article, "What separates the best customers from the merely satisfied," Magids, Zorfas, and Leemon (2015b) more clearly state that "Customers connect emotionally with brands when the brand resonates with their deepest emotional drives – things like a desire to feel secure, to stand out from the crowd, or to be the person they want to be" (p. 3). In their work, they differentiate the satisfaction of customers from the emotional connection of customers. They determined that "highly satisfied customers often have low emotional connection" (p. 3).

Businesses working to improve experiences for their customers focus attention on the emotions of the people who buy their products. The designers working with these businesses strive to create what they describe as meaning by appealing to the emotions of customers. As one designer expressed it, "It's no secret among designers that if you create an experience that connects with users on an emotional level, you've succeeded. Emotion is what makes an experience an experience. Emotional reactions create bonds between users and products, signifying that are experiencing something memorable" (O'Grady, 2015).

Service designers often talk about creating exceptional experiences in their effort to connect with customers. O'Grady explains that delight, for example, is something that customers feel "when all the elements work well together." As her company focuses on delighting their customers, they are striving to understand "how delight feels and how to create experiences that evoke delight" (O'Grady, 2015). She expands on this idea by explaining that the effort to evoke delight led the company to creating experiences that are "magical and meaningful" (O'Grady, 2015). The design effort in this case is aimed at "how the experience should feel as a whole, rather than what it should do." The company defined delight as consisting of these components: "benefit, ease and positive emotion and developed a means for measuring their progress in producing the components that would create delight for the customer" (O'Grady, 2015).

Magical and meaning are used together to describe experiences that achieve what the designer and the company are striving to produce for the customer. As O'Grady explains, "An experience feels magical when it seems to know what the user wants and automatically delivers on that need without being asked. An experience feels meaningful when it feels relevant, right for me, and human. These two elements work together to create an emotionally rewarding experience. Meaning makes magic believable and valuable. Magic deepens meaning and often makes it more noticeable" (O'Grady, 2015).

From the perspective of meaningful healthcare experiences, emotions associated with memories are foundational to the development of beliefs, values, and principles of people receiving healthcare services. Because of this, if the care process and the interaction with the people delivering care are aligned with the beliefs and values of the people receiving care, it is likely that the emotions that underlie those beliefs will reflect that alignment. As Frijda, Mesquita, and Bem (2000) describe it, "Emotions involve beliefs; they include the formation of beliefs and they often stimulate the elaboration of these beliefs" (p. 52).

Since emotions have their origins in the memories of past experiences, assessing the beliefs and values of people receiving care and people delivering care and working to design process that aligns with these should result in more positive emotions and more meaningful healthcare experiences. This approach reflects a more deliberate effort to understand the origin of the emotions and beliefs that people have about healthcare experiences and what makes them meaningful through co-design and experienced-based design of services. The outcomes as reflected in the emotions of the people involved may offer a way to evaluate how closely beliefs and values are aligned for all those involved in the delivery of healthcare services.

Power and Meaningful Experience Design

Michel Foucault (1995), a philosopher, focused much of his philosophical writings on the nature of power, specifically in analyzing prisons, mental hospitals, and sexuality. Foucault contended that "What is power is the question at the center of everything" (Foucault, 1995, p. 41). He expanded on his concerns related to power. "And to be more specific: how is it exercised, what exactly happens when someone exercises power over another?" (p. 41). Foucault stressed that the typical view of power as strictly prohibition or preventing someone from doing something was inadequate. He believed that the true nature of power cannot be identified until "the strategies of power – the networks, the mechanisms, all those techniques by which a decision is accepted and by which that decision could not but be taken in the way it was" (p. 41) are acknowledged.

We can begin to appreciate the sense of what Foucault was suggesting by examining the way power is manifested in healthcare and how power influences the design of meaningful experiences. It is important to recognize that healthcare continues to operate on the basis of traditions from the twentieth century and reflects the architectural designs and the views of management and medicine from those periods. Current structures in many places continue to be the architectural expressions of science and organizations at an earlier stage. The buildings consist of multiple layers of subdivisions of space in a reductionist design that mimics the scientific view and the bureaucratic structure of an organizational chart. Control of movement and access is an important part of the design. In conception and operation, healthcare organizations often continue to share characteristics with penal institutions.

For the people who are required to stay in a hospital, the perception of lack of power to manage themselves and to make decisions is reinforced in subtle ways. The people delivering care control the processes of care and as a function of these processes manage the schedules and the treatments whether it is administering medications or performing procedures or obtaining specimens. Scheduling the activities of the people receiving care and restricting certain movements and behaviors while requiring other response contributes to a pervasive sense that the individual receiving care has entered an alien environment in which the normal rules of society and the personal life no longer apply. Whether it is clothing, equipment, sudden changes in the room, or sudden room changes, events occur within the hospital that are driven by hidden forces. When explanations are requested by people receiving care, the responses may be limited due to time or simply too complex for the people delivering care to fully address.

Limiting and sharing information in a language that is unfamiliar creates the impression reminiscent of the medieval church in which the Mass was conducted in Latin which most people did not understand. People receiving care are often required to quickly sign complex consent forms that are difficult for even knowledgeable people to interpret. They receive information about their stay in the hospital, their room, their rights and responsibilities with the expectations that they will be accepted and followed without resistance as the way things are done.

At the same time, most healthcare organizations have not arranged systems to respond to requests for information that are outside of the routine of the organization. Even though the cost of care can be very high, they are not able to provide an accounting of the costs of the care during the stay. Though there is a strong potential for harm from either infections or medications or the quality of the care, they are not able to offer information on the safety of these concerns. The requests for information and the lack of information together contribute to a sense of powerlessness within the confines of the hospital.

The people delivering care operate within a sphere with structures dominated by the professions ranging from the independent profession of the physician to the dependent professions of nursing, pharmacy, and various therapists. They have identification and clothing that appear to signify either status or function, but often the meaning of the designations is not discernible by the people receiving care. Due to specialization of medicine and surgery in the twentieth century, physicians exercise their control over the people receiving care in unpredictable arrangements. Hospitalist physicians or nurse practitioners control much of the hospital care but they are superseded by the surgeons or intensivists whenever there is a need for additional care. The radiologist, anesthesiologist, gastroenterologists, and other supporting physician specialties contribute mysteriously but may exercise significant power in the care process behind the scenes. The various divisions that deliver the care may not communicate with each other very well and may not provide the person receiving care with any information. This is perhaps most clearly expressed in situations in which people receive large bills for services by physicians outside the network of their insurance coverage. These services were provided without the knowledge of the person who is required to pay the bills.

Nursing often serves as interpreters for the people receiving care and are often asked to serve as advocates for them when they become confused or have trouble interpreting the activities around them. As a dependent profession, nursing is often caught between the physicians and physician assistants and the administration of the organization and the support services. In attempting to serve as advocates for people receiving care, nursing often extends itself beyond its realm of influence and the results are a sense of powerlessness on the part of nursing and other support staff that is ultimately communicated to the people receiving care.

Power in the form of physical domination is often communicated unintentionally by people entering the personal space of someone lying in bed or in a recliner and standing over them. Providing information within the context of this spatial arrangement may convey an expectation of compliance and may produce a sense of vulnerability in the person receiving the information. Moving closer into the intimate space of a person receiving care may create a higher level of stress depending on the familiarity between the people and goal of the interaction.

The hospital as a sociotechnical environment creates the impression for people receiving care that the technology has become a significant influence on the delivery of care. As the people delivering care spend more time focused on monitors, pumps, computer terminals, and other devices, they may struggle to redirect attention toward the people receiving care. This creates the impression that the technology is vitally important to the delivery of care, but people receiving care have no ability to enter the technical aspects of the process and no ability to interpret the significance of what is happening. Often the record and the results of care are contained in the technology but there is no way to access it. In a more personal sense of powerlessness, the equipment in the room may create signals and alarms that cause the people delivering care to react in a way that is beyond the control or may not be understood by the people staying in the room.

In addition to the more obvious ways in which power is part of the healthcare experience, there are the more subtle influences that arise when there are cultural differences between people delivering care and the people receiving care. Most organizations have developed specific ways to respond to obvious cultural differences concerning diet and languages and familial relations. The expression of power is often most pervasive when conflicts occur between the beliefs, values, and principles of people receiving care and those delivering care. It is in these moments that organizational and professional power may be used by the care providers to overcome the resistance in order to facilitate compliance.

In considering all the ways that power may be expressed within the hospital and other healthcare settings, it is clearly an environment in which the effort to produce meaningful experiences must include recognition of the subtle but nonetheless significant undercurrent of power. It is important to remember that the people delivering care as well as the recipients of care may be subject to the effects of positional and professional power. This may result in ethical dilemmas that create moral stress for the people involved.

Meaningful experience design creates the opportunity for the identification of those situations in which people receiving care and those delivering care may encounter power from a variety of sources and in a variety of forms. Recognizing when power is shaping the experience and subverting the alignment of beliefs, values, and principles is an important aspect of the design of meaningful healthcare experiences.

Generations and Meaningful Experience Design

Since the 1990s, the concept of generations as a means for understanding American culture and society has been very popular. In 1991, *Generations: The History of America's Future, 1584 to 2069* by Neil Howe and William Strauss provided a very elaborate scheme for organizing patterns in the generations of Americans that they believed were not only descriptive of behaviors and views but also predictive of future generations. An article in the *Harvard Business Review* in July–August 2007 by Howe and Strauss, titled "The next 20 years: how customer and workforce attitudes will evolve," offers an example of the way their original work was applied. As they state in the article, "Generations follow observable historical patterns and thus offer a very powerful tool for predicting future trends" (p. 42).

Howe and Strauss expanded on the historical significance of generations in several ways. They concluded in 2007 that they could identify 2007 six distinct generations of Americans: GI Generation, Silent Generation, Boom Generation, Generation X, Millennial Generation, and Homeland (which later became iGen or Generation Z) (p. 42). In addition to these generations, they also developed designations for generations depending on whether they came of age during or after a period of national crisis or during or after a period of cultural renewal or awakening describing them as "Prophet, Nomad, Hero and Artist generations" and using these metaphors as predictors for the future (p. 45). The work by Howe and Strauss received mixed reviews but served to popularize the idea that generations offered a powerful tool for businesses and service organizations to understand their customers better and gain insight into their expectations and needs.

Karl Mannheim (1972), a German sociologist writing in the early twentieth century, developed a systematic assessment of the way in which cohorts of people born during the same period can share values and perspectives. Mannheim viewed generations as "one of the indispensable guides to an understanding of the structure of social and intellectual movements" (Mannheim, 1972, pp. 286–287). The "sociological problem of generations" as Mannheim described in 1923 was that "a commonly accepted approach did not exist," and he felt that sociology was the discipline best equipped to address this problem (p. 287). He, therefore, undertook the task of attempting "to work out in formal sociological terms all the most elementary facts regarding the phenomenon of generations" (p. 288).

According to Jane Pilcher in her article "Mannheim's sociology of generations: an undervalued legacy" in the *British Journal of Sociology* in 1994, Mannheim's work "has been described as the seminal theoretical treatment of generations as a sociological phenomenon" (p. 481). The value of Mannheim's work, according to Pilcher, is that it "locates generations within socio-historical contexts and moreover is part of a wider sociological theory of knowledge" (p. 482). It is the socio-historical understanding that makes generational differences important for understanding and designing meaningful healthcare experiences.

Mannheim (1972) turns away from the view that "there is a secular rhythm at work in history" (p. 286) and views attempts at explanations for historical development as unknown and prone to "imaginative speculation" like the broad sweep of history espoused by Howe and Strauss (p. 286). Instead, he uses a systematic method to "define and understand the nature of generations as a social phenomenon" (p. 290).

Mannheim (1972) starts simply in describing the way individuals identify with each other. Individuals can be grouped into class structures, and these are defined by the "changing economic and power structures in society" (p. 290). They can be located within generations based on biological factors of life and death and aging. "Individuals who belong to the same generation who share the same year of birth are endowed to that extent with a common location in the historical dimension of social process" (p. 290). Building on the concept of a common location, he adds that "Only where contemporaries definitely are in a position to participate as an integrated group in certain common experiences can we rightly speak of community of location of a generation. Mere contemporaneity becomes sociologically significant only when it also involves participation in the same historical and social circumstances" (p. 295).

In addition to the specific historical and social circumstances, Mannheim (1972) emphasizes that experiences early in life are particularly significant. "In estimating the biographical significance of a particular experience, it is important to know whether it is undergone by an individual as a decisive childhood experience, or later in life, superimposed upon other basic and early impressions. Early impressions tend to coalesce into a natural view of the world. All later experiences then tend to receive their meaning from this original set… This much, however, is certain, that even if the rest of one's life consisted in one long process of negation and destruction of the natural world view acquired in youth, the determining influence of these early impressions would still be predominant" (p. 295). The predominance of early influences is what makes the years of birth of a generation so important relative to major events during the period that could be influential.

Individuals who were born in the same year and experience the same events have the potential to become a generational unit. However, Mannheim (1972) argues that it takes more than similarity. "To become really assimilated into a group involves more than the mere acceptance of its characteristic values – it involves the ability to see things from its particular aspect, to endow concepts with its particular shade of meaning and to experience psychological and intellectual impulses in the configuration characteristic of the group. It means further, to absorb those interpretive formative principles which enable the individual to deal with new impressions and events in fashion broadly pre-determined by the group" (p. 306).

Finally, Mannheim (1972) observes that not every generation location or age group "creates new collective impulses and formative principles original to itself and adequate to its particular situation" (p. 309). Mannheim argues that the development of the unique generational unit results when the tempo of change is different. "When as a result of the acceleration in the tempo of social and cultural transformation basic attitudes must change so quickly that the latent continuous adaptation and modification of traditional patterns of experience, thought and expression is no longer possible, then the various new phases of experience are consolidated somewhere, forming a clearly distinguishable new impulse and a new center of configuration" (p. 309).

Pilcher (1994) summarizes Mannheim's theory of generations as "constituting individuals by historical dimensions of the social processes that predominated in their youth that then forms social generations. Individuals are shaped by the socio-historical location and through their less or greater participation in the events of the time" (p. 491). In concluding his analysis, Mannheim states that "The phenomenon of generations is one of the basic factors contributing to the genesis of the dynamic of historical development. The analysis of the interaction of forces in this connection is a large task in itself, without which the nature of historical development cannot be properly understood. The problem can only be solved on the basis of a strict and careful analysis of all its component elements" (p. 320).

In seeking to translate the work of Mannheim and others in understanding the sociological implications of generations into contemporary practice, the Pew Research Center offers the modern perspective on the use of generations as a source for understanding changes in society. The Pew Research Center in its 2015 paper "The Whys and Hows of Generations Research" points out that the identification of an individual's age denotes two important characteristics of the person. The first is their place in their individual life cycle. Based on age, they can be viewed as children, adolescents, adults, or elderly persons. Each age group has certain activities that occur based on age, and these may change for a variety of reasons. Age also provides the means for aligning the individual with other individuals in their age cohort. This can be useful in understanding how a cohort is responding to changes and the degree of variation that may occur within the group. Finally, a generation serves as a way of grouping people born within a 15–20-year span into a group for study (Pew Research, 2015, p. 1).

The Pew Research Center (2015) uses designations similar to those developed by Howe and Strauss to set up their generations but with different intentions. An important difference between the Pew Research approach and Howe and Strauss that exemplifies the current approach to generations as more scientific is that it "involves tracking the same groups of people on a range of issues, behaviors and characteristics" (p. 2). Baby Boomers, according to Pew Research, is an example of a generation "that is largely delineated by demography" in that it is distinguished from other generations by the very large increase of births that occurred following World War II (p. 2). Conversely, Generation X is defined by the small number of births that occurred during the years between 1965 and 1980 (p. 2). The Millennial generation is the "echo boom" of the Baby Boomers and is also defined by demographics (p. 2). Early generations such as the Silent generation and the

Greatest generation are defined based on the crises associated with their birth years. The Greatest experienced the mobilization and fighting required to win World War II. The Silent endured the Great Depression and World War II and are distinguished by their civic-mindedness and cooperative demeanor (p. 2).

In researching how groups may differ from each other, the Pew Research Center (2015) assesses life cycle effects, cohort effects, and period effects. Examples of life cycle effects would be differences between older and younger people due to their place in their life cycles. "Period effects are seen when events and circumstances (for instance wars, social movements, economic booms or bust or technological breakthroughs) as well as broader social forces (such as the growing visibility of gays and lesbians in society) simultaneously impact everyone, regardless of age" (p. 4). Finally, cohort effects may reflect the influences of "unique historical circumstances" that affect an age cohort during a formative period in their development (p. 5).

In comparing generations, the Pew Research Center (2015) breaks out American generational cohorts as follows, and there is general agreement among most researchers about the approximate timeframes for each generational cohort:

Silent Generation: 1928–1945
Baby Boomers: 1946–1964
Generation X: 1965–1980
Millennials: 1981–1996
Generation Z: 1997–2012

A consensus has not been developed about the generation that comes after Generation Z, but Generation Alpha or Generation Glass has been suggested as a possible designation for everyone born after 2010. Generation Glass arises from the introduction of the iPad in 2010 (Bologna, 2019).

Based on their research, Pew Research (2015) has identified differences between the various generations. The Millennial generation is the most racially diverse adult generation compared with Generation X, Baby Boomers, and the Silent Generation (p. 9). Of the number of adults who had married, Generation X had a much lower marriage rate than Baby Boomers and Silent generations (p. 10). The Silents are the generation most likely to identify as Christian compared with Millennials and Gen Xers (p. 11).

Jean M. Twenge (2014), a professor of psychology, has spent many years researching, analyzing, and writing about generations and her approach represents the way in which social scientists, in general, are working to understand people within the context of their various birth year cohorts. The first edition of her book, *Generation Me* (her designation for Millennials), was published in April 2006. According to her Preface for the revised 2014 edition, the original edition in 2006 drew on fourteen studies on generational differences, based on data from 1.2 million people. Her revised edition was based on a total of more than thirty studies incorporating responses from 11 million people (2014, p. 4). In her studies, she uses "nationally representative surveys (including high school students) providing a view of the entire generation" (p. 3).

Drawing from this data, she generalizes the results in her books and articles. She has recently focused her research on Generation Z or "iGens" as she calls them who were born after 1995 (Twenge, 2017a, Location No. 64). She specifically identifies this generation with using smart phones during their formative years since the first iPhone appeared in 2007 and the avalanche of technological innovations that created the social networking environment of the current age. Twenge describes recognizing "shifts in teen behaviors and emotional states in 2012" (2017) that were dramatically different from preceding generational data. She concluded after further research that 2012 marked the point when "the proportion of Americans who owned a smart phone surpassed 50 percent" (2017). The presence of the technology in the lives of the iGeneration made their experiences as a generation "radically different from those of the generation that came of age just a few years before them" (2017).

Mannheim (1972) set forth the importance of understanding the way in which generations of people develop their understanding of themselves and their times as an aspect of the sociology of knowledge. What is the role of this information in the design of meaningful experiences in healthcare? Age has always been important clinically in understanding anatomical and physiological processes that people may experience. As research such as that performed by the Pew Research Center (2015) and psychologists such as Jean Twenge (2014, 2017a) continues to produce credible reports on important characteristics of people that are derived from their early life experiences as well as their place in their life cycle, this information should be useful in understanding the influences from meaningful experiences in healthcare organizations. Meaning in life for people receiving care and people delivering care arises from the meaning frameworks that are shaped by beliefs that arise from memories of experiences and other sources of information. Generational differences provide important insights into the beliefs, values, and principles that shape the meaningfulness of healthcare experiences and affect the way in which people delivering care work together and relate to the people receiving care.

Summary

Meaningful healthcare experience design requires an awareness about a variety of areas that affect human experiences and their meaningfulness. Proxemics, emotions, power, and generations are four factors examined in this chapter that are often overlooked in considering the dynamics at work in healthcare experiences. Their influence is often subtle, and the implications of variations can often be challenging to interpret. However, as noted in this chapter, the importance of these influences is significant in understanding the beliefs, values, and principles of the people involved and the healthcare organizations delivering services.

In the design of healthcare experiences and in working to improve experiences, an important indicator that may point to concerns in these aspects is in the emotional responses of the people involved. When these factors are viewed by the people involved as appropriate or understandable or not a concern, then there is probably alignment between the people involved and the organization around the factors presented in this chapter. However, if conversations about beliefs, values, and principles lead to individuals commenting on issues related to intimate or personal space, to a sense of powerlessness, or to an impression that there was a disconnect between the people involved in an encounter, then it is important to explore the nature of the lack of alignment. The emotions displayed in this discussion may indicate the degree in which there is a lack of consensus on how the meaningfulness of the experience. This can lead to additional exploration of what concerns should be addressed to improve the experience.

DESIGNING MEANINGFUL HEALTHCARE EXPERIENCES

2

Chapter 5

A Healthcare Experience

Healthcare experiences that we share with family and others are typically presented as a story because it is as a story that we are able to create a sense of the connections between the events and the feelings that together form the memories and meanings of what occurred. The following story depicts a common healthcare experience that may help to illustrate the way meaning is created within the social and technological context of our lives today.

Once upon a time, there was a baby, a mom, a physician, and a vaccine. Though the baby is the one responsible for the story, the baby was really just along for the ride. Mom had scheduled a checkup with the pediatrician and the busy morning had gone pretty well. The house was clean, the traffic was light and, most importantly, the baby was settled into the car seat and enjoying the ride.

Arriving at the doctor's office, Mom disengages the futuristic car seat/baby carrier and walks into the office with baby swinging like an oversized tote. As she opened the door, the typical pediatric office of colors, kids, moms, a few dads, and noise opened before them. Registration went smoothly with the office reviewing information the mom had sent online the week before in preparation for the visit. The insurance information had been updated and everything appeared to be in order. The mom rocked the car seat with her foot as the checked messages on her smart phone. She had a part-time business selling athletic wear and she tracked orders and inquiries through her social network connections. After a few minutes in the waiting room, they were called and the mom and baby headed to the back to the examination rooms.

The medical assistant led them to the room as greetings, questions, and answers were exchanged. All is going well and a pediatric nurse practitioner (NP) comes into the exam room with a bit of a rushed demeanor from her busy morning. With a quick smile to the mom, she introduces herself as an NP who has recently joined the practice. The mom expresses surprise as she has seen physicians in previous visits. The NP reassures her that she has been practicing for years and is very qualified for the well-child visit. Mom is put at ease and the NP turns to the baby and her smile grows as she interacts with the baby who is also smiling. As she goes through the examination, she asks the mom questions and documents in the computer the information about the baby's progress. The baby is actually enjoying the attention, and everyone is doing well.

As the NP progresses to the end of the exam, she looks at the screen where she has been documenting the results of the exam and sees a flashing alert that indicates that it is time for a vaccination. Mom states simply that she's thought about the vaccinations and doesn't want her baby vaccinated. There is just the slightest pause and the NP states, still looking at the screen, it will only take a moment to get it ready and it is standard practice to administer vaccines as scheduled. Mom states again that she doesn't want the vaccination for her baby.

Turning her face from the screen to the mom, she looks at her intently and asks why she would not want her baby protected by a vaccination. The very small exam room begins to grow suddenly darker. As the mom begins to explain that she has researched vaccinations online heard from some other moms in her social network about the dangers of vaccines. She doesn't want to risk it. The NP says she understands there are people who are against vaccinations, but online information is often incomplete and the best scientific medicine studies indicate that vaccinations are important protections to prevent illness in children and to prevent the spread of illness. Surely, she wants the vaccination to protect her baby.

Quietly, the doctor asks the mom does she place her confidence in scientific medicine or the online antivaxxer moms? In that moment, twentieth-century medical science encounters twenty-first-century postmodern mom. The baby is being very quiet. Mom starts to pick up their belongings and place the baby in the carrier as the NP continues to insist that it really is important for the baby needs to be vaccinated and it would be irresponsible of the mom not to comply. Mom maneuvers past the NP to the door and leaves without stopping at the desk on her way out.

The NP returns to her office to compose herself and cannot believe the mom could be so foolish. A few days later, the mom calls the hospital and complains about the way she was treated during the visit. The NP reported the interaction to the medical director for the practice. Within a week, the pediatricians in the office came up with a policy that parents who will not have their children vaccinated will need to find another practice in order to protect other children who come to the practice from exposure to communicable diseases.

The interaction in the office between the mom and the NP it the type of healthcare encounter that is repeated millions of times every day around the world. The parts of the interaction that are evident to an outsider consist of the person receiving care and the person delivering care and the place where they meet. Each of them brings to the encounter a vast array of influences that may or may not be visible and may or may not be present in their minds at the moment they meet. Through their conversations and expressions and gestures, they seek to communicate their thoughts and feelings to each other. The nature of the illness, the hopes, and expectations of both participants come out as they exchange information and through physical contact.

In the current sociotechnical epoch of healthcare, it is important to recognize that the social environment and the technological environment are shaping the information available to the people involved and their views. This is at the heart of the encounter between the people described above. In the story, there is a disagreement between the NP and the mom on the importance of the baby receiving a vaccination. It is useful to look at this specific question from the perspective of each person and the organization.

Beginning with the mom, it is clear from the story that she cares about her baby and wants what's best. She is willing to be an advocate for her baby even in a situation where the power of the practitioner can sometimes seem overwhelming. This commitment is part of her views of meaning in her life and comes from the meaning frameworks that have been shaped by her community and the family she grew up in. She believes that it is important to take her baby for well-child checks as part of caring for her. She values good health for her baby, and her goal is to do what she can to enable her to have a good life. All of her care for her baby is based on her identity as a mother and the responsibilities of being a mother. These beliefs, values, and principles are part of the meaning framework. These beliefs, values, and principles arise out of her social environment and support for these influences are the basis for a meaningful healthcare experience.

As a mom in her early 30s, she is very adept at using her smart phone and accessing sources of information outside of her own community. This technology has become an important part of her life and the way in which she understands and navigates through the "noise" of modern life. She has a part-time business that is based on Internet sales and she actively promotes her athletic wear on social media sites. She advises other women on where to find the best quality and values in athletic wear and how to care for their clothes. She enjoys watching podcasts and producing podcasts for her own social network sales. When she needs information, she is most often searching online and has come to feel that she can recognize a reliable source and where to go for answers that will be useful. The comments she has read about vaccinations were not part of her physical community but emerged from her online connections. She found them to be persuasive.

The NP is in her late 40s and has a number of years of experience first as a pediatric nurse and then as a certified pediatric NP. Though not from the immediate community, she has spent her life in pediatric practices in similar locations. Through her years of practice as well as her training as an NP, she values scientific medicine as the foundation that has proven to be effective in healing illness and injury and in promoting health. Her extensive training and her knowledge of studies related to vaccines and the potential for adverse reactions to vaccines give her confidence that she is justified in questioning the mom's views and strongly recommending her own. Her experience and the studies she has researched have led her to rely on standard medical texts and sources as the most reliable sources of information.

As an NP and as a mom, herself, the meaning frameworks for her have been shaped by beliefs that developed over the years of training and experience. She believes that she is able to provide good care to her patients and accurate, reliable information to their parents. The values important to her are to recognize the needs of her patients and to provide the right care. It is a fundamental principle in her life to contribute to the well-being of her patients in whatever possible so that they receive the benefits of good health.

During her years in practice, she has had to move from a healthcare that world of paper and pen to a world based on the electronic medical record. The transition has not been easy, and even in its current form, it is a mixed blessing with as many problems as benefits. The computer provides access to information, but often in ways that are not easy to access and the interface with the system is not like the forms she used in the past. When she should be facing the patient or parent and focusing on their needs and concerns, she finds herself entering numerous "clicks" to unrelated questions and trying to get the right information up on the screen. Entering information is problematic with delays in the way screens appear and the long pauses following requests. Often, she feels that the technology is an obstacle to good care and maintaining it requires that she stay long after the patient has been seen to update her documentation or to respond to the never-ending prompts and alerts. As she considers meaning in work, she feels that she is given the authority for self-realization in shaping most of her work. Because she works directly with patients and their parents, she sees the broader purpose that brings a sense of significance to what she does. However, the technology does not contribute as it should to her sense of meaning in work.

The organization, itself, is part of the sociotechnical environment that surrounds the mom and baby and nurse practitioner and brings its own influences. The current state of American healthcare care is portrayed in this simple scenario of a mom and a baby and a physician or nurse practitioner. The healthcare organization has created a delivery process involving a healthcare professional, office staff, office facility, and all the necessary support services. The beliefs, values, and principles of the organization are embedded into everything arranged for the visit.

The facilities themselves such as the campus and grounds with signage and parking and access routes, the building and its overall structure and design including building materials, colors and architecture, and means of movement within the building. The office and waiting areas and their signage, décor, materials and colors, and the sounds reflect decisions made by the organization. The office equipment such as technology for the records and registration and communication within the office and to the outside. The examination rooms in size and configuration and design and colors and décor reflect the organization.

The processes designed by the organization to facilitate the work reflect the organizational influences. Embedded in these processes are the beliefs, values, and principles of the organization and the organizational structure. At some point, in the past, each step of the process that occurs when a patient contacts the organization to arrange a visit has been determined by the part of the organization responsible for the delivery of the office visit. Each step can be traced back to a decision made by someone in the organization that either consciously or unconsciously expresses the nature of the organization. The hierarchy of authority and decision making within the organization produce the reality of the facilities and the processes that occur within them either through specifically determined actions or assumptions that were implemented or lack of attention which resulted in a spontaneous arrangement to meet needs in the moment. The value stream of the organizational process encompasses all of these aspects of the organization and expresses the beliefs, values, and principles of the organization.

Each person from the receptionist to the medical assistant to the nurse and the nurse practitioner employed by the organization to participate in the delivery of the service brings to their work in the organization their beliefs, values, and principles and expresses them in the context of their activities every day. From the moment the worker encounters their first awareness of the organization, the relationship between the worker and the organization as an entity begins to develop. Meaning in work becomes an integral part of the beliefs, values, and principles of the worker and the way the worker relates to their coworkers, the organizational structure and the work, itself.

The hiring process, the orientation process, the work environment and schedule, the pay and benefits, and all of the other aspects of the worker's relationship to the organization ultimately are reflected in the ways the worker contributes to the organization and to those who receives the services of the organization. The worker's specific activities as reflected in job description or direction of supervisors or coworkers or based on the workers' own ideas and routines form the expression of the engagement of the worker with the organization to produce one part of the overall experience of healthcare service delivery. It is in this context that the worker's beliefs, values, and principles are expressed. Since the nature of work and the worker within the organization is to repeat the majority of the work on an ongoing basis, the meaning in work of the worker is reflected over and over again and directly affects the meaning of the experience of the patient and coworkers involved in with the worker. At the same time, the relational elements expressed by the recipient of the service contribute directly to the meaning of the experience for the worker.

From the moment that a person as a patient or customer or consumer becomes aware of the organization or has an interaction with someone associated with the organization, their beliefs, values, and principles as they relate to the organization begin to take shape. All of the activities at each touchpoint in which the recipient of the services engages with the organization and the workers, the elements of a relationship – emotions, communication, knowledge, trust, etc. – become part of the way in which the service becomes meaningful to the person receiving the service. All of the activities associated with setting up the appointment, coming to the facility, providing and receiving information and receiving the final services and processing payment contribute to this impression.

The relational elements of greetings, conversation, and expressions or caring and compassion and concern exhibited by the organization's workers contribute to the creation of the meaning of the experience for the recipient of the service. The mom has followed the process of making an appointment, arranging her own schedule and preparing transportation to the office. The meeting between the mom, baby, and practitioner followed routine in all respects except the ending. The mom, relying upon her own sources of information, makes a decision that is significantly different from the advice of the professional. It is at this point that the mom's beliefs, values, and principles about medicine and being a mother in this community confuses the practitioner who had assumed they shared a common set of beliefs, values, and principles. Just as the organization and the professionals reflect much of the traditions and history of the twentieth century, the mom reflects the new perspectives that have arisen with the advent of new technology, new sources of information about health, consumer-oriented retail services, and changing status of professionals. Since the physician and the organization did not foresee and plan for the clash of values, beliefs, and principles, the encounter becomes challenging for everyone involved and no longer represents a meaningful experience that either is likely to want to repeat.

For the mom and the practitioner, the anger they feel at the end when the mom walks out is a result of the conflict between the beliefs of the mom and the principles of the practitioner. For the mom, it is not a question of whether her information is correct. She has been persuaded by her online contacts and she is not asking for additional information from the practitioner. The conflict is with her belief that when she requests something different from a service provider such as a pediatric office, the office should agree to her request. This view of the way services are provided arises out of a transactional relationship based on the marketplace view of healthcare. It is a product offered for sale and the customer makes the purchase decision.

For the practitioner, the advice she gives is authoritative because of the medical science behind it and it should be accepted. To reject the advice is to reject the science and the practitioner's role as the authoritative source of information. This violates the practitioner's principle that healthcare is based on the science of medicine. The tradition of medical science and the role of professionals have been refined in America for more than a century and is an accepted principle that is incorporated into the training of practitioners. To reject it is dangerous from the practitioner's perspective.

For the organization, the conflict between mom and the practitioner requires a resolution because the mom called and complained about the visit and the physicians in the pediatric practice requested that the Chief Medical Officer approve a policy that requires parents who do not permit vaccination of their children to seek care elsewhere to prevent unvaccinated children from coming to the office. The complaint and the request by the pediatricians and the anger expressed about the issue have raised the alert for the organization that the process of care in this case has broken down and requires attention. For the organization, this process failure conflicts with the organizational value that people receiving care and people delivering care have a meaningful healthcare experience that they are willing to repeat.

The Chief Medical Officer refers the situation to the ethics committee to investigate and develop recommendations because it appears to be a conflict between beliefs, values, and principles. The ethics committee interviews the mom and the nurse practitioner and identifies the lack of alignment between the mom's belief about the role of the person delivering the care and practitioner's principle related to medical science and the welfare of people receiving care. The recommendation was for the organization to acknowledge the lack of alignment between beliefs and principles and to redesign the process.

The request for the redesign of the process is referred to the Quality Council which includes representatives from the patient and family advisory council and the ethics committee. The design of the new process incorporates information about vaccines into the prenatal materials the obstetricians distribute and information about the pediatric practices via their websites, patient portals, and social media. Practitioners in the future specifically address vaccines in the initial visits and offer information about adverse reactions. This information affirms the role of parents as decision makers but also indicates that the practice will refer patients and parents to other sources of care if they choose not to vaccinate their children to prevent the spread of disease.

People receiving care, people delivering care, and the healthcare organizations share a partnership in creating meaningful healthcare experiences in the sociotechnical epoch of American healthcare. Recognizing that meaning in healthcare experiences emerges out of the alignment of beliefs, values, and principles is important for organizations that develop the processes for delivering healthcare. Utilizing organizational resources such as the ethics and quality structures to support the design and improvement of meaningful healthcare experiences represents a way to promote experiences that people find meaningful and that they are willing to repeat in the future.

Chapter 6

Healthcare Service Processes from a Sociotechnical Perspective

Healthcare service delivery processes are unique among services. If we consider these services from a social and a technological perspective, we begin to understand the complexity and the uniqueness that is inherent in healthcare. This uniqueness begins with the actual physical nature of the recipients of the services who are often in the care of the people delivering the services whether in a hospital, a skilled nursing facility, or clinic. They require a certain environment and certain provisions in order to remain viable. Extremes of temperature or pressure or light or darkness or pleasure or pain or noise or filth or lack of water or food work against all the efforts of healthcare services. People receiving care cannot be exposed to psychological extremes of isolation, crowding, silence, neglect, or abuse without harm to their mental state that, again, works to thwart the best purpose of healthcare services. All the services to be delivered must be provided in a way that is commensurate with these considerations.

Beyond the essential physical and mental provisions, people receiving healthcare services must be served in a way that is consistent within the established standards of the family and community and state within which they reside. The services must be delivered in a way that respects the family standards related to age, gender, birth order, role in the family, and particular preferences of the individual and family concerning deference in decision making and privileges and other cultural and religious customs and practices. Community standards also apply to the way services are delivered with regard to race, ethnicity, wealth of the individual or family, prerogatives of lineage, status, and rank or position within the community as well as connections with people in positions of power and prestige within the community. Lack of regard for these aspects of the lives of the people receiving care transforms healthcare services into moral and cultural battlefields that can disrupt the delivery of services and cause increased suffering.

People providing healthcare services also occupy a unique status in relation to the person receiving care. Depending on their role in delivering healthcare and their status in the family, the community, and the state in which they reside, people delivering care enter into the intimate space of people receiving care to examine them and to perform any number of actions that in and of themselves would be considered either inappropriate or illegal if performed by anyone else. This privilege of access is governed by the consent of the people receiving care and their family, community and institutional rules and regulations, professional standards, state and national legal provisions, and the personal moral and ethical principles of those delivering care. Within this matrix, there is a constant sense that healthcare services involve the people delivering care with the people receiving care in a unique relationship during specific times in their lives and careers. This relationship, whether short or long, pleasant or unpleasant, helpful or harmful, sad or joyful is permeated by meaning in the lives and in the work of those involved.

All the elements of healthcare services mentioned above are foundational to the delivery of healthcare services and to the meaningfulness of the services to everyone involved. It is important to remember that healthcare is dynamic and is evolving constantly in terms of the social aspects as well as the technical. Healthcare services in America evolved from homes and almshouses and dispensaries to hospitals and offices to retail pharmacies and most recently to online virtual visits and consultations. As the healthcare services evolved, the societal structures evolved. Initially, people receiving services were identified as a patient in the original sense of someone suffering and the person delivering the healthcare services viewed them in a paternal light in terms of the exchange of information and the cost of the services delivered. The poor who received care were charged less but expected to accept what was offered as charity. Those who had the means to pay for the care they received were patients as well but as customers of the people and institutions delivering services. They exercised the rights of the customer to choose care providers and sites of service whether homes or institutions.

In America, as opposed to other countries, the role of the hospital as the pivotal point of the overall care of sick and injured people in the country grew. It developed the technological and human resources to work through a fragmented care process that had frequently failed to care for people, particularly the poor and minorities. It became the protector of people who had no other resources or were unable due to mental illness and disability to manage their own affairs. For those with resources, a growing diversity of care sources developed that were more convenient, easier to access, delivered services faster, and with less complexity. Hospitals became the place of last resort due to the cost, inconvenience, and the potential for harm or additional illness.

As hospitals became the place to receive care, new methods of paying for care appeared in the twentieth century in the form of employer or government provided insurance, the recipients of services reverted to the patient status with care and services provided as directed by their insurance coverage. The people delivering healthcare services followed the guidelines of the insurance coverage and cared for the patient in a way required in order to receive payment. The insurance company had become the customer and the patient received the services as directed by the insurer. Patients accepted the care they received, and the insurer paid the bills. For insurance companies, the person receiving care was a consumer of healthcare services and the costs of their care were the medical losses of the insurance company and the employer.

Patients with insurance became particularly important to hospitals after World War II. With the advent in the 1980s and 1990s of care management of insured patients, the length of stay for patients became an important indicator for the quality of care as well as the costs of patients. The cost of the room was initially the major concern, but later the continuing cost of medications, treatments, and the threat of additional illness from extended hospital stay incentivized hospitals to find ways to discharge patients as quickly as possible.

As insurance changed and more of the costs of healthcare were passed on to the people receiving care, their relationship changed again and the people receiving care became customers. They were encouraged to actively seek out certain services as customers. This mixed identity of patient, customer, and consumer pervades and distorts the relationships of people receiving care and people delivering care and creates confusion and is a detriment to the pursuit of meaningful healthcare experiences.

The poor who had no place to go after discharge from the hospital created a growing problem for hospitals that needed some way in which to discharge the patients to open their beds for other patients. With growing concern about cost and the disposition of patients, hospitals and insurance companies created case managers to assist patients with the arranging for their departure from the hospital. These arrangements became more complex as the commercial and governmental insurance became more complicated and the options for care became more diverse. Hospitals formed a critical component of the overall social safety net of American society. Individuals who had no resources and became ill were brought to the hospital and it was up to the hospital to design a discharge that was safe. Social workers and case managers took on the role of designing and managing the cost and humanitarian aspects of the care of patients as they prepared to leave the hospital. Nursing evolved to focus more on the acute care and the management of clinical care in the hospital, while case managers and social workers took over the more personal aspect of the welfare of the patient in recovery and afterward.

Healthcare service processes changed as technology changed throughout the twentieth century. What began as two people sharing a story as confidants and seeking meaning from each other changed with the introduction of technology. Technology in the form of mechanical devices came between the people receiving care and the people delivering care and separated them. Rather than two people sharing a story, the person receiving care became the object for examination and the person delivering care became the person interacting with the technology. Each technological innovation created an additional separation between the two.

The stethoscope led to a 12-inch separation between the physician's ear and the patient's chest and led the physician to converse with the heart and lungs rather than the patient who was informed of the conversation later. The X-ray machine and the laboratory interacted with the patient and delivered a picture or test results to the physician without any contact with the patient. The technology associated with the delivery of surgical services shaped the workflow of hospitals and the introduction of technical devices into patients in orthopedics, cardiac surgery, vascular surgery, and other procedures shaped the recovery experiences and life expectancies of people receiving the devices.

People delivering care viewed the technology as the primary focus as the machines became more integrated into the healthcare processes. Intravenous infusions of medication represented one of the earliest introductions of technology to the nursing functions. Nurses were responsible for the timely administration of medication as ordered by the practitioners. With IV medication administration, the management of the rate of flow and the replenishing of the IV fluids became a nursing responsibility. In the same way that the stethoscope separated the physician from the patient by introducing a piece of equipment as an intermediary, the IV administration of medications over time shifted the nurses' attention from the patient to the operation of the IV. Rather than waking the patient to give a pill or administer an injection and engaging with the patient, the IV permitted the nurse to enter the room, check the fluid levels and rate of administration, and leave without engaging with the patient. This process of extending the capabilities of nurses through the use of technology continued as computers and electronic monitoring became available. Nurses were able to monitor patients electronically and to document results of treatments without engaging with patients. It also permitted individual nurses to monitor the care of more patients which reduced the attention paid to individual patients and the level of contact with patients. As electronic monitors and smart pumps became routine parts of care, the nurse's attention drifted more and more toward the monitoring equipment and management of the technology pump and less and less on the patient.

In the 2000s, patient healthcare records and other forms of healthcare information were migrating from paper to electronic forms. For many hospitals, the transition to an electronic medical record was a paralyzing experience because of the effort required to create the electronic record and the workflow changes required to use it. The use of the electronic medical record reshaped many healthcare service processes that had been in existence for decades. For hospital medical staff and nursing staff that depended on frequent documentation and access to information, the changes in workflows required for the electronic medical record altered many aspects of their work in significant ways. At times, it was simply a matter of documenting in a new location. At others, it is an entirely new level of documentation requiring new sources of information as well as new ways of documenting.

With the advent of the Internet and the use of electronic communication systems as well as the development of smaller, portable computers in hospitals, it became possible for computers to go to the point of care and to be used near the patient. This appeared to offer a very efficient way to collect clinical information in examining and talking with the patient and then documenting the information in the computer in the room. However, an amazing transformation took place. The computer became the new patient and focus of attention shifted away from the patient in the bed. Forms in the computer provided guidance for the nurse's assessment or the physician's documentation. In completing the forms, the nurse would often face the computer and ask the patient questions while entering the responses. For the patient, the nurse's attention was much more focused on the computer and what she was documenting than on the patient and the patient's concerns. The decreased eye contact and facial expressions made the conversation more impersonal even though the questions were being asked and answered and documented. This same process occurred with the physician who was likewise focused on documenting in the computer while asking patients questions. The lack of focus on the patient was not intentional but really a focus of asking the nurse or physician to use the technology in the room to document the examination. The ability to save time became an overriding concern for nurses and physicians who typically had more work than time to do it and needed ways to leverage more time out of changes in workflows. The computer documentation process offered the potential for time savings but required a multitasking approach to the interview rather than simply listening to the patient and then completing the form.

Together, people delivering care and people receiving care along with clinical and business technology work to arrange for the delivery of services in and out of the hospital. Just as the computer sitting between the people becomes a third person vying for attention, it is important that organizations recognize the effect of technology on healthcare service processes and the meaningfulness of the experience. Within this sociotechnical environment consisting of people from various perspectives with diverse forms of technology will emerge the meaningful experiences of healthcare in the future. In order for this to happen, it is important that design of the healthcare service process gives equal weight to the beliefs, values, and principles of the people as it does to the technology. Without this, the people will be marginalized and the technology will create an environment that may appear to be functioning but in reality is not creating the meaningful experiences that are necessary for healthcare to fulfill its mission or to enhance the health and lives of people receiving care and the people delivering care.

Healthcare service processes are at a critical juncture with expanding numbers of disciplines involved and the increasingly pervasive role of technology in shaping the processes and the experiences. The sociotechnical nature of healthcare services represents an important consideration in meaningful experience design. The social aspect of the relationship between the people receiving care and people delivering care and the technical aspects that are incorporated into the healthcare organization workflows and use of technology must be included in the design of meaningful healthcare experiences.

Chapter 7

The Three Value Streams of American Healthcare Experiences

A "value stream" is a useful metaphor for the invisible activities of an organization that produces products or services. The term "value" points to whether the steps in a process are useful in accomplishing the goals of the process. The image of a stream brings to mind flowing water moving from point to point continuously in a smooth motion. In manufacturing and other industries, the concept a process consisting of steps that move smoothly along has been a powerful image of production. Its most graphic representations in the early twentieth century were the conveyor belt and assembly line. Henry Ford's assembly line pulled the car along as workers assembled the vehicle. The worker remained in one place and repeated the same actions with each car. This permitted the assembly line to operate efficiently and produced a consistent product at the end of the line.

American healthcare's tradition never included the image of an assembly line for patient care. The classic image of medicine was The Doctor, a picture by Sir Luke Fildes created in 1877 that was used by the American Medical Association in its effort to promote the professional status of the physician. The central image in the picture is a well-dressed man with a concerned expression staring intensely at a sick child as the parents watch in the background. The setting is the family home. The message is that the man as a physician shares the family's concern for the sick child. It is an emotionally powerful image and specific to the people involved as if to say that the physician treats all his patients this way.

By the third decade of the twentieth century, however, the passive, watchful waiting of the Fildes picture was replaced by the rapid movement of patients in and out of operating rooms as surgery became the healthcare equivalent of an assembly line and the technology of well-designed patient flow became very important. The operating room emerged as the surgical workshop and surgical patients from all classes of society began to be admitted to the hospital for surgical procedures. Surgeons needed to be able to perform surgeries on a scheduled basis and they needed the operating room to be set up with appropriate supplies and equipment and the room prepared for maintaining an aseptic environment. They needed the nurses, anesthesiologists, and other staff for the surgery to be available at the same time to perform the surgeries. The patients had to be scheduled to arrive at the hospital and to be prepared for the surgery and for post-operative care. All these activities and people and materials had to be arranged to be present at the time the surgeon was prepared to perform the surgery. Once the surgery was done, everything that was done for the surgery had to be removed, and the preparations for the next surgery initiated. The hospital and the surgeon needed a way to make all of these things happen so that surgery could be performed each day for as many patients as were scheduled to have surgery. This was one of the earliest applications of the concepts associated with a value stream in healthcare.

Value streams officially appeared in American healthcare with the arrival of the Toyota Production System or "Lean manufacturing" as it was referred to in America. As a result of increasing concerns about quality and costs, American healthcare organizations explored industrial methods beginning in the 1980s, but embraced specifically as Lean methodologies in the early 2000s. Toyota was recognized as producing high quality with lower costs by removing waste or non-value-added activities from processes. This appealed to American healthcare organizations because insurers and agencies were promoting continuous improvements as a part of hospital operations, and quality and cost had become important value metrics. A number of agencies and consultants created healthcare programs using the Toyota Production System as the model and providing it to healthcare organizations.

Taiichi Ohno was the principal architect of the effort by Toyota to remove as much waste as possible from the production process in order to keep costs low and to reduce the time from the order for a car to its final delivery as short as possible. Ohno's basic idea was that the production process should include only steps that add value to the car production process and that the customer is willing to pay for. In analyzing the production step by step, Toyota worked to identify every step in the process and to determine whether it added value or did not. Non-value-added steps were to be removed. Value-added steps were to be retained. Because Toyota viewed the manufacturing process as a continuous flow, the steps formed a stream. The goal was to create a value stream in which all the steps forming the stream were value-added as much as possible. Toyota and later American Lean use the metaphor of value streams for this process improvement methodology.

Many healthcare organizations worked hard to implement Lean throughout their organizations but translating the concepts and the methodology proved difficult. Healthcare is a service rather than a specific, tangible product. It is a service that requires customization for each person receiving care. Manufacturing was able to control for quality and cost by standardizing the product and the production process to eliminate waste and defects and to accelerate production. The product of healthcare is the health or condition of the patient and the production method is the diagnosis and treatment to achieve a health status or condition that is acceptable to the physician and the patient. Both the product and the production process are not easily standardized due to the complexity of human anatomy and physiology as well as the individual practice patterns of autonomous professional physicians.

In addition to the variability between the outcome of the patient's condition and the production process, the problem of aligning the concept of value-added with a specific customer is equally problematic in healthcare. Both the patient, as the product and the customer, and the physician as the process owner and the final determiner of quality compete from the hospital's perspective for the title of "customer." American healthcare has typically defaulted to the physician as the customer because they write the orders that create the production and they are the loudest voice in terms of whether they are satisfied with the hospital's efforts. The customer, on the other hand, is the one whose health is changed and is ultimately the one who possesses the outcome of the services provided.

Given these concerns about the manufacturing concept of a value stream, can the metaphor apply to healthcare? I believe that the value stream can be a very important metaphor for healthcare, but it needs to be re-interpreted to correspond to a service that is very different from manufacturing and from non-healthcare services. The principal service provided by healthcare organizations is the experience that is created and shared by the people who deliver care and the people who receive care as they interact within the context of the healthcare organization's process. Healthcare experiences as well as hospital processes can be viewed as a series of activities or steps that move continuously in a flow.

There are three important distinctions when applying the metaphor of the value stream to healthcare experience. The first distinction is that healthcare experiences consist of not one value stream but three. The patient has a value stream of steps as part of the interaction with the healthcare organization. The organization has a value stream that is similar to the more traditional value stream in which the steps are a series of activities provided by the organization. The final value stream is the healthcare worker's value stream. These three value streams begin separately for each healthcare experience but ultimately merge to create the experience and then diverge when the experience has finished.

The second distinction in the value stream for healthcare experiences is that the steps that make up each of the streams are evaluated based on three criteria. The first criterion is that the steps in the value stream accurately reflect what is happening in the sequence of activities. The second criterion is that the individual value stream aligns with the beliefs, values, and principles of the perspective they represent: patient/customer, healthcare worker, and organization. The third criterion is that any conflicts or lack of alignment between the beliefs, values, and principles of the patient, healthcare worker, and organization are identified at the point where the three value streams merge.

The third distinction is that improvement in the meaningfulness of the healthcare experience that is produced from the convergence of the three value stream is an experience-based, co-designed change that reflects all three perspectives. The experience must be meaningful in terms of acknowledging the beliefs, values, and principles of all three participants and achieves a high level of alignment through the recognition and respect for the perspectives in each value stream. The inclusion of the perspectives of the three value streams offers the best approach for creating a merged value stream that accomplishes the essential work of the encounter in terms of the practical medical aspects. At the same time, the synergy of the shared beliefs, values, and principles offers the best potential for creating a meaningful experience that all three participants are willing to repeat in the future.

Since the 1990s, healthcare organizations have tried to improve quality and reduce costs by designing more efficient processes that accomplish the work that needs to be done. Unfortunately, in the effort to make improvements, healthcare organizations often design processes that are not workable for either the people receiving care or the staff involved. This occurs for a variety of reasons that relate to underlying influences that are not drawn out and addressed during the improvement process. Conflicts between departments or conflicts between professional staff and other workers or conflicts between patients and staff or simply too much work and too little time with too few resources all form common reasons why process improvements fail.

The result is a new process that the staff undermines within a relatively short period of time and returns to simply doing things the way they were done in the past that feels more comfortable than the new process. Sustainability is the most underrealized quality improvement goal in healthcare. Process improvements are not sustained because they do not address the basic beliefs, values, and principles of people receiving care, workers, or the organization. At the same time, changes in processes often create experiences that people are not willing to repeat daily because they are not meaningful. This results in the staff and recipients of care avoiding the processes and either locating new places to get care or simply not following through what is required for the process to work. This is the ultimate failure of American healthcare's efforts to improve.

A good way to understand the relationship for the three value streams is to imagine three streams in a forest. Each one originates at a different point in the forest and somewhere further downstream they flow together to form a larger stream. The origin of the streams represents not just the start of the process design or improvement that is the point of creating a value stream but represents the origin of the beliefs, values, and principles that are inherent in the streams. This origin may be an individual such as the patient. It may be an organization such as the hospital or physician office. It may a combination of organization and individual such as the healthcare worker. By identifying the origin or source of the three important perspectives of beliefs, values, and principles, their presence in the value stream and their influence on the creation of a meaningful experience design become clearer. This is critically important in the co-design of the experience that occurs when the three streams merge.

The origin of the organizational process value stream lies in the organization itself and its relationship to the community and to its medical staff. If the organization was started years before by a religious group or community group, this will continue to influence the value stream of the organization. If the organization has struggled in the past financially, if it has frequent turnover of leadership or problems with the community or has had a difficult relationship with the medical staff, these factors will also influence the value stream. In addition to the historic influences on the organization, its current situation shapes and influences the value stream. Depending on competition in the market and the intentions of the organization to grow and expand, there may be significant emphasis place on the latest technology or new construction or new services. If the organization's leadership has embraced the latest improvement initiatives and is striving to be perceived as a leader in quality and improvement, this will influence the value stream.

The origin of the patient's value stream lies in the life of the patient and the current state of the patient's situation. All the socio-demographics of age, gender, marital status, religion, education, work, and income shape the patient's beliefs, values, and principles and become part of the stream. Where the patient grew up and current residence as well the patient's health history and past experiences with healthcare organizations and health providers become influences in the stream. The flow of activities of the patient's value stream prior to the appointment becomes an influence that is incorporated into the value stream.

The healthcare worker's value stream influences the experience that occurs when the three streams merge, but it is perhaps the least recognized or appreciated of the value streams. The healthcare worker's value stream incorporates elements of the other two streams in the influences that shape the beliefs, values, and principles that are part of this third stream. The worker's socio-demographics and relationships within the community are important influences within this stream as with the patient. In addition to these influences, the worker's relationship and experiences with the organization as an employee contribute to stream. Finally, it is the healthcare worker who is present at the merger of the three streams who is most influential in the way in which the three streams come together. The worker's awareness of the influences that are part of the organizational stream and the patient's stream as their own is important in understanding the way in which the three streams will form a meaningful experience.

The merger of the three streams occurs within the context of the organization process that is designed to provide the specific service that the patient needs. The point where the streams merge represents the focus of traditional quality improvement in manufacturing and healthcare. This is where the patient directly encounters the organization's processes and where the organization directly encounters the patient. It is within this context that the organization typically tries to understand and respond to the needs of the patient. It is also the context within which the patient most frequently experiences problems with the way the organization is attempting to provide the service. Improvement, therefore, often focuses on what the organization and the patient find problematic during this encounter and what can be one to fix it. Unfortunately, the real problem may be that the organization's beliefs, values, and principles are not in alignment with the patients' views. If that is the case, even when the actual process functions as the organization designed it and the patient actually receives the basic service that was expected, the experience is not viewed as meaningful by the patient. The reactions of the patient during the encounter with the healthcare workers involved may also not have resulted in a meaningful experience for the worker. This may create a distaste for the work and for the patients and even a sense of moral stress because of the way the encounter was handled.

If we use a patient visit to physician's office as an example, many aspects of the interaction between the patient and the healthcare worker in the context of the organizational process are visible and recognizable and viewed as common to many other processes and experiences. Hidden beneath the surface of the more common aspects are deeper elements that are not often recognized but which play an important role. One way to describe these hidden elements would be think of them as beliefs, values, and principles that operate in the minds of the patient and the healthcare worker, and within the designs of the process created by the organization.

In simple terms, beliefs are aggregations of memories that are considered to be true by either the worker or patient. Beliefs can be as simple as a patient trusting that by arriving a few minutes early for an appointment, the physician will see the patient at the appointed time. This belief may have its origin in past experiences of the patient unrelated to the current situation, but it is applied whenever the patient has any type of appointment with a healthcare organization. For healthcare workers, the belief may that a good evaluation will result if the worker is pleasant to everyone regardless of whether the appointments occur on time or not. Beliefs held by the organization also influence the situation, but their presence is actually in the design of the process. The belief that the patients will come to the office for care if the registration process is efficient is incorporated into the steps of the registration process by the group that was appointed to set up the office when it was first opened.

In addition to beliefs, all three value streams are influenced by the values of the patient, worker and organization. Values relate to the goals and sense of purpose that underlie what people are doing. The patient may value a timely appointment and that provides the motivation for arriving for the appointment early. The worker may value a promotion that could result from a good evaluation. That value may serve as the reason that the worker is always smiling at everyone. The organization may value a sufficient revenue stream to ensure the cash flow to sustain the office practice and this motivates the organization to design the most efficient registration process to only meet patient expectations but also to accommodate as many patients as possible each day.

Along with the values and beliefs of the patients, workers, and the organization, each stream is influenced by the principles that are part of the flow. Principles are comprehensive and fundamental laws or rules that form the basis for decisions about whether something is good or bad or how something works. For the patient, a principle could be that each person is responsible for maintaining their health and by seeing her physician on a regular basis to protect her health she is doing the right thing. For the healthcare worker, a principle may be that working to support a child in college is an obligation that must be fulfilled. Finally, the principle underlying the organization's value stream may be that protecting the safety of patients and healthcare workers is the highest priority in the design of all processes.

In pursuit of understanding the fundamentals of American healthcare, the realization of the complexity of the value streams that form the experiences of patients and workers needs to be recognized. Patient come into the healthcare experience with their unique blend of beliefs, values and principles. The healthcare worker participates with a similarly unique set of hidden concerns. And, finally, the organization introduces its beliefs, values and principles into the experience through the design of process and the training of the staff. The challenge for everyone involved is to work together to create a meaningful experience that satisfies the beliefs, values and principles of each while and that each is willing to repeat in the future.

In order to create a meaningful experience, each participant much be involved in the design of the experience. Each set of beliefs and values and principles must be recognized and acknowledged. Finally, the activities of each associated with the process must be considered within the context of the value stream as influencing the perspectives of the participants. Only in this type of co-design can a meaningful experience be created designed (Figure 7.1).

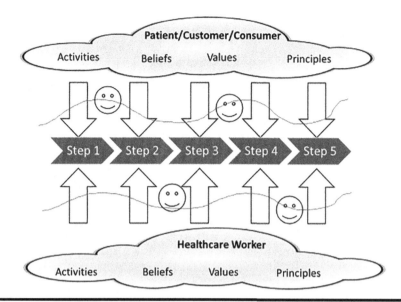

Figure 7.1   Meaningful Healthcare Experience Value Streams. This diagram illustrates the three value streams in their complexity. The work process in the center forms the structure for the activities that occur. The healthcare worker and the patient/ customer create their value streams out of their own encounters with the work process and their interactions with each other. It is in this context that a meaningful experience design comes to life and becomes an important goal of quality and process improvement. If the value streams conflict or if they are not in synch or supportive, the experience becomes less meaningful and may become a negative experience. When this happens, the people involved, and the quality professionals need to recognize that the dysfunction lies within the principles, values, and beliefs influencing the value streams.

Chapter 8

Organizational Process Value Stream

Of the three value streams that form healthcare experiences, the organizational process values stream is often the first place that the design or improvement begins. This is the value stream that incorporates the specific steps required to deliver the service. It is the stream that most resembles the improvement tradition of manufacturing and is the most familiar to people who have been involved in organizational process improvement in the past. It is important, therefore, to understand not only the specific steps of the process but the way in which the beliefs, values, and principles of the organization and the people who deliver care are integrated into the stream and, therefore, into the creation of a meaningful experience. The people receiving care and the people delivering care meet in the context of the organizational process value stream and react to the influences, beliefs, values, and principles that are part of that stream. This is often the place where lack of alignment between the influences in the three value streams occurs, but it is also the place where it can be most difficult to identify the issues that need to be addressed.

It is helpful to consider the organization from a broader perspective when trying to understand the organizational process value stream. This broader perspective includes the history of the organization and the history of the specific areas included in the value stream. American healthcare organizations emerged historically from needs within specific communities and, therefore, tend to reflect the beliefs and values of the community. Each organization also has its own history shaped by the way it was founded, who was involved, and the way in which the initial building and organizational structure were set up. If there were specific situations in the past in which the organization experienced a crisis or had a sudden change in senior management or financial struggles, these all contribute to the way the organization operates today and should be identified and acknowledged as influences on the organizational value streams. These may seem to be distant memories that no longer apply to contemporary situations, but memories are the basis of beliefs and beliefs are the basis for meaning frameworks not just in people but also in organizations. Bringing at least a superficial awareness of the history of the organizations' creation and operation offers important insights that can be important to understand the value stream.

The administrative bureaucracy's own history and culture contribute to the development of organizational process value streams. Most organizations have a mission that describes the reason the organization exists. It also has a vision of what it is trying to accomplish or become as an organization. Organizations post lists of values reflecting the way in which the organization intends to act and promotes the conduct and behaviors of employees that are considered consistent with the values. These values may reflect more general business type values that are considered to be appropriate or they may be very specific to the community and organization and based on historic incidents or issues that shaped the culture. The degree to which these fundamental elements of the culture are routinely displayed or addressed in everyday activities varies by organization. Recognizing the extent to which these are active is important in understanding the culture as it influences the value stream.

In the same way, the department or operational areas that are included in the process have their own history and may have their own mission, vision, and values. This history should not be minimized because the capacity of these operational areas to accept changes and to commit to new ways of achieving meaningful experiences lies in its history and development in the past. The directors and managers in the departments may be able to provide this history or interpret it and what it means in the current environment. The history of the mission and vision and the policies and procedures related to the services involved may also provide insights. It is important to understand this background information related to organizational processes because the departmental dynamics incorporated into the process are often far more complicated than is initially apparent.

Since healthcare organizations typically consist of two major divisions, the administrative bureaucracy and the medical staff structure, it is important to understand the organizational process value stream relationship to the medical staff and clinical practitioners and the way the service developed from their perspective. Just as senior management and department directors can provide the history of the areas, the members of the medical staff that are involved offer important insights into the way value streams originated and changed over time. Often, the medical staff members have more history to offer than the directors who tend to change more frequently. The clinical staff can share situations in the past in which the beliefs, values, and principles in three value streams were not aligned and the problems that arose from those situations. They may also have insights into the ethical issues that developed in the past in which staff felt moral stress.

Organizational process value streams draw their inspiration from the culture and aspirations from a variety of sources. The actual leadership style offers important indications of the beliefs, values, and principles that may be incorporated into the organizational process value stream. If it is an older centralized management style in which control predominates and innovation is the prerogative of senior management, then the value stream that emanates from the administrative structure will reflect this perspective. This will come out operationally when decisions are pushed much higher into the organization to obtain consent. If the leadership has been in place for an extended time, the influence may be more deeply felt and more a part of the assumptions that the group working on the value stream brings to it. Comments such as "this is the way it is done here" are expressed as a way of resisting changes rather than seeking alignment of beliefs, values, and principles. If the leadership has changed recently or frequently or the organization has undergone a merger or affiliation, then the culture and its values may be in transition as well. This situation makes it even more important to search for the perception of beliefs, values, and principles in order to gain as much understanding as possible of what values are influencing the value stream.

The history of process improvement in the organization and departments is an important consideration particularly in the approach to the organizational process value stream. So much of the drive in American healthcare in the early stages around improvement related to compliance with regulatory agencies that were imposed from outside of the organization and the community. These external requirements for improvement often created a cultural reaction of simply finding the best way to comply rather than to embrace the philosophy of improvement as a vital part of the operations of the organization. Depending on where the organization and specific departments are in their understanding and acceptance of the basic concepts associated with improvement will have a significant influence on the organizational process value stream. Value streams require a more advanced perspective of the relationship between operational activities and the beliefs, values, and principles because the goal is the creation of a meaningful experience. This is not as concrete as checking the box that a specific task was performed. For organization and staff that are struggling with negative feelings toward improvement due to lack of knowledge or bad experiences, meaningful healthcare experience design many prove difficult.

Many hospitals focused only on compliance with the requirements due to staffing issues and lack of other resources to facilitate additional changes or lack of leadership interest in promoting additional changes. Other hospitals, however, move to create specific cultural changes to support broader changes associated with quality and process improvements. Some hospital retained consultants who promoted Six Sigma and Lean methodologies and supervised large projects that could be identified as making a difference in the quality as well as reducing costs. In some of these organizations, the methods for improvement and the specific beliefs, values, and principles of these methodologies became part of the organizational value streams. Staff were trained in methodologies and the organizations promoted their use and acceptance. In some organizations, advancement was based on participation in the specific improvement methods and initiatives. For the organization with leadership and staff engagement in training and using specific quality and improvement methodologies, it is important to recognize these as part of the value stream.

With the emphasis on cost reductions as well as improvement, many healthcare organizations focused on patient safety as a particular area for change. Following the 1999 Institute of Medicine report *To Err Is Human*, the need for greater insight into the risk inherent in healthcare processes pushed organizations to find new ways to identify potential harm and to change processes to reduce the likelihood that patients and staff would be hurt. Many of these methodologies emphasized the importance of a culture of safety in which communication between all members of the staff is encouraged. The use of aviation techniques such as crew resource management promoted teamwork. High reliability promoted mindfulness and resilience. Just culture promoted a method for addressing adverse events by increasing awareness of the role played by processes as well as individual accountability. Each of these methodologies advocates a variety of beliefs, values, and principles associated with the way organizations work, the way processes function, and ways that people relate to each other. If an organization has embraced these methodologies and promoted their implementation, then the beliefs, values, and principles need to be recognized in the organizational value stream.

The promotion of a higher level of engagement with people receiving care became a new initiative in healthcare as The Centers for Medicare and Medicaid Services (CMS) and other payers began to survey patients' perceptions of care to assess organizational improvement. CMS uses the Hospital Consumer Assessment of Healthcare Providers and Systems (HCAHPS) for surveying patients about their perceptions of care and communications. Other companies provide surveys based on patient satisfaction and encouraged hospitals to take specific steps to improve their scores. For many hospitals, the need to improve scores to satisfy payers or to meet the expectations of governing boards led to expanded efforts to address patient complaints, to respond to patient suggestions and recommendations, and to create opportunities for patients and families to speak directly to hospital staff about their experiences.

Out of these efforts, the stories of patients began to appear and the perspectives of patients and families about their care began to enter the awareness of hospital leadership and governing boards. Responding to these stories fed the interest to better understand the nature of patient experiences and how hospitals could partner with patients to improve care, reduce harm, and to recognize the concerns of patients as valid expressions of hospital quality. Patient and family advisory councils emerged and became important resources for hospitals to engage with patients in a neutral environment and to also orient former patients to the way hospitals work and to encourage them to participate in the life of the hospital on committees and in reviewing changes to add the patient perspective. When hospitals have these types of programs in place, their beliefs, values, and principles should also be incorporated into the value streams of organization processes.

Since the early 2000s, technology has become increasingly important to the understanding of the way organizational processes work and the way that the technology shapes the services and affects the healthcare workers and patients that are involved. Sociotechnical concerns related to technology are important to identify and the influences of technology in understanding organizational process and the beliefs, values, and principles that were part of the decisions to acquire and implement the technology. Regulatory agencies have been major influences in providing funding and requirements for the implementation of electronic health records and other forms of technology in healthcare organizations. Due to the influences of the technology on the workflows of healthcare workers, these initiatives have not always been positive experiences of organizations and their workers. Physician burnout is one of the recent manifestations due to the practitioners attempting to adapt to the technology while at the same time maintaining their beliefs, values, and principles concerning patient care. In some case, the stress has resulted in ethical issues regarding what values are to be given priority.

Considering the issues associated with the evolving sociotechnical healthcare environment, some organizations have taken the ethical aspects of work into consideration as they have approached organizational processes. Ethics committees in healthcare in the past have often limited their work to clinical ethics in which the concerns were most often providing ethical consultations to patients and staff in cases in which end of life, clinical trials, or care issues created conflicts that were difficult to resolve. Ethics committees are beginning to recognize their role in assisting staff in resolving ethical conflicts that relate to work and technology. If new technology slows down the processes of care and clinical staff are unable to perform as they believe they should, then they may find themselves struggling ethically. These types of situations highlight conflicts or lack of alignment in organizational process value streams and will need to be a consideration in their design and improvement.

Chapter 9

The Value Stream of People Receiving Care

Healthcare experiences occur within the routine reality of our lives. They may happen suddenly or be planned months in advance. They may pass quickly out our current attention or escalate into questions of life and death. They may continue for months during recovery or for life as grieving and remembrance. Our health and our healthcare always have the potential to become problematic in relation to our routine reality, so we are continually re-evaluating our thoughts around it. This lack of predictability plays an important role in the development of the value stream for people receiving healthcare services and the desire for healthcare experiences to be meaningful.

In most cases, the value stream of a healthcare experience for people receiving care begins with a thought or idea. This occurs when a reminder appears on a calendar in your phone or computer that alerts you to schedule a healthcare appointment or to remind you of one that is already scheduled. Your spouse or mom or friend asks if you have addressed some minor health issues or taken steps to get your flu vaccine or a blood pressure check. At that moment, a cascade of memories and evaluative thoughts move from the background of your mind to become part of your current reality. You think about your current health, your past healthcare experiences, and what you anticipate from the upcoming visit. These thoughts along with memories will continue to evolve and will expand as you take steps to engage with the healthcare organization or to make plans for the visit and all of this will become an important part of what you consider when you eventually determine whether the experience created by your value stream has been meaningful.

Value streams of people receiving care incorporate beliefs, values, and principles that are part of their everyday life as members of a family, a community, and as participants in other societal and cultural aspects of life. The type of community, city or town, urban or rural, section of the country all play a part in influencing their value stream. At the same time, the individual's status within the community is influential. People who are long-time members of the community view healthcare organizations that developed in their communities differently from newcomers. Employment, financial security, insurance, and other economic factors shape views of healthcare and its associated costs. People within a community make decisions about where to seek healthcare and when it is necessary depending on their ability to pay for the care. Gender, age, ethnicity, religion, race, and other characteristics of the people receiving care also play a role in influencing the value stream associated with healthcare. All these aspects of life contribute to the memories that form the beliefs of people along with the views of life in general. From these influences, the meaning frameworks shape the different components of meaning in life and their beliefs, values, and principles.

Healthcare value streams of people receiving care begin in the distant past with the very first encounter with American healthcare that can be remembered. This encounter may have occurred as a child with an illness and a visit by or to a family doctor. It may have involved a first injection or childhood illnesses or injuries that led the first visit to a hospital which often becomes a part of the family's memories as well as the individual's. If the visit to the emergency department was a particularly traumatic injury or resulted from a dangerous illness, the memory may be recalled and discussed on the anniversary of the event or at family gatherings. Often, the care processes and the perceptions concerning the event may be the basis for future views of hospitals or healthcare in general. These events can become important influences in the creation of beliefs, values, and principles of the person receiving care and their family.

In addition to memories of past interactions with healthcare organizations, some people are frequent recipients of healthcare services. Not dissimilar from healthcare workers who develop their value streams everyday along similar paths from the day before, the frequent users of healthcare represent a group that has established very well-defined value streams of beliefs, values, and principles that they associate with healthcare and which are part of each visit that they experience. Because of the frequency in which these recipients of care experience the value streams of the organization and healthcare workers, they may enter their latest encounter already sensitized to areas in which the beliefs, values, and principles in their value stream were not compatible with the organization and the healthcare worker in the past. They anticipate that conflicts will be a part of the experience and are preparing for the interactions to be more about defending important aspects of their value stream rather engaging with the organization and worker to develop a meaningful experience. If, however, they have found their value stream to blend well with the organization and workers, then the expectation will be that they will have a meaningful experience and the interactions will be affirming and supportive rather than conflicted.

The initial contact with the healthcare organization via phone or email or physically arriving at the organization begins the process of the integration of the three value streams for the recipients of care. As they progress through the value stream established by the organization for the delivery of care and as they interact with the healthcare worker's value stream, there is a continuous evaluation of whether the value streams of the organization and healthcare worker are in alignment with the value stream of the recipient of care. Each interaction with a healthcare worker like each step in the process is filtered through the beliefs, values, and principles of the patient. This may not be a conscious effort or maybe very conscious if there have been incompatibilities in the past. If everything appears to correspond with care recipient's value stream, then the visit progresses as an evolving meaningful experience. If interactions or steps in the process occur that do not seem to be consistent with the values stream of the person receiving care, then this may result in questions and expressions of concern clarify the inconsistencies. It may cause the recipient of care to withdraw from the interactions either physically by leaving or mentally by simply following whatever is requested and not resisting or engaging beyond what is required.

When the visit ends, the person who received care returns goes through a period of reflection as part of returning to the routine reality of life. The recipient of care may discuss what happened with family and friends. This reflection may also be a time of personal reflection in which there is no discussion. The reflection represents the final stage of the value stream for this healthcare encounter. In this reflection period, the beliefs, values, and principles that they perceived in the organizational process value stream and the value stream of the healthcare worker are compared to the beliefs and values and principles in the value stream of the person receiving care.

If there is a perceived consistency between the three values streams, then the visit was a meaningful experience. If, however, there were inconsistencies or conflicts, then it is likely that the recipient of care may not consider the visit to be a meaningful experience. It is possible that the level of meaningfulness will vary depending on the degree of inconsistency or conflict. This is all part of the reflection part of the value stream. If the experience was found to be sufficiently meaningful, then the person receiving care will be willing to return to the organization and to work with the healthcare workers in the future. If the experience was not meaningful, then other care options and other healthcare organizations may be considered.

Though healthcare in some aspects may seem very similar to other retail sales encounters that people have every day, the reality is that healthcare is intrinsically different and this is the reason why a clear understanding of the three value streams and the creation of a meaningful experience are so important. As much as many people would like to redefine healthcare services as a commodity that can be received in an impersonal manner, the nature of healthcare is inherently personal. The focus is on the physical and/or mental status of the individual seeking care. At each step of the process, the recipients of care and the healthcare workers interact closely with each other and the nature of the interaction engage their beliefs, values, and principles and those of the organization. There is no way to minimize this closeness and deliver healthcare services.

The need for meaningful experience design in healthcare truly arises from all the factors that are working within the very nature of healthcare. The intensely personal interactions between recipients of care and healthcare workers and the sharing of very personal information and feelings amplify the need for clarity about the influences at work in the value streams that shape these interactions. Identifying and defining these influences that interact in the three value streams and then making this information an integral part of the design of healthcare experiences may seem excessive, but the nature of health and healthcare as different from the routine reality and its role in the development of meaning in the lives of the people involved makes this type of analysis and design work necessary.

Because healthcare is so personal and because beliefs, values, and principles find expression in our health more than in other parts of our lives, the understanding of the influences in value streams is important to learning how the three entities fit together in order to create meaningful experiences. For the healthcare worker and the recipients of care, the willingness to come together again in the future to deliver and receive healthcare services is based on the meaning that both have drawn from the experiences they have had together. The worker is faced with the creation of meaning daily with a broad range of people. The success of the organization in designing a meaningful experience in which the workers find meaning in their work as it relates to the organization's processes is critically important in shaping the ability of the worker and the recipient of care to come together in a meaningful experience. And, finally, it is the meaningful experience design that facilitates the blending of the three value streams that all the participants find support and affirmation. They are willing to repeat the experience because they found it meaningful.

Chapter 10

The Value Stream of People Delivering Care

The value stream of people who deliver care is the least understood and most problematic of the three value streams. The value stream of the people receiving care and the organizational process value stream are the two streams that appear most clearly in the traditional understanding of the delivery of healthcare services. It is the value stream of people delivering care that is hidden because the healthcare worker is subsumed into the organizational process, and their beliefs, values, and principles are lost in the much larger concern for the organization's delivery of services.

The reason for the neglect of the healthcare worker's value stream was a result of industrial quality viewing the worker as a component of the organizational processes. The activities of the worker were standardized within the process steps of the organization, and the individual worker was expected to complete the work as it was designed by management or by the improvement team. Within a manufacturing environment, the view of the work as designed according to the best practice and the worker as performing the work repeatedly to execute this best practice was considered the basis for reducing costs and waste and improving quality. In the Toyota Production System, workers were encouraged to identify ways to improve processes continuously, but they were expected to perform the work in an established way until those suggestions had been incorporated into the work and the best practice had been changed officially.

The delivery of healthcare services requires that the value stream of the people delivering the care be recognized as a vital component of the creation of the meaningful healthcare experiences that are the essence of the services delivered. This value stream is formed by the activities of the people delivering care based on their beliefs, values, and principles as expressed in the work that they perform. Their value stream then converges with the organizational process value stream and the value stream of the people receiving care. Meaningful healthcare experiences are created as the value streams of the people delivering care and the people receiving care converge within the healthcare organization's process value stream and the beliefs, values, and principles of all three align and support each other.

It is important to recognize that the value stream of the people delivering care incorporates three perspectives. Each healthcare worker pursues meaning in their own life. Their beliefs, values, and principles formed through their lives are integral to their views about meaning in life. At the same time, they are working to find meaning in work through their experiences as participants in the organization. Workers seek meaning in work through the sense of their own significance that they find in self-realization, which is expressed in shaping the work and delivering services in the manner that they feel is meaningful. They also seek significance in the broader purpose of their work that comes from the way it contributes to the well-being of the people who receive care but also in viewing the work as a way to support their families and making their community a better place. Finally, the healthcare worker is the interpreter of the organizational process to the people who receive care. As the workers interact with the people receiving services and other workers, they interpret the beliefs, values, and principles integrated into the work by the organization and shape the experiences in light of these influences. Given the very significant role that the people delivering care play in the creation of meaningful healthcare experiences, it is important that their meaning in life and meaning in work and their interpretation of the organizational process align in order to support the value stream of the people who receive care.

The value stream of the people delivering care originates outside of the organization. It begins with worker's personal history, education, and prior work experiences. Their pursuit of meaning in life and meaning in work often draws them to healthcare for personal reasons that come out of their past life experiences. Their education is frequently a combination of the general education common to most people and the specialized education associated with healthcare. Healthcare workers, particularly those providing clinical care, are part of traditions that have their own values that are incorporated into the education and training of the practitioners. These may vary depending on the institution that provides the education. Within these educational organizations, the relationship of their students to other healthcare practitioners is often based on history and traditions that are incorporated into the training.

For dependent practitioners, the relationship to independent practitioners such as physicians who generate the orders that direct the patient care is often an important element of their education and the traditions of their professions. Their training may also be designed to comply with state and federal regulations that govern the performance of their work as pharmacists, nurses, and therapists. There are beliefs, values, and principles that are incorporated into their education and that then become a part of the influences that are part of the value stream they create.

Past work experiences are also important contributors to the beliefs, values, and principles of healthcare workers because of the very personal nature of the work. Healthcare workers are often in situations in which the care and the outcomes involve strong emotions and memorable encounters with patients and with other workers. Particularly traumatic or painful patient care events may have long-lasting effects on the beliefs, values, and principles of healthcare workers. These become part of the background that contributes to their value stream prior to its introduction into the current experience.

Healthcare workers not only relate to the organizational processes based on their history, education, and work experiences but also as members of particular departments within the organization. Since organizational processes are shaped by the dynamics of individual departments, so the workers as member of the departments incorporate the departmental perspectives into their own work. Relationships within the department are important in shaping the way in which the workers relate to the work and their views of the organization itself. If the department is understaffed or stressed due to lack of other resources, this will shape the views of the healthcare worker toward the organization and the organizational processes. If the department's management is supportive and engaged with the workers as they perform the work, this will also shape the perspective of the workers. The relationship of the management of the department to the broader organization exerts significant influence on the healthcare worker's pursuit of meaning in work.

In the current healthcare environment with the increasing emphasis on cost reduction and quality improvement, healthcare workers are key participants in the design of the organizational processes. In this endeavor, the workers often receive training related to process design and improvement and the importance of identifying the customer and the needs of the customer in the delivery of healthcare services. This training becomes part of the healthcare worker's perspective on the organizational process and their own role within that process. The use of Lean techniques for designing and improving organizational processes places an emphasis on the steps required to accomplish the work and the completion of the work without errors and within the specified time. Most healthcare processes are sociotechnical in nature in that technology and people are integrated into the design and the functioning of the process. Within this environment, the relationship of the workers to the technology and to the performance of the work should be given a high priority. However, it is often the technology rather than the experience of the worker that is given the priority and this can create ethical issues as the works attempt to adapt to the technology.

As the healthcare worker engages with the organizational value stream by fulfilling the steps required in the process, the beliefs, values, and principles of the organization and those of the healthcare worker come together. In the initial engagement with the organizational process, the healthcare worker looks for the alignment with their own beliefs, values, and principles and those incorporated by the organization into the design of the process. The interaction between the influences inherent in the worker's value stream and those inherent in the organizational value stream creates the context for the experience of the worker with the work that is being performed. Where the beliefs, values, and principles align, the healthcare worker is able to participate in the work with a sense of understanding of how the work is to be performed. The worker translates the influences detected in the work through an interpretive process that is the basis for understanding the work process and the creation of a meaningful experience within the context of the engagement with the work.

If the worker is unable to find a meaningful correspondence through the interpretive process, then the worker begins to look for ways to workaround the lack of alignment. The goal for the worker is to find a way to reduce the conflict between the beliefs, values, and principles perceived in the organizational process and the worker's own beliefs, values, and principles. The lack of consistency between the worker's value stream and the organizational process may take a variety of forms.

The work as designed may not match the professional education and training the workers have received. They may view the performance requirements established by the organization as incongruous with their training.

The workers may be asked to assume more responsibility for the work than seems appropriate to regulations governing their practice. The workers may feel that the volume and speed required to perform the work is inconsistent with the quality they feel is necessary. If there is technology involved, the worker may not feel properly trained or experienced to use the technology successfully. The technology, itself, may require the worker to perform the work in a way that seems inconsistent with the worker's beliefs, values, and principles. The relationships between the workers, other disciplines, and the people receiving care may be perceived as inappropriate or inconsistent with past work experiences.

In attempting to resolve conflicts between the value streams, the health-care worker may accept the situation and ignore the concerns because the job is important for other reasons such as supporting their family. This approach often results in an ongoing sense of conflict that creates both physiological and mental stress for the worker and may ultimately create a sense of moral stress. The worker may seek out ways to resolve the conflict by engaging with leadership in the department. This may come in the form of questions about the organizational process, clarification of expectations of the worker by management, and complaints and requests for changes in the process.

Depending on the reaction of management, the situation may be resolved sufficiently for the worker to move forward or the worker may feel more needs to be done. If the worker continues to feel that the interaction with the organizational process is not working, then the worker may seek to encourage other workers to speak out and may look for ways to create a different work process that is more acceptable. The worker may add or remove steps in the organizational process to make it function in a more meaningful way for the worker. These changes often occur without soliciting approval but simply by the worker making the changes in a way that is designed to avoid detection by management.

Since the healthcare workers are most of employees of the organization, the quality of their experiences with the organizational process is particularly important to the overall meaningful experience design because as employees they are most commonly the interpreters of the organizational process to the people receiving care. If employees are struggling to find consistency between their value stream and the organizational process value stream, they will not be able to guide patients in their interpretation of the process they encounter at the hospital or physician office and how it fits with their own value stream. It is not helpful if workers are struggling to find a meaningful experience in the work while the people receiving care are seeking to find meaning in the organizational process and the interaction with the healthcare worker.

People receiving care arrive with the expectations that those delivering care are able to provide them with a meaningful experience. If they turn to the healthcare worker close at hand for help in finding that meaning and the worker is unable to help because of struggles to understand it themselves, then the experience is less meaningful. In cases such as this, the worker and the patient may seek to align their own frustration with the lack of meaning that they are both experiencing in the organizational process. Such a shared experience does not reinforce a desire on the part of the people receiving care to have similar experiences in the future. It reinforces the healthcare worker's sense that the organizational process value stream is not working.

When the value stream of people delivering care is aligned with the beliefs, values, and principles of the organizational process value stream, the people receiving care can ask questions and the healthcare worker can guide them in identifying the alignment with their beliefs, values, and principles with those of the organizational value stream. In this way, the interaction would help to confirm for everyone the meaningfulness of their experiences within the context of the organizational value stream.

The organizational process value stream and the value stream of people delivering care blend together with the value stream for the people receiving care as an arrangement designed by the organization to deliver a healthcare service to a patient. These three streams flow into each other as the healthcare worker arrives at work and enters into the organizational process as part of a routine that repeats over and over again and engages with the people who are receiving care. This repetition represents a strength and weakness in sustaining value streams that create meaningful experiences. The strength in the repetition is the familiarity as the steps that occur every day are well known. However, the repetition of this interaction between the organization's value stream and the healthcare worker's value stream holds a hidden danger if it is not meaningful for the worker. Repeating a series of steps that are meaningless eventually becomes an exercise in mindlessness rather than meaningfulness. The healthcare workers sense a disconnect between themselves and the work. The organizational process steps become simply an endless series that are repeated hour by hour, day by day, and week by week.

Healthcare workers find meaning in work when they are able to create a sense of personal significance in the self-realization that comes from exercising autonomy in the work and the way the work is performed and seeing a broader purpose in the work as they relate it to contributing to their sense of the world. This meaning in work is a vital part of the way that healthcare workers express their beliefs, values, and principles in their value stream. If the work, however, that is repeated every day does not contribute to the healthcare worker's sense of meaning, it may actually create feelings of irritation, anger, and moral stress due to a lack of alignment between the values of the organization and the values of the worker as expressed in their value streams. It is in this context that healthcare workers find that the conflicts between their own values are violated by the values of the organizational process. At the end of each shift, the worker leaves feeling like a battle has been fought simply to maintain their integrity and to accomplish what they feel is the meaningful work they were trained to do.

It is vitally important to meaningful healthcare experience design that the organization recognizes the existence of the healthcare worker's value stream and the important role it plays in creating meaningful experiences for the people receiving care and the delivery of services. The people delivering care are more than participants in the organizational processes. Their ability to find meaning in work and meaning in life through the alignment of their value stream with that of the organization serves as the foundation for the convergence of the three value streams as they guide the people receiving care in interpreting the alignment between their needs and the services offered by the organization. The successful blending of the three streams is the basis for sustaining the design of the organizational process. When the person delivering care and the person receiving care find an alignment between their value streams and the organizational process value stream, their interaction becomes meaningful to them. It is this meaningfulness that is important to the sustainability of the design of the process and for the willingness of the worker to engage with the process repeatedly day after day.

Chapter 11

Meaningful Healthcare Experience Design Map

Organizations design meaningful healthcare experiences and improve them by researching, documenting, and analyzing all the elements that form the value streams of the people receiving care, the people delivering care, and the organizational process value stream. The Meaningful Healthcare Experience Design Map (Figure 11.1) is a tool that can be used to gather information. The map facilitates the evaluation of the value streams to enable teams to design meaningful healthcare experiences by providing a visual representation of the value streams, so everyone involved in the meaningful experience can contribute their perspective to the design or improvement of the experience.

The Meaningful Healthcare Experience Design Map draws inspiration from a number of sources. It is formatted similarly to the customer journey map used in design thinking in that it incorporates emotions as well the activities associated with each of the value streams into the map of the process. The design map also brings the influence of a service blueprint into the map by incorporating the healthcare worker's value stream as an important element in the overall development of a meaningful experience. The patient's activities and the healthcare worker's activities follow the sequence of the organizational process steps that are similar to the flowchart of industrial quality. However, it is important to recognize that the activities for the patient and the healthcare worker as part of their value stream begin before the point where the two merge with the organization's value stream to create the meaningful experience and continue after it.

Meaningful Experience Design Map Name:											
Time/Day											
Factors: Proxemics, Power, Generation											
Care Recipient Beliefs, Values, Principles											
Care Recipient Emotions											
Care Recipient Actions											
Organizational Process Steps											
Organizational Beliefs, Values, Principles											
Worker Actions											
Worker Emotions											
Worker Beliefs, Values, Principles											
Factors: Proxemics, Power, Generation											

Figure 11.1   Meaningful Healthcare Experience Design Map. This map is a combination of the customer service journey map, the service blueprint map, and a process map. It includes space for the activities, beliefs, values, and principles for each value stream; additional factors such as proxemics, power, and generations; and space for noting emotions for the value streams of people receiving and delivering care. In the center is the organizational process map around which the other two flow with space for beliefs, values, and principles.

Though meaningful experience design draws from these various sources, it is a unique approach that is specifically designed for American healthcare. This uniqueness includes a recognition that recipients of care, healthcare workers, and healthcare organizations approach healthcare with beliefs, values, and principles that must find a point of alignment to create a meaningful experience. These meaning in life values for the recipients of care and the healthcare worker and the organizational values are identified as stories are shared reflecting each perspective. The experience-based co-design approach that has become a part of the patient experience movement of healthcare is represented in the sharing of these stories in order to facilitate awareness and understanding by everyone involved. It is important when considering the meaningfulness of a healthcare experience from all the perspectives become part of the mapping process.

The design map documents a number of aspects of the three value streams that are important. The beliefs, values, and principles that influence the three streams are documented along with the steps of the process for the people receiving care, the healthcare worker, and the organization. It is important to recognize that different beliefs, values, and principles are engaged at different points in the process. Along with these influences in the value stream, the map tracks the specific activities of the people involved at each step in the organizational process to show not only the organizational process but also how those steps are interpreted and reflected in the activities of the worker and the patient.

The emotions experienced by the recipients of care and the healthcare workers at each step along the organization's process are documented for two reasons. The first is to assess their reaction to the actions required by the organization. The second reason is to determine their reaction to the beliefs, values, and principles expressed at each step by the organization and by the other person. If the influences of the three value streams are aligned, then there should be a sense of meaning between the three entities and a sense that the experience is progressing in a way that is either acceptable or at least understandable. By comparing the emotions of the people receiving care to the people delivering care and the alignment of the beliefs, values, and principles of the three value streams at each step, specific opportunities for creating more meaningful experiences can be identified at points where these influences are not in alignment.

Using the map to analyze the experience of the healthcare worker and the recipients of care in the context of the organization's process offers the opportunity to bring together the three perspectives and to identify points where there may be real lack of alignment and find ways to improve the alignment to facilitate a more meaningful experience for both the worker and patient. These discussions provide insights into the ways in which the merger of the values streams affected the patient and healthcare worker that they may not have realized. Often the reactions of people during a healthcare experience arise from beliefs or values or even principles that they may not have realized were involved in the situation. By bringing these to the surface and discussing their relevance to the situation, the participants can develop a deeper understanding of their own thoughts and feelings and move toward creating a more meaningful experience.

The organizational process is in the center of the map because it forms the interface between the healthcare worker and the people receiving care. The map provides space for documentation of the steps in the value stream and the time tracker at the top of the page provides an indication of the amount of time required for each step. Below each process step is the space for documenting the beliefs, values, and principles that were incorporated into the overall process and into each step in the process. Since it is ultimately the organizational process that creates the context for the experience, it is important that thoughts behind each step in the process are identified. These thoughts may offer important insights into whether the steps are actually useful as well as how well the steps align with the value streams of the worker and the patient. It may be in these thoughts that are in the background to the organizational process design that the key issues are hidden.

The sources of information about the organizational process beliefs, values, and principles begin with the original documentation of its design and any policies and procedure describing its operation. It may be that there are existing documents that provide quantitative as well as qualitative information about the process itself and its design from past minutes of committees and other groups. Interviewing leadership responsible for the process may provide additional insight into the steps as originally designed and as modified over time. Critically important in the research about the process is any indication of how this process and particularly the steps involved flow out of the beliefs of both past and current leadership as well as the organization's values and principles that guide operations. Documenting these provides a basis for evaluating the alignment between the organization and the workers and recipients of care and their views about the process. Once the organizational process and the influences in its value stream are captured on the map, this provides the basis for discussions with the healthcare worker and the patient.

The healthcare worker is an important source not only about the way the process is currently operating but about the beliefs, values, and principles that underlie it. Asking healthcare workers to provide their assessment of the organizational process and value stream in relation to their work provides an important source of information on the way the process actually is performed. Encouraging them to tell stories about their experiences with the process and with people receiving care, patients provides valuable information on the beliefs, values, and principles that underlie the worker's approach to the process. Observations can also pick up important information about the process and the worker's engagement with it. Other sources include general organizational information such as human resources data on absences, turnovers, and exit interviews of workers involved with the process. Risk management documentation of complaints and incidents may reveal important patterns that create potential harm for workers and patients but which are neither seeing nor acknowledging. Compliance issues may also provide useful information. Above all, asking the workers to share not only their experiences but their feelings and emotions related to each step in the process provides valuable insights that then become source material for the future co-design of the experience.

Since meaning is created through the shared experiences of everyone involved, all of the stories and all of the voices are important. In terms of the fulfillment of the promise which is built into the delivery of healthcare services, it is the recipient of care who is most dependent upon the structures designed by the organization and the healthcare worker and most able to provide information that leads to the design of meaningful experiences for all concerned. Like the healthcare worker, the patient's value stream precedes the point where the three merge. These preliminary activities often set up expectations. In order to capture the origin of the beliefs, values, and principles incorporated into the value stream of the patient, the full story of the patient's experience is needed even if it begins years before.

As someone outside of the organization who is a member of the community, the patient brings the culture of the community into the experience and is in turn shaped by the values and perspectives of the community. Capturing not only the activities of the patient throughout the value stream but also the emotions that are engendered at each step offers indications on how meaningful the recipients of care finds the current process and what steps are most likely to represent opportunities for improvement. As with the healthcare worker, the voices of the people receiving care come through interviews and stories and are supplemented by observations.

Body language and emotions offer important insights into how the patient perceives what is happening but also how closely it matches what was anticipated. Additional sources of patient information include surveys that patients send in and any complaints or suggestions about the process. All of these combined with information about the socio-demographics of the patient provide useful information.

As information is gathered and documented in the meaningful experience map, it forms the basis for the co-design process that follows. Once all three value streams are documented, representatives from all three perspectives can come together to review and evaluate the information that has been gathered. In the evaluation process, the stories will be shared and the discussion of alignment of value streams will be an important focus. Are the organization's beliefs or values or principles the same as those of the healthcare workers and the people receiving care or are there significant differences. As the value streams merged into one stream in the organization, what was the meaning that emerged out of the combined stream for the recipients of care and the healthcare worker as they experienced each other and the organizational process? Out of these and other questions, the representatives of the three value streams are looking for points of consensus and points of divergence in the fundamental perspectives that they each bring to the discussion.

Ultimately as they share their thoughts and feelings and hopes, their reflections on the meaningfulness of the convergence of the three value streams and what emerged from the convergence into a single stream will guide the experience design effort. This same approach is used in experience-based co-design of the delivery of healthcare services throughout the organization. Through these efforts, it is hoped that healthcare will become a meaningful experience for people receiving care and workers and support quality of life and meaning in life for everyone who comes to the organization for care (Figure 11.1).

IMPLEMENTING MEANINGFUL HEALTHCARE EXPERIENCE DESIGN IN ORGANIZATIONS

3

Chapter 12

Meaningful Experience Design as the Foundation of Healthcare Quality

As American healthcare has evolved in the early twenty-first century, it has grown more complex. This complexity has shifted the foundation for producing high-quality healthcare from the development of facilities and technology and the quantification of processes to the creation of meaningful experiences by the people delivering care and the people receiving care as they interact in the context of healthcare organizations. The construction of healthcare facilities and the development of new technology continue to be an important part of healthcare, but they in themselves will not produce the quality of healthcare necessary to meet the needs of the future. Their purpose lies in supporting the creation of meaningful experiences as the basis for achieving high-quality healthcare.

The relational basis for healing and healthcare was minimized as hospital-centered technology became the focus in the twentieth century. Quality was equated with increasing technological sophistication and intensification. However, as America achieved unparalleled levels of mechanization in its hospitals, it was found that quality did not increase with the number of computers, smart pumps, MRIs, and scanners. Additional layers of technology added cost but did not produce commensurate levels of quality. The addition of more and more technology increased the level of complexity and increased the potential for harm to patients and healthcare workers. Electronic information systems diverted the attention of the people delivering care from their patients to data input in computers. The meaningfulness of the work diminished and the ability to engage with the people receiving care and to think outside of the programmed clinical support systems. This reduced the capacity to anticipate problems and to respond effectively to reduce harm.

Having come to the realization that layers of technology increase cost without necessarily producing the quality sufficient to warrant the high cost, healthcare organizations began to look for ways to reduce costs even as they sought to understand the nature of healthcare quality. The number of places in communities and around the country where healthcare can be obtained has expanded enormously while at the same time the importance of finding ways to connect the information systems in the many locations delivering care has also become more important. Many of these changes find expression within the context of population health as the focus of healthcare organizations and payers. With the diversity of locations, services, demographics, and care providers, a crucial question becomes how is the delivery of healthcare services to be coordinated to provide the patient and family with the care that they need in a way that they can access and afford it and provide them with the information to help them sustain or improve their health in the future.

In many communities, hospitals and other healthcare providers are partnering to create a continuum of care in which the patient's information is accessible from multiple points in the continuum, and there is support to guide the patient to the appropriate services as they are needed and to follow the patient until they are at their baseline or sustainable level of care. Within the context of this continuum, the patient and the care providers regardless of where the care is delivered need to the healthcare experience designed so that it is meaningful to them. The meaningfulness of the healthcare experience plays a significant role in the willingness of the patient and the healthcare worker to desire to participate again in the future but also to ensure that the patient is willing to follow the care plan that is agreed to in the experience.

As American healthcare evolves out of the hospitals as the single place for care and expands to form a continuum of care in partnership with businesses and agencies in communities and across the country, the design of a meaningful healthcare experience becomes of paramount importance for ensuring that patients, healthcare workers, and organizations operate from a common foundation. The foundation is created as patients, workers, and organizations come together to create meaningful healthcare experiences based on awareness and respect for the beliefs, values, principles, and activities that shape and influence their separate value streams. Out of this awareness, the blending of the three value streams during a healthcare experience occurs within the context of an organizational process that has been designed to align the influences within the three value streams so that they blend in a way to produce a meaningful experience for everyone involved.

Whether defined as a hospital, regional healthcare system, or a national organization, the characteristics associated with complex systems have become important considerations in the delivery of healthcare. These systems are complex because they are made up of numerous points that are connected and rely on information within the system to coordinate their activities continuously. All the points of contact need to share a common vision or understanding of how they relate to each other and to the world at large in order to maintain the identity of the system. Part of the reason for the importance of the connections and the common sense of the system among all the participants is that the system is constantly adapting to changes in its environment.

As services are delivered and patients and families engage with the system, the system responds and reacts to the interactions that occur. These interactions result in information that is shared within the system and all the connected locations and individuals need to be able to respond to the interaction wherever they occur. Since the number of interactions that occur between the complex system and its environment may be very large and may happen very quickly, the individuals involved must make decisions about how they are to respond without waiting for approval or supervision. This ability to adapt quickly without guidance from a central leadership is important to the survival of complex adaptive systems. It requires that all the participants have strong awareness and understanding of the goals of the system the ways in which they facilitate the systems response to the environment.

Functioning as a complex adaptive system is challenging for American healthcare even it offers opportunities for finding new ways to meet the needs of patients and healthcare workers. The structure that is still the most common in hospitals and healthcare organizations originated in the early twentieth century as an outgrowth of scientific management. It is a hierarchical structure in which the prestige and power are placed at the top of the organization and the rest of the organization takes its direction and reports its activities from the top. The organization is divided into departments based on reporting status to various ranks of management. The reporting process flows down from the top in the form of directives and requirements and flows up in the form of reports on the progress in meeting the directives and requirements. This bureaucracy is designed to promote accountability and to hold individuals personally responsible for results through a system of individuals who have responsibility.

Complex adaptive systems, however, require accountability that is based on the acceptance of a common mission and vision and values as the guidance and the willingness of everyone in the system to shape their work around those common values and beliefs. Since the changes in the complex system occur so rapidly that there is no time to refer it to a central leadership of a bureaucracy, the individuals who are at the interface with the environment must adapt on their own and maintain the consistency to the overall mission and vision. This is challenging for American healthcare and is an area in which meaningful experience design plays a key role.

Part of the reorientation to quality that is required in a complex adaptive system is the ability to understand how quality is created within the context of a meaningful healthcare experience. Quantification was the focus of healthcare quality in late twentieth-century healthcare because this was the basis for quality in manufacturing and manufacturing was the model. If specific activities or outcomes occurred at the right frequency, then quality was delivered. Reducing healthcare quality to such simplistic metrics was part of a learning curve for healthcare and the result was an increasing awareness that this approach was not useful. Patient safety failures dramatically demonstrated that as healthcare processes increased in complexity, the quantification of quality into simplistic measures offered little benefit. This approach resulted in significant waste of time and effort by healthcare workers and governance and was demoralizing in that it did not produce the anticipated results. The quality of care in the sociotechnical world of healthcare could not be converted to these simple metrics.

Complex adaptive systems incorporate sophisticated technology, but their true form lies in the relationships between the individuals that connected by the technology. Meaningful experience design becomes significantly more important within complex adaptive systems due to the role that beliefs, values, and principles play in the way the organization, worker, and people receiving care interact. Due to the rapid pace of healthcare interactions in complex systems, the healthcare worker and the recipients of care often face situations in which creativity and the ability to solve problems are required. As people engage with each other in environments that are rapidly changing, the unanticipated is very likely to occur. When it does, the healthcare worker and the people receiving care need to be able to creatively interact to solve problems based on a common understanding of their beliefs, values, and principles. For this reason, the co-design of healthcare experiences through the use of meaningful experience mapping uses information from the people receiving care, healthcare workers, and the organization to create the foundation for solving problems and designing experiences to be meaningful to everyone involved.

In designing meaningful experiences for people receiving care and people delivering care, the measures that are developed for assessing the quality of the experiences are an important consideration. How does the organization assess whether the experiences of people receiving care are meaningful to them? How are the experiences of the people delivering care evaluated from a quality perspective? And, finally, the organizational process designed to deliver the services to the people receiving care must contribute to the meaningfulness of the experience. How is this to be determined?

In the simplest terms, the most important measure is the meaningfulness of the experience to two people involved. Within the concept of meaningfulness, the alignment of the beliefs, values, and principles of the three value streams that compose the experience are important process measures that are evaluated at each step in the delivery of the service. Following the delivery of the service and the completion of the interactions of the people involved, the outcome measures for the meaningful experience focus on the willingness of the people receiving care and the people delivering care to repeat the experience. The organizational process for delivering the service may have measures that quantify certain characteristics of the service, but these measures are important only as they relate to the meaningfulness of the experience for the people receiving care and the people delivering care. If the organization, itself, needs to quantify certain aspects of the service for its own purposes that is an internal quality assurance measure rather than a measure of quality in relation to the healthcare worker and the recipient of care.

Meaningful healthcare experience design is foundational to the development of new ways to deliver healthcare services and it requires new ways to understand and measure quality. As Avedis Donabedian, an early healthcare quality pioneer, so insightfully expressed it, "Systems awareness and systems design are important for health professionals, but they are not enough. They are enabling mechanisms only. It is the ethical dimensions of individuals that are essential to a system's success. Ultimately, the secret of quality is love. You have to love your patient, you have to love your profession, you have to love your God. If you have love, you can then work backward to monitor and improve the system" (Mullan, 2001, p. 140). Creating meaningful experiences for people receiving care and people delivering care is an important step forward in fulfilling the true measure of quality expressed by Dr. Donabedian.

Chapter 13

Aligning Organizational Structures for Meaningful Experience Design

Meaningful healthcare experience design focuses on helping the people who receive care and the people who deliver care to understand what is most meaningful to them as they engage with each other in creating a healthcare experience. The source of meaning in a healthcare experience is the same as the source of meaning in life. Psychologists view meaning in life as consisting of the components of comprehension, purpose and significance, or mattering (Martela & Steger, 2016; George & Park, 2016). When individuals feel that these areas in their lives are meaningful for them, then they experience a sense of well-being and meaningfulness about their life.

For the purpose of meaning in healthcare, these components have been simplified to beliefs, values, and principles but the goal is the same. Organizations design or improve healthcare services processes through quality improvement programs and structures. Healthcare experiences that people find meaningful support meaningfulness in their lives by aligning the beliefs, values, and principles of the people receiving care and the people delivering care with the actual work to be done. Meaningful experiences can be defined simply as experiences that the people involved are willing to repeat.

The initial step in meaningful design is for the organization to take seriously the discovery of the beliefs, values, and principles of the people involved in the care processes. This begins with identifying existing structures in the organization that can be used to coordinate the design or improvement of healthcare experiences with organizational processes. Management at the organizational and department level needs to be a part of this as well since the beliefs, values, and principles of the organization are manifested in the organizational process that forms the context for the interaction between the people.

As has been discussed, meaningful experience design focuses on the blending of three value streams. Within each of these streams are activities, beliefs, values, and principles that influence the value streams and contribute to the creation of the meaningful experience as the streams converge. Though there are a variety of ways in which support for meaningful experience design can be structured, the three value streams must be addressed as well as responding to other factors that influence them.

First, the organization needs a way to bring together the people receiving care to express their beliefs, values, and principles and to describe their experiences. Second, there needs to be a way for the people delivering the care to express their beliefs, values, and principles about the work they perform and their interactions with the people receiving care and other workers. Third, the organization must have a structure where the beliefs, values, and principles of the organization are actively discussed and applied to the design of processes. Finally, a structure is needed to respond to the conflicts between the beliefs, values, and principles that influence each of the value streams and to find ways to align these influences so that the experiences of the people involved are meaningful and consistent with the needs of the organization.

Structure for People Receiving Care

People who have had healthcare experiences, whether good or not, find it difficult in many instances to express precisely what happened and what they would like to do to make it better. At the same time, there are people who are angry about their experience and to verbalize their feelings and reactions to their care and then walk away. Meaningful experience design requires time and effort to think deeply about the people involved and their health.

Some of the basic issues that need to be addressed in developing a structure that enables people who have had care to collaborate with people who can make changes in organizations include creating points of contact to facilitate conversations with people; helping people to express their thoughts and feelings about their care in a way that helps them to uncover the beliefs, values, and principles that were part of what they experienced; and finally, to engage with others in imagining what type of experience would be meaningful for them. This approach to engagement with people who have received care is challenging because they focus on the raw experiences or as they occurred without analyzing the underlying elements that influenced their own reactions.

One way to support the participation of patients in the co-design of meaningful experiences in healthcare is through a patient and family advisory council (PFAC). Massachusetts General formed one of the earliest PFACs, the Children Family Advisory Council, in 1999. In 2010, the State of Massachusetts required hospitals to establish PFACs. By 2015, over 2000 healthcare organizations had PFACs (Wachenheim, 2015).

PFACs are an important first step in creating an ongoing dialogue between those who receive care and those who deliver care. Organizational leadership will need to recognize and support the effort necessary to set up the PFAC and recruit and train members as well as support staff. Composed of people who have received care and family members who supported people who received care, PFACs require a selection process that includes information about the interested person and an interview process. PFACs also have hospital representatives as members. PFAC members are trained as volunteers and are oriented to the structure and operation of the organization. The selection process focuses on the interest in the hospital of potential members, their desire to work to improve the organization, their willingness to promote more meaningful experiences for themselves and future patients, and their ability to donate time to the organization. Through regularly scheduled meetings, PFACs develop a familiarity with the organization and between the members. This helps to provide an environment within which the discussion of beliefs, values, and principles can become a regular part of meetings.

The members of the PFAC form an important resource for the organization by providing people who have received care to offer their views and insights as members of organization committees and in improvement initiatives. As the organization begins to take seriously the development of meaningful experience design, PFAC members will be asked to participate in the ethics committee. The ethics committee serves an important role in the design and improvement of meaningful healthcare experience by providing expertise in recognizing and addressing conflicts between beliefs, values, and principles that may undermine the meaningfulness of experiences. PFAC members offer the voice of the people who have received care to clarify their beliefs, values, and principles and to promote understanding on how these may conflict with people delivering care and the organization. Through this exchange and the assistance of the ethics committee, the organization can find ways to reduce or eliminate the conflicts by aligning the beliefs, values, and principles of everyone involved. PFAC members are also able to speak to the conflicts with organizational beliefs, values, and principle that may not be recognized by the organizational leadership.

As members of the quality committee and as members of the community, representatives from the PFAC have an opportunity to provide important insights into the way in which processes are perceived by people receiving care. As the organization seeks ways to create more meaningful experiences, the PFAC members can offer suggestions and recommendations and promote dialogue by sharing experiences. They can also bring out beliefs and values associated with the processes under consideration that the organization may not realize are important to the people receiving care. By engaging with PFAC members as part of the ongoing improvement of care, the organization's leadership can expand their awareness of the concerns of those receiving care and the views of the PFAC itself on the performance of the organization.

Perhaps even more importantly, PFAC members can support other people who have received care in helping them to express their beliefs, values, and principles as participants in efforts to improve the meaningful experiences of particular groups of patients. It is in this liaison role between the organization and the people receiving care that the PFAC members represent an important voice in shaping care that will be meaningful for people in the future. Because of their role as members of the community as well in the organization, they can help others articulate their thoughts about their experiences as they are perceived by the community. Being able to create an environment where people who are unfamiliar with the organization feel that they have someone who understands their perspective can be a tremendous help in encouraging them to openly and honestly express their beliefs, values, and principles. This will enable the improvement effort to move forward more quickly and with a stronger sense that the people who received care are able to relate their views without concern that someone will criticize their comments.

Structure for People Delivering Care

A critically important part of meaningful experience design is the alignment of the beliefs, values, and principles of the people delivering care with those of people receiving care. Assuming that the people delivering care have the same fundamental beliefs, values, and principles as the organization would be an unfortunate assumption that can undermine the effort to create a more meaningful experience. Creating a structure that supports the people who deliver care in participating in the work of identifying the beliefs, values, and principles that are part of the process can be challenging. As employees, they may feel that honestly expressing their views can be interpreted as being disloyal. They may fear that they will hurt their relationships with other workers or their prospects for future advancement if they speak honestly when there are conflicts.

The value stream for healthcare workers differs from that of the people receiving care. The people delivering care as part of the organization are also seeking to find meaning in work as well as meaning in life through their value stream. Meaning in work adds a new dimension of significance to their value stream. Significance in meaning in work consists of two components. It comes from a sense of personal significance the workers find through self-realization and a broader purpose in their work. Self-realization comes from the autonomy and freedom to shape the work and deliver the services in the manner that they feel is meaningful. They also seek significance in the broader purpose of their work that comes from the way it contributes to the well-being of the people who receive care but also in viewing the work as a way to support their families and making their community a better place.

An important part of the creation of meaningful healthcare experiences is the recognition of factors that are hidden within the actual processes of work that nonetheless threaten the meaningfulness of the experience. These factors may include elements of the sociotechnical nature of the work in which technology has been implemented that changes the organizational process and this in turn changes the workflow of those delivering care. Though it may not be apparent to those unfamiliar with the workflow, the introduction of technology can create a variety of stresses that challenge the worker's ability to deliver services in a way that supports their sense of meaning in their work. Workers may experience moral stress in trying to fulfill competing demands on their time and attention (Berlinger, 2016). Seeking to alleviate the stress may cause the work to develop unethical workarounds or unsafe changes in the process in order to achieve the required goals. The exercise of positional or professional power by individuals in the department or organization may create impediments to the worker finding meaning in the work or meaning in the experience with the results that people receiving care also do not find the experience meaningful. Moral stress represents a serious conflict in values, beliefs, or principles that can hinder any efforts to create more meaningful experiences. It may also prevent those who are delivering care from being open and honest about underlying issues and lead to ineffective improvement efforts.

Most organizations have groups of employees who are involved in promoting workplace safety. These employees may be a valuable resource in working with other employees who are participating in meaningful experience design. It is also possible that representatives from various departments may be brought together to form a taskforce and to be trained in the basics of meaningful experience design to serve in helping other employees who are involved in working on the redesign of processes. This group could become a subgroup of the quality committee that can be called upon to assist as needed based on their profession and experiences. The training will involve developing an understanding of the tools that are used in meaningful experience design and a deeper understanding of the importance of the alignment of the beliefs, values, and principles as part of value streams and the convergence of value streams as meaningful experiences.

Organizational Structure

The quality program in its generic form in most healthcare organizations includes a plan for organizational improvement approved by the governing body. The plan requires senior management to appoint a committee or a council with approval of the governing body to oversee the implementation of the plan for improvement throughout the organization and to receive reports on the improvements on a regular basis for reporting to the governing body and agencies. The plan typically sets forth the way in which the organization would make improvement on a continuous basis. This would include the reporting structure from the council to the various functions and departments in the organization and then to individual improvement efforts and projects. The plan described the way in which the mission, vision, and values of the organization are to be operationalized in the improvement efforts and the methodology for improvement that would be used to ensure consistency throughout the organization. The frequency of reporting on the results of the improvements to the oversight committee and the governing body would also be included in the plan.

For most organizations, the Quality Council and improvement structure offer a very viable structure for supporting meaningful experience design. The Council usually includes senior management and reports to the Board. The members are well versed in improvement methodologies and are familiar with the organization on a global scale due to the wide range of reporting on quality issues. The committee is supported by the quality or performance improvement staff and has additional administrative resources should the need arise. In most respects, the Quality Council is the easiest and most logical place for the organization to operate its part of the meaningful experience design structure. Adding members to the Quality Council from the ethics committee members as well as PFAC will be an important step in preparing the Quality Council for meaningful experience design. Patient representatives can be drawn from the PFAC to provide assistance in understanding patients' perspective on beliefs, values, and principles. Finally, representative members of the ethics committee should be included on the improvement committee. These representatives will be able to facilitate Quality Council understanding and engagement with conflicts that may result from lack of alignment in beliefs, values, and principles.

The most challenging aspect for the quality committee in anchoring the meaningful experience design effort lies in the understanding of the beliefs, values, and principles that the organization contributes to the process value stream. While the mission, vision and values of the organization may be clearly displayed and widely recognized, the actual operation of these fundamental values in a value stream may be unclear. It may also be difficult for the members of the quality committee to recognize or accept that the organization's beliefs, values, and principles may actually be in conflict with those of the people receiving care or even those delivering care. An important initial task for the committee will be to focus on the beliefs, values, and principles as the essential elements of the design of organizational processes. This is important because meaningful experience design is based on the alignment of the organization's fundamental beliefs, values, and principles that are part of the process value stream with those of the value streams of the healthcare workers and the people receiving care. This represents a significant change for most healthcare organizations and a challenge for the improvement structure. Strategic objectives are often identified by healthcare organizations to operationalize its mission and vision. These objectives define what the organization hopes to accomplish within a specific period of time. It is within the context of the mission, vision, values, and strategic objectives that the underlying beliefs, values, and principles can be found.

For meaningful experience design to become part of the improvement structure of the organization, the improvement plan and the council or committee that oversees the plan must accept specific definitions for the beliefs, values, and principles that are to be identified in the design and improvement efforts as inherent in any organizational processes. The most difficult aspect of this modification to the improvement plan for the committee will be to understand itself and the organization sufficiently to be able to identify these influences. Since the beliefs, values, and principles that are chosen for inclusion in the plan will be operationalized through experience mapping throughout the organization, it is important that the selection represent the views of management and the organization. As part of departmental improvements or larger improvement initiatives that involve process changes to design meaningful experiences, the mapping of organizational beliefs, values, and principles will start with those identified in the plan and then adapt them to the specific process design that is the focus of the improvement.

It is important that the improvement committee recognizes the significance of the three value streams as equally important to the design of meaningful experiences. There will always be a tendency within the organization to view the organizational process value stream as the most important because it defines the steps in the actual processes for the organization to use to perform the work. Though the organizational process creates the context for the meaningful experience to occur, the process value stream will be interpreted by the healthcare worker and will be blended with the healthcare worker's value stream and that of the patient to form the meaningful experience. The ultimate goal of the meaningful experience design is for the organizational process to function in a way that support the healthcare worker and the patient in finding alignment between their beliefs, values, and principles as they work together to accomplish the steps in the organizational process. Even if the steps are fulfilled, if the worker and patient were not able to align the influences in their value stream with those of the organization, then the experience will likely not be meaningful and the process will have failed in its primary purpose.

As meaningful experience design initiatives at the department or project level come to the improvement committee for review and evaluation, it will be important for the committee to carefully consider how the three value streams blend to form the one value stream of the meaningful experience. A key part of this evaluation will be a review of the value stream mapping that incorporates the activities, beliefs, values, and principles of all three value streams. Understanding the alignment of the influences within each of the value streams and any conflicts that may have occurred and how they were resolved provides valuable insights for the committee to consider. The healthcare worker representatives and recipient of care representatives may find important points within the review of the meaningful experience map that can be applied in other areas and that may be helpful for the PFAC to review. The ethics committee representative may find that the conflicts between beliefs, values, and principles between the three value streams offer opportunities for the ethical evaluations and possible recommendations.

It is possible that in the process of designing meaningful experiences that the people involved in the design work may need assistance. The improvement committee can help to facilitate the provision of additional resources for the work. The ethics committee can provide ethics consultations to help to resolve issues concerning lack of alignment between the three value streams that cannot seem to be resolved by the team working on it. The PFAC can assist with issues related to the people receiving care. Issues pertaining to conflicts between the value streams may be referred to other committees or departments as needed. The healthcare worker can appeal to improvement committee for human resources assistance or other resources if needed to address conflicts between the worker value stream and the organizational value stream.

Meaningful experience design is different from the improvement work in the past that drew its inspiration from industrial quality. It includes the steps in the process and the satisfaction with the outcomes of a service, but the focus is on the meaningful experience that emerges out of the convergence of the three values streams. The design involves the actual co-design of the experience by the healthcare worker and people receiving care within the structure of the organizational process as the service is created, delivered, and received by the people involved. This is much deeper level than most improvement projects, but it is the level that is most appropriate to the intensely personal nature of the production of healthcare and receipt of healthcare.

Since healthcare services are evaluated by the people receiving care based on the way the care was delivered as well as by the result of the care, the people delivering care and the recipients of care must have an alignment of their beliefs, values, and principles sufficient to enable them to share an experience that is meaningful and that they are willing to repeat in the future. Understanding how to work at this level of engagement will require improvement committees and organizations to develop new perspectives about the work of improvement that delves deeper into the hearts and minds of workers and patients.

Co-designing meaningful healthcare experiences is the work of quality and improvement for the twenty-first century and it will challenge the ability of organizations to stretch to accomplish it. Improvement efforts to date by healthcare organizations have not been generally viewed as achieving the success that is needed to deliver high quality of care at affordable costs. Meaningful experience design pushes improvement efforts into new areas with the hope that by recognizing the true nature of healing as an experience and designing experiences to be meaningful that healthcare can finally make real progress in realizing its goal of truly meeting the needs of patient and healthcare workers (Figure 13.1).

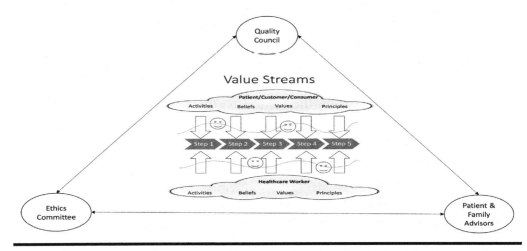

Figure 13.1   Organizational structures supporting meaningful healthcare experience. The triangle represents the relationship between the structures in healthcare organizations that can help to create and support meaningful experiences in the interactions that occur within the context of processes. The Quality Council is the source of the design and operation of the industrial process in the center of the figure and the work activities of the healthcare worker within that process. The Patient and Family Advisors work with the healthcare workers to help them understand how the patient/customer views and experiences the process and the interaction with the healthcare worker. The ethics committee helps to uncover and explain the values, beliefs, and principles (represented in the clouds) that are influencing both the patient/customer's experience and the healthcare worker's experience as they interact in the process. The process inside the triangle has three parts or three value streams: the numbered steps in the center represent an idealized process that incorporates all the values of industrial quality; the patient/customer cloud represents all that the patient/customer brings to the engagement with the industrial process in the center; the healthcare worker cloud represents all that the healthcare worker brings to the engagement with the industrial process; and the arrows crossing the process flow represent the interactions between the patient/customer and healthcare worker as they meet at different point along the path of the process.

Chapter 14

Introducing Meaningful Healthcare Experience Design into Healthcare Organizations

Steps	Activities
1	Senior leadership appoints a small Taskforce to explore meaningful experience design and to develop a proposal for leadership to review and approve
2	Integrate organizational structures to support meaningful experience design
3	Develop training materials for meaningful experience design
4	Identify opportunities for using meaningful experience design
5	Initiate the first meaningful experience design project
6	Complete the initial meaningful experience design project
7	Report on the initial project and lessons learned
8	Improve the meaningful experience design methodology
9	Train more groups and initiate new design and improvement projects
10	Conduct quarterly and annual reviews of the program

Step 1 – Senior Leadership Appoints a Small Taskforce to Explore Meaningful Experience Design and to Develop a Proposal for Leadership to Review and Approve

Meaningful experience design is a new approach to design and improve healthcare services. As with any significant change in an organization, it needs the approval and support of the senior management. This is particularly true when the focus of the improvement is on developing experiences that the people receiving care and the people delivering care find meaningful. An integral part of this process involves beliefs, values, and principles that the leadership supports and expects to be represented in the processes that the organization designs to deliver services.

The membership of the Taskforce should be a relatively small group but needs to incorporate certain perspectives to accomplish the work. At a minimum, the membership should include a senior manager, a quality representative, a patient experience representative, a medical staff representative, a nursing service representative, a social services representative, and a member of the ethics committee. Since the work of the Taskforce will require time away from existing responsibilities, there should be support for these members to take time away from their routine responsibilities to participate in this work. The amount of time required for the Taskforce to complete its work will vary.

In developing the proposal for senior leadership, the Taskforce needs to consider whether the basic structures exist within the organization to implement meaningful experience design. The three essential structures are a viable quality program that includes an organization-wide improvement plan and reporting process; a committee or program for engaging with patients and recipients of care to involve them in improving services and experiences; and an ethics committee or ethical consultation program in which an experienced group of people assists with resolving ethical conflicts in clinical services and organizational practices.

Critical points that the Taskforce needs to consider as it reviews the literature and evaluates meaningful healthcare experience design for the organization involve the following questions:

■ Is there evidence that the organization has a history of progressively increasing the level of engagement with people receiving care with the goal of involving them in improving quality?

- Is there evidence that the organization has a culture in which the people delivering care are encouraged to actively participate in quality improvement and their views and concerns are solicited and respected?
- Has the organization's management demonstrated over a period of time a strong commitment to its ethical principles and moral values in its corporate compliance practices, in its relations with people receiving and delivering care, and in its clinical practices?
- Is there an agreement in the Taskforce that the meaningfulness of a healthcare experience is a valid measure of the quality of healthcare services?
- Can the Taskforce members agree that creating meaningful healthcare experiences represents a worthwhile organizational goal because it strengthens the relationship between the organization and the recipients of care, creates a work environment that promotes retention of healthcare workers, and contributes to the well-being of the people involved in the experience?

Once the Taskforce has reviewed the literature concerning meaningful experience design, assessed the availability of supporting organizational structures, and considered the critical questions about the organization's culture in relation to the meaningful experience design program, then the views of the Taskforce about pursuing this type of program should be presented to senior management. If the proposal is to move forward and senior management supports the initiative, then the people assigned to implement the meaningful healthcare experience design program as a part of the overall quality program can move on to the following steps.

Step 2 – Integrate Organizational Structures to Support Meaningful Experience Design

Meaningful experience design is an improvement methodology and needs to be incorporated into the organization's performance improvement program. The plan should be modified to describe the meaningful experience program as a methodology and describe the way it works as a component of the overall program. The initiation and reporting of meaningful experience design projects should be consistent with other improvement projects.

The plan should include a description of the alignment of the three structures of the quality committee, the ethics committee, and the patient experience or engagement committee as essential elements of the meaningful experience program. It should specify that representatives from each of the committees are members of the other committees. This representation signifies the integration of quality, ethics, and patient experience as essential elements in support of meaningful experience design.

The plan should also include the acceptance and use of the meaningful healthcare experience design map as an improvement tool in the organization. There should be a description of the tool and the way it is used to support the meaningful experience design. It should include the provision that the map is to be used in a manner similar to other quality improvement tools and techniques.

Once the performance improvement plan has been modified to include the meaningful experience design elements, it should be submitted to senior management and to the three committees that serve as support for the methodology for their review and approval. This is important because the methodology requires the active participation of the three support structures in the work of meaningful experience design.

Step 3 – Develop Training Materials for Meaningful Experience Design

Developing materials to use in guiding the work of meaningful experience design is the next step after the structure has been set up. Even for people with experience in healthcare quality improvement and process improvement, the new elements in meaningful experience design require additional time and training to ensure everyone understands them and can work effectively together. The important elements requiring training are as follows.

Description of the Overview of Meaningful Experience Design

Meaningful experience design has distinctive features that need explanation for the people engaged in it. Elements of the overview include the definition of meaningful experience design; the reporting processes through the quality structure; the interpretations of beliefs, values, and principles as influences in value streams; the role of the ethics committee and patient engagement committee to support this work; the way in which people delivering care and the people receive care work together to map the value streams that form the meaningful experience; and the ways that changes are approved and implemented.

Meaning, Beliefs, Values, and Principles

Of all the elements in meaningful experience design, beliefs, values, and principles have the greatest potential for confusing people. It is not that these terms are unusual to most people. They are terms that are widely used in daily conversation. However, these terms have specific meanings associated with this improvement methodology which makes them different from common conversational usage. The struggle that is most likely to occur regarding these terms is the role they play in the way an organization delivers care and how they contribute to the concept of a meaningful experience.

The training related to these terms should provide a brief discussion of the background including the uniqueness of healthcare experience in life, the work in Positive psychology on meaning in life, and the application of this work to meaning in healthcare and meaningful experience design. Part of the training will be to provide simple definitions of these terms as interpreted by the organization. This is an important aspect of meaningful experience design, and it is important that everyone understands what these terms signify. This book provides the information needed to create training materials on meaning, beliefs, values, and principles.

People Delivering Care

Training should provide an understanding of the role of people who work within the organization as people delivering care and their part in the design and creation of meaningful healthcare experiences. This training should include the concept of the value stream of the people delivering care; the way their beliefs, values, and principles influence the value stream; and the way their view of meaning in work influence it.

An important part of the training related to the people delivering care is to explain their role in interpreting the influences in the organizational process value stream as part of their interaction with the people receiving care. It should also include a description of the creation of the meaningful experience through the convergence of the value streams and the alignment of the beliefs, values, and principles of the people involved.

People Receiving Care

As with the people delivering care, the people receiving care represent a broad designation that includes anyone who is the recipient of a service and is part of the creation of meaningful experiences. People receiving care includes all individuals who receive services at the organization regardless of their activities and the services or whether their role is as patients, customers, or consumers.

The training for people receiving care is more an invitation to share their experiences and their beliefs, values, and principles as part of the improvement effort related to a specific service. It should include simple explanations of the role of beliefs, values, and principles in experiences, value streams as a way of thinking about the way the experience occurs and the improvement work of aligning influences between the three value streams to create a meaningful experience.

Organizational Processes and Process Improvements

Meaningful experiences are created through the interactions of people who are receiving care and the people who are delivering care as they interact within the context of a process that has been designed by the organization to deliver a service or to accomplish a function. Organizational representatives who participate in meaningful experience design will need training in understanding organizational processes as a key aspect of meaningful experience design. This training should include explanations about the sequence of steps or activities that are at the center of the organizational process. An important part will be the identification and understanding of the organization's beliefs, values, and principles that were incorporated into the original process design and its operation. The organizational process value stream and the beliefs, values, and principles that form it play a significant role in the meaningfulness of the experience for the people receiving care and the people delivering care. They will also need orientation to the improvement of the process related to waste, efficiency, and effectiveness as well as the alignment of the influences in the value stream.

Mapping Meaningful Experience Value Streams for Design and Improvement

Probably the most important training associated with the design and improvement of meaningful experiences is learning to use the meaningful healthcare experience design mapping tool. This is also the aspect of the work that will require the most time and the most involvement by everyone associated with the effort as described in the following discussion. The outcome of the value stream mapping will provide information that will guide the analysis of the alignment of beliefs, values, and principles as well as process steps to identify opportunities for improvement.

The value stream mapping tool is designed to align all three value streams: people receiving care, people delivering care, and the organizational process. For the three value streams associated with the people, the map provides for documentation of activities and the beliefs, values, and principles that are associated with each activity. The value stream mapping for the people involved also includes space for documenting their emotions as they experience each activity that forms a step in the process. By viewing the beliefs, values, and principles for all three value streams and the associated emotions for the people involved, it is possible to identify conflicts that represent opportunities for improvement.

A variety of techniques are used to gather the information associated with each value stream. For the organizational process, the steps in the process are identified by the people who perform the work. This information can be obtained in meetings through flowcharting and by observing the work as it is performed. This part of the map is then compared to the way in which the organization originally designed the process to understand how close the current practice is to the original design. This is also the point at which the owners of the process describe the beliefs, values, and principles associated with each step in the process from the organizational perspective.

For the value streams of the people receiving care and the people delivering care, the steps that they follow include not only the actual participation in the steps of the organizational process but also the steps that come before and after the convergence of the value streams into a common flow that creates the experience. The information for these two value streams comes from interviews with the people involved, and these may be videoed or transcribed for review in the future. Along with the actual steps that they take in their value streams, documenting the feelings associated with each step and the beliefs, values, and principles associated with the activities provides the necessary information for mapping their value streams.

Once the information for the three value streams is aggregated in the map, it is reviewed and confirmed as accurate by the people involved. Not only will the map serve as a valuable tool in assessing the meaningfulness of the experience but the act of creating the map offers an opportunity for people receiving care and people delivering care to think about the experiences and their feelings and the way that their beliefs, values, and principles were engaged.

As part of the training of the meaningful experience value stream mapping, all the participants should be oriented to the way opportunities for improvement appear in the mapping process. Once the value stream mapping has been completed, the analysis of the alignment of the beliefs, values, and principles between each of the value streams provides the insight needed to make the experience more meaningful for the people receiving care and the people delivering care. The training focuses on identifying the points where emotions are negative for the people involved and where the descriptions of the beliefs, values, and principles indicate the most significant lack of alignment between the three value streams.

Implementing Improvements

Finally, the training should include orientation to the way in which improvements will be implemented once the need is identified. Once the mapping has been completed and the points in the value streams that indicate a lack of alignment due to emotions and descriptions of beliefs, values, and principles, the work of improving the meaningfulness of the experience begins. The interviews and the insights into the value streams offer the information needed to identify the points for improvement and the types of improvements that may be needed.

Improvement work follows similar patterns to other types of improvements with the addition of the structures that have been created to support the work of meaningful experience design. Where there are points where emotions are negative due to lack of alignment of the beliefs, values, and principles, the ethics committee and the ethics consultation process may be helpful in uncovering ways in which improvements can take place. Through additional interviews around specific issue using the ethics consultation approach, specific improvements may be identified. At the same time, the representatives from the patient experience or engagement committee may offer additional insights into the ways to improve the experience of the people receiving care.

For the people delivering care, additional insights may be obtained from other groups of people working in the organizational process associated with the experience. Also, there may be department directors who are able to provide information that could be helpful. Working with a variety of sources to clarify what was found in the value stream mapping related to the people delivering care is a useful part of developing ways to improve the experience. It is important to prioritize the various opportunities for improvement and to recognize when creative approaches to changing the organizational process and addressing the lack of alignment may be helpful.

Improving the alignment for the people receiving care may focus much more on the organization helping them to clearly define what their expectations are for the experience. Because the value stream for the people receiving care originates in the community from very diverse points, much of the alignment work is in understanding common perspectives from the community concerning the nature of the experience they are expecting. This may reflect the history, socioeconomic issues, and concerns from diverse groups of people with different backgrounds. It may also reflect a lack of awareness of either limitation within the organization or specific requirements for the service that need to be met. The organization may identify ways in which people receiving care can be informed and can receive ongoing updates to help them create a more realistic alignment of their beliefs, values, and principles as they engage with the organization around specific processes and services. It is at this point that groups working on engagement with the people receiving care can be most helpful.

At the same time, the points that demonstrate a lack of alignment between the organization's process and the beliefs, values, and principles may be opportunities for improvement on the part of organizational representatives. There may be specific beliefs or values or principles inherent in the design of the process that the organization may need to re-evaluate. These may reflect older perspectives or views that are no longer current in the organization but that remained embedded in the process from the past. It may be that the beliefs, values and principles that are incorporated into organizational processes have never been clearly identified and need to be addressed to make the processes more meaningful for people receiving and people delivering care. When issues of this type are brought to the attention of management through the meaningful experience design process, it is important for people in positions of authority to actively participate in defining the current beliefs, values, and principles and applying these to the process to improve the alignment between the value streams.

For the people delivering care, the lack of alignment between the value streams may identify a variety of opportunities for improving the experience. Beliefs, values, and principles that are incorporated into the value stream of the people delivering care may originate from diverse sources such as professional education received at different schools, organizational training that has not been updated or no longer accurately reflects the process, work-related issues such as staffing, materials and leadership that have evolved over time and no longer meet the needs of the people receiving or the people delivering care.

For the people delivering care, there may be moral stress associated with the lack of alignment of beliefs, values, and principles. This may be due to conflicts between the three value streams that need to be addressed or it may be due to repeated attempts by the people delivering care to address issues and leadership failed to respond. Moral stress often has its source within the organization in the way in which power is expressed between the people delivering care and the leadership. It may also indicate deeper conflicts in which between the needs of the people receiving care and the inability of those delivering the care to meet those needs for a variety of reasons. The ethics committee can be especially helpful in cases in which this type of lack of alignment has resulted in moral stress.

Once opportunities for improvement are identified, it is important to consider creative ways to approach the alignment issues between value streams. Beliefs, values, and principles reflect personal perspectives that require more customized approaches to improvement. Improvement methodologies such as design thinking emphasize empathy and the development of prototypes that enable improvement teams to learn from the responses of the people as they interact with prototypes. A traditional Plan-Do-Study-Act approach can also be used to plan and track improvements in processes when the work is clearly defined, and the results are quantitative more than qualitative.

Reporting on Improvements

Training should also include the reporting on improvements for meaningful experience design and the process that it follows. Meaningful experience design reports through the exiting quality structure to ensure that the improvements are tracked as part of the overall quality program and the leadership and board are kept informed of the work by teams using meaningful experience design. This reporting also enables the organization and the supporting structures of the ethics committee and patient and family advisory council to benefit from learning about the alignment issues associated with the value streams that meaningful experience design uncovers. This information is particularly important because it highlights potential conflicts or changes in the beliefs, values, and principles of people delivering care and the people receiving care as well as within the organization's own processes.

Step 4 – Identify Opportunities for Using Meaningful Experience Design

Once training materials are available, the next step will be the identification of an initial opportunity for using meaningful experience design. This initial effort will be used to evaluate the best way to conduct the project and the organization's response to this type of improvement. This is an important first step for introducing this approach to improve experiences for people.

The quality committee with the assistance of representatives from the ethics committee and patient engagement committee should identify a care delivery process that needs improvement and is an important contact point between people receiving care and people delivering care. It should be a point of contact in which the people receiving care are frequently in touch with the department to enable the Taskforce to identify individuals who have a personal interest in improving the care they receive and are willing to work with the improvement group. An example of this type of environment would be a family practice or internal medicine office associated with a hospital or part of a large multidiscipline practice group.

Once the process for the initial project has been identified, a survey of potential team members including the people delivering care and the people receiving care along with the management in the area and potential group members should be conducted. If it appears that there is interest, the concept should be presented to the quality committee as a proposal. If approved, the project would move forward.

Step 5 – Initiate the First Meaningful Experience Design Project

The initial meetings of the group working on the first meaningful experience design project would focus on the training materials. Once everyone is reasonably familiar with the concepts and process and the basic format of the meaningful experience value stream mapping technique, the team can begin to develop the organizational process flowchart of the specific steps and to arrange the interviews with people delivering care and people receiving care.

The focus in the interviews will be to develop the steps in two value streams and then associate the beliefs, values, and principles with those steps. The emotional responses will follow to complete the essential elements of the value streams. After completing the mapping and identifying points in which emotional responses indicate lack of alignment and where there are clear conflicts in the value streams, the team can begin to evaluate possible ways of addressing these issues with support of the ethics committee and patient and family advisory committee. As the team moves to development of improvements and creative prototypes to make the experience more meaningful, the quality committee should be updated on the progress that is being made any roadblocks that are delaying the project. Finally, a proposal for improvements can be rapidly tested.

Step 6 – Completion of the Initial Meaningful Experience Design Project

When the first meaningful experience design team project has been completed with plans for implementation, the team should take time to evaluate the project from the perspective of their experience as members of the team. It would be useful to cover some of the same elements used in the meaningful experience design project to assess the work of the team and their ability to make progress in the various phases of the project. This should also include the beliefs, values, and principles of the team members as team members and their emotional responses to the work of the team at different points in the project.

Step 7 – Report on the Initial Project and Lessons Learned

An important part of the work of the Taskforce and the first meaningful experience team is to develop a presentation of the work they performed, and the lessons learned for presentation to the quality committee, ethics committee, patient and family advisory committee, medical staff executive committee and board. The goal of the presentation is to review the process, to share lessons learned, and to describe the overall sense of this method for improving the experiences of people receiving care and people delivering care. An important part of the presentation will be to discuss what was learned concerning the beliefs, values, and principles of the people involved and how these new insights can be helpful in creating more meaningful experiences in the future for recipients of care and the employees who are delivering care. It will also be important to discuss how the methodology was used to evaluate the work of the team and what was learned about making the methodology more meaningful in the future.

Step 8 – Improve the Meaningful Experience Design Methodology

Improving the meaningful experience design methodology and the experiences of team members involved in the work will always be a part of performing the actual improvements. This begins with the assessment by the first team of lessons they learned and what they would do differently in the future. An area of interest would be the processes followed in selecting and working with the people who receive care and the people who deliver care and encouraging their participation in the work of the team. The ability of the team to be open and supportive in asking for information about beliefs, values, and principles and sensitive to the emotional responses of the people involved in the processes can be critically important to gaining the insight need to create more meaningful experiences.

The fundamental differences between meaningful experience design and other methods of improvement revolve around the way in which people find meaning in their experiences. As part of the work of the team, learning how to find effective ways to encourage and support people in talking about their beliefs, values, and principles and the emotions they feel when there are conflicts or lack of alignment are essential to the future success of improving experiences and to the organization in its efforts to improve overall.

Step 9 – Train More Groups and Initiate New Design and Improvement Projects

Once the meaningful experience design team has reported off on the project, training can begin to establish more permanent arrangements for requesting and initiating additional meaningful experience projects across the organization. With the assistance of the quality committee, request forms and orientation materials can be developed and distributed to promote this method of improvement and to encourage directors and managers to consider projects in their areas. People who have had experience in using the methodology should be included in future teams to provide support for the next generation of teams using meaningful experience.

Step 10 – Conduct Quarterly and Annual Reviews of the Program

Once the meaningful experience design methodology has been implemented, the quality program should conduct quarterly and annual reviews of the work and the findings. Because this methodology uses a unique tool and the concepts of meaning, beliefs, values, and principles, it has the potential of uncovering unique aspects of the organization and the relationships between the people delivering care and the people receiving care. Identifying new findings that provide important insights into the way healthcare services are delivered and received makes meaningful experience design an even more valuable methodology for the organization to use.

Chapter 15

Orienting People Who Deliver Care to Meaningful Experience Design

Once the organization has approved the use of meaningful healthcare experience design as part of its quality improvement program, the education of people who deliver care is the next step. Their training will be like any quality improvement methodology. The best place to start is often with the various layers of management staff who are responsible for the operations in the various departments and divisions. Regularly scheduled management meetings may provide an appropriate forum for introducing meaningful experience design and answering questions. Once the management members have been oriented, they can provide training to their departments. The following training will be the same for both management members and department members.

The initial meeting will be used to familiarize everyone with the existing quality improvement structure and plan. Since meaningful experience design is an improvement methodology, it is part of the overall quality plan. In introducing meaningful experience design as a new method for improvement, it is important to explain that it offers additional benefits that are not available in other methods of improvement. Many healthcare workers have only a minimal understanding of the concepts associated with improvement. The focus of the introduction will be to develop a common understanding in the group of the way in which improvement opportunities are identified both as departmental initiatives and as larger projects. The reporting process will also be helpful for the group to review to understand the relationship between those who are working on improvements and the management of the organization and the governing body or board.

Once the group is familiar with the basics of improvement in the organization, they can proceed to the new methodology for mapping improving meaningful experience. The simplest way to present the meaningful experience map is to explain that it is a methodology that is designed to create healthcare experiences that the people receiving care find meaningful and worth repeating and that healthcare workers find meaningful and worth repeating. Since healthcare organizations want people to return for care and they want their employees to find their work meaningful and worth doing every day, improving the experiences of people receiving care and people delivering care makes sense. It is also the best way to sustain improvements in healthcare services.

Working with the group, use the mapping tool to highlight the three value streams and to focus on the activities that are captured as part of each value stream. Most people will be familiar with and comfortable talking about experiences such as the activities associated with a visit to a physician's office or having an outpatient surgical procedure. The group should develop the initial list of activities associated with the organizational process, the healthcare workers' activities, and the recipient of care activities. The management representatives can document the organizational process steps as the patients and healthcare workers document their activities. Once the general steps in these processes are identified, then a picture of the three together along a common timeline can be developed to show what happens in each at different points. It is important to include the parts of the value streams that occur prior to the healthcare worker and person receiving care converging at the organization and after the convergence as these are important in understanding how each of the participants in the value streams begins their process and reflects on it after it is over.

Once the steps in the processes are documented, then the group should come together to discuss the other parts of the experience map. In developing an understanding of the emotional state, beliefs, values, and principles, the discussion between all the members of the group will be helpful in building a common understanding. These concepts will need some explanation on how they are defined and why they are included in the design of meaningful experiences. One of the important developments in quality improvement that occurred in recent years through design thinking is the realization that as people experience processes related to services, their emotional state at different points in the experience can be important to their perception of the product or service. This is particularly true of an intensely personal experience such as occurs with healthcare. However, most healthcare organizations are just beginning to think in terms of documenting the emotional state of people receiving care and incorporating that into the understanding of the design of the processes of care.

Thinking about the emotional state of the person receiving care may not be difficult for the group to grasp once it is presented since most people have experienced healthcare services. They have feelings about healthcare experiences and going to see a physician or nurse practitioner particularly when it may involve a serious health problem. The anticipation of the visit, sitting in the waiting room, going through the visit, and then returning to home are all familiar steps in the process with associated emotions that the group can recognize. A more unique aspect of the experience map will be the documentation of the emotional state of the healthcare worker during their participation with the patients in the process. Most improvement efforts recognize the importance of the worker's knowledge of the process and ideas on ways the process can be improved. However, most do not recognize that workers along with recipients of care experience changes in their emotional state during the course of the process. This is an important aspect of meaningful experience design because the meaning of the experience forms in the emotions of the healthcare worker along with the person receiving care. Documenting changes in the worker's emotional state is an important part of identifying opportunities for improvement in the experience. Once the group has a chance to discuss this aspect of the experience map, the inclusion of the worker's emotional state will probably seem as reasonable as documenting the emotions of the patient.

Once the activities associated with the process and emotional states of the patient and healthcare worker at each point are documented, the final step may be the most challenging for the group. The idea for including beliefs, values, and principles as influences that shape healthcare value streams arose out of the realization that healthcare is a unique experience for most people. Its place in the ordered reality of our lives is problematic. This makes healthcare unique even when compared with other personal services which are important for healthcare workers to realize. Meaningful experience design focuses on the alignment of beliefs, values, and principles at different points in the experience. These influences are often unspoken and hidden as the recipient of care and the healthcare worker go through the steps of the process, but their role in the creation of a meaningful experience is critically important because they influence the emotions and sense of meaning experienced by the participants.

The group will initially discuss the concepts of design and meaning as they apply to meaningful experiences. They will discuss how best to define beliefs, values, and principles as influences within the context of the convergence of three value streams. The group will consider how different beliefs, values, and principles may influence the emotions of the people receiving care and healthcare workers at different points in the value stream. In identifying these influences at different points, the group will consider how they align or do not align in the three value streams. Alignment would be viewed as supporting the experience as meaningful for the people involved. A lack of alignment would be viewed as creating a conflict that needs to be addressed to work toward a more meaningful experience.

Once the group has completed the meaningful experience map, the next step is to identify opportunities within the map for improvement. Opportunities for improvement initially will follow the usual process improvement methods for identifying steps in the process that are not adding value or that may not be working well. Once the basic process steps have been identified for improvement, the group will consider the emotional state and the alignment of beliefs, values, and principles. Exploring the ways in which conflicts in beliefs, values, and principles would appear and what would result will help the group to recognize why these aspects are part of the design process.

When potential conflicts are identified as lack of alignment between the belief, values, and principles in the value streams, it is important for the healthcare workers to understand that ethics committee can offer some insights into resolving these conflicts through ethics consultation process. Conflicts in processes are not dissimilar from conflicts that occur in the determination of end of life care or other healthcare decisions. When these conflicts occur, the ethics consultations can be very helpful to clarify the values that are in conflict and what would be the best way to resolve them for the patient to receive appropriate care. In the case of processes, when the people receiving care and the healthcare worker are in conflict, it compromises their ability to work together to create a meaningful experience. Bringing these conflicts to light is an important part of the meaningful experience design mapping process. As the group identifies these influences in the three value streams, ethics committee representatives can help them work toward a resolution.

After identifying opportunities for improvement, the group will use the typical improvement methodology. For process steps, the typical Plan-Do-Study-Act process of improvement or whatever the organization uses can be implemented to make the changes and test the changes. For other changes in the processes related to the emotional state and to conflicts in beliefs, values, and principles, the group will offer observations about the lack of alignment and negative emotions and recommend ways to align beliefs, values, and principles that may help. Evaluation tools for monitoring improvements in patient and healthcare worker emotional states and acceptance of recommendations for aligning value stream influences will be used to demonstrate improvements and for standardization and follow-up.

Chapter 16

Inviting People Who Receive Care into Meaningful Experience Design

If patients are to take an active role in the design of meaningful experiences in American healthcare, then American healthcare needs to transition from an activity based on physicians and hospitals to service delivery focused on people receiving care and their experiences. However, this transition presents a unique problem because of the nature and role of recipients of care. They are not typical customers, and healthcare is not a typical service. Simply applying the usual standards for service and the common understanding of customers to people who receive healthcare leads to serious confusion and a sense of disorientation.

Once a healthcare organization has determined to use meaningful experience design to improve the care and experiences of people receiving care, it is important for the people on the patient and family advisory council (PFAC) or other patient engagement committee to have at least an overview of the way that the methodology works and the importance of having people who have received services participate in the improvement. The representatives of the PFAC that are trained in meaningful experience design should take the lead in explaining how it works and encouraging the members of the committee to provide assistance when recipients of services are needed for the work.

Once a service or point of interaction between healthcare workers and recipients of care is identified for improvement, then people who have experienced this service or point of care need to be found. The director or manager of the department or service will need to be involved in identifying people who have received services who may be interested in improving the experience. It can be helpful if members of the PFAC can participate with the people involved in setting up the meaningful experience design project in reaching out to people who have used the service and inviting them to share their thoughts on the particular service.

PFAC members can also serve as intermediaries in contacting patients for possible inclusion in the project. By using the PFAC, the recruitment becomes more of an invitation from someone who does not work for the organization but is actively involved in improving services. This can make the people who have received care more comfortable about participating and help to build awareness about the PFAC as well. Also, as patients agree to participate in the meaningful experience design, the PFAC can support them and their understanding of the hospital and help with their orientation.

Recipients of care who participate in meaningful experience design will need some help in understanding the basic concepts such as the value streams that represent the three perspectives of the interaction that is at the center of design project. Meetings of the meaningful experience design group working on the project offer opportunities to share some initial aspects of the three value streams and for the participants to get to know each other's perspective a little better. It can be helpful to people to share their stories of the services they received. The story can be either videoed or recorded to save time and serve as a valuable reference as changes are proposed. For example, their life in the community and early experiences with physicians or healthcare organizations provide valuable insights that may be further developed once the basic aspects of the story are added to the experience map. It will also be helpful to share the organizational process value stream to remind them of the different steps in the process.

Once the person who received care has provided sufficient information to graphically represent the value stream of their experience, these can be added to the experience map with the organizational value stream and the healthcare worker's value stream. The mapping should also include any indications from the patient's story of feelings or emotions that were associated with steps in the value stream or interactions with people. Though the person may not realize it, the emotions that occur at each point in the value stream offer insights into their beliefs, values, and principles.

The most important, but probably the most difficult, aspect of engaging with people who received services will be encouraging understanding and sharing of beliefs, values, and principles. Most people move through the experiences of their day dealing with the emotions that are produced due to interactions and steps in their activities. However, they typically do not consciously trace these back to fundamental beliefs, values, and principles. Rather, these important influences operate behind the scenes intuitively. Though they exert significant influence over the emotions of people, awareness of these influences may be quite minimal. Engaging with people in meaningful experience design requires that these important aspects of their value stream are brought to the surface in order to understand how they influence emotions and experiences. This requires an orientation to help them associate their feelings with underlying beliefs, values, and principles.

Once their activities associated with the value stream and emotions are captured on the map, it is time to explore with the patient the beliefs, values, and principles that may be the source of the emotions. It is important that the patient understanding there is no judgment associated with either the emotions or the beliefs, values, and principles. Building this information into the experience map helps the group working on the project to look for alignment or lack of alignment between the patient's value stream influences and those of the organization. Negative emotions may highlight points in the process where the patient's beliefs, values, and principles are not in alignment with the healthcare worker's or the organization. This would indicate an opportunity for evaluating the influences in each value stream and identifying where there is a lack of alignment. If it is a simple adjustment in the process to bring the influences into alignment, then this can be noted and an improvement identified for a Plan-Do-Study-Act test of change in the future. However, if there is a serious conflict between the value stream influences, then it may be helpful to engage the ethics committee and PFAC to evaluate the conflict and to offer some assistance in working on a resolution to bring the influences into alignment.

Helping the people to understand the roles and processes of the ethics committee as with other aspects of the meaningful experience design project will be important to their participation in resolving conflicts in value streams. Most people do not have experience in formally working through ethical conflicts, particularly involving emotions. Once the conflicts have been assessed and resolutions agreed to by the group working on the project, it will be important to share these findings with the PFAC and the ethics committee and as part of the reporting on the project to the quality improvement structure. It will be important to reassure the people who are describing their reactions to the services they received that this process is not a judgment of beliefs, values, and principles, but an effort to create meaningful experiences by aligning these in the three value streams. This insight is very valuable to the organization and to the healthcare workers and appreciation for the willingness of the people to share their feelings and other influences should be communicated throughout the project.

When the project is concluding, it is helpful to describe the improvements to the people who participated as recipients of care and shared their feelings and beliefs, values, and principles. Meeting with them to learn from them what they thought of meaningful experience design and any insights that could be shared on what could be improved in training, orientation, and participation would be helpful. By repeatedly involving recipients of care in meaningful experience design projects, organizations create a valuable conduit of information about the beliefs, values, and principles of the people they serve and how these can be incorporated into the value streams of the organization and the healthcare workers to create more meaningful experiences in the future. The engagement of people who receive care and people who deliver care together in meaningful experience design is in itself a major step forward for healthcare organizations in creating the future of healthcare based on meaningful experiences that promote healing and a healthier work environment.

Chapter 17

Improving the Meaningfulness of Healthcare Experiences

American healthcare is in a period in which the delivery of healthcare services is changing as technology and communication change. The move from hospital-based physicians as the center of the delivery system to a continuum of care powered by new ways of communicating and methods of treatment will accelerate as cost and quality continue to be important drivers of change. Designing meaningful experiences throughout the continuum of care and adapting those experiences to meet the needs and expectations of people receiving care and people delivering care will be an important aspect of the quality of care in the future.

Healthcare is fundamentally different from other services, and it will be held to a higher standard even as the effort to equate it to other types of services increases. Through meaningful experience design, the people and organizations delivering healthcare services are able to continuously evaluate the way in which the value streams of people receiving care and people delivering care interact with organizational processes across the spectrum of services and delivery locations.

In order to improve the meaningfulness of experiences, healthcare organizations will need to continuously monitor the way in which the value streams evolve and the people interact. The best indication of a decline in the meaningfulness of the healthcare experience lies in the interactions that occur at the point of convergence of the three value streams. A secondary source of information is the period following the convergence in which the people receiving care and their families go through a period of reflection on their experience and make decisions about whether to repeat experiences or change service delivery providers.

Data collection and data analysis have always been problematic for healthcare. Healthcare professionals and healthcare processes have always focused on the actual delivery of care. Once the crisis is over and the healthcare issue has been addressed, the person receiving care leaves and the people delivering care move on to the next crisis. This production system left little time or interest in gathering data about the experience or analyzing what happened in the past.

Creating meaningful healthcare experiences requires a reorientation to the collection of information about the experience at the time it occurs in order to assess whether it was meaningful and whether the patient and the healthcare worker are interested in repeating the experience again. This also means that the locus for improvement and innovation in care moves from the central leadership to the points of care. If the components of a healthcare meaningful experience are the three value streams, then monitoring the experience is monitoring the quality of the convergence of the value streams and evaluating that experience.

In the design of meaningful experiences, the alignment of beliefs, values, and principles is the important consideration. The emotional reactions of the healthcare worker and the recipient of care as they engage to create the experience is an important point for assessing the quality of the experience. Building into the organizational process the means for assessing emotions at different points in the convergence of their value streams offers a real-time method for identifying opportunities for improvement. This type of data gathering has usually been viewed in healthcare as a distraction and not really part of the care process. When the focus is on the meaningfulness of the experience, then evaluating the emotions of the participants is an important part of the experience and the best way for the organization to identify opportunities for improvement.

Using the meaningful experience map as a guide, people receiving care and people delivering care will be asked as part of their engagement with each other to provide information on their feelings at the time. Using a map with key touchpoints identified and offering simple metaphors to assist in the description of the experience, will encourage the people involved to describe what they are experiencing. This becomes an important source of data for evaluating individual experiences. At the same time, an important part of the work of management will be to review the data on a continuous basis in order to identify points in which the responses are evidencing a lack of alignment in the value streams and adjustments are needed. If the need is urgent, management provides space and time for the healthcare workers to review the responses from people receiving care and their own responses and to look for particular issues that may be causing problems that need to be addressed immediately.

For anyone who has worked in healthcare in America or has been involved in quality improvement in healthcare, the idea of capturing data about the work at the time it is performed has always been a distant fantasy. The rush of activities has always worked against the ability to improve. The professional aspects of healthcare in which clinicians from various disciplines are working with patients created obstacles to rapidly identifying and addressing quality concerns because of the difference in perspectives and the lack of common vision between the disciplines.

The important difference in meaningful experience design lies in the common focus on the experience. Each discipline within the healthcare delivery system is expected to meet the standards of care defined for its practice. This is assumed and evaluated differently from the experience. The goal of creating a meaningful experience is something that is common to all healthcare workers and all the people who receive care and can be evaluated and improved by working on the alignment of beliefs, values, and principles that form the experience. The initial work is in the design of the experience. In this design process, the ability to document the experience as it is occurring is built into the organizational process value stream for the healthcare worker and the people receiving care. Emotions associated with the points of interaction provide insight into the alignment or lack of alignment of the beliefs, values, and principles that were originally designed into the experience.

Creating a real-time data collection process and a rapid response to issues identified in the data relates to the focus on the experience. Having a bad day at work would seem to be a usual part of every person's experience of work. However, because of the importance of meaningful experiences within healthcare, a bad day for healthcare workers and people receiving care means that the quality of the healing experience was compromised and the goals of the organization to create meaningful experiences was not accomplished. The emphasis on the experience as the purpose of the engagement between the recipients of care and healthcare workers creates the impetus for the organization to support and sustain the achievement of meaningful experiences as the goal of the work.

As data are collected throughout the healthcare delivery system and improvements are made, the aggregate of this information is pooled and evaluated in the quality structure. Lack of alignment in beliefs, values, and principles that are identified and resolved offers important insights. Reviews of these changes by the patient and family advisory council, the ethics committee, the quality improvement oversight committee, and summarized for the board provide valuable information on the relationship of the organization and its workers to the people receiving care and to the community. Out of these reviews, the organization may identify ways in which its beliefs, values, and principles may be revised or clarified to better align with those of the healthcare workers and people receiving care. The reflection on the stories and events and feelings that characterized these events become moments in which the management of the organization can share in the experiences and learn from them.

Redefining quality as a meaningful experience and the design of meaningful experiences as improvement challenges much of the tradition of healthcare. If healthcare is to fulfill its role of delivering high-quality care that actually creates an experience that promotes healing, then this will mean rethinking the way that healthcare experiences are designed to focus on beliefs, values, and principles as well as the service. It will mean creating time in the actual experience for the recipient of care and the healthcare worker to express their thoughts about the experience. It will require the organization to respond quickly to a breakdown in the alignment of the value streams in the same way that a response is needed if a clinical process is failing to improve the patient's condition. And, it will involve the management of the organization in seriously considering its beliefs, values, and principles as the foundation for aligning with the workers and the patients.

Quality in the future for healthcare organizations is the creation of meaningful experiences that patients and healthcare workers are willing to repeat. The wonderful thing about this approach to quality is that it will engage everyone involved in healthcare in the design and improvement of experiences in which people connect with each other and share their beliefs, values, and principles. The meaning that emerges out of the convergence of the value streams promotes healing and an affirmation that people caring about each other contributes to making life more meaningful. Finding ways to make this a reality for everyone in healthcare is what makes healthcare a desirable profession. Work is simply a search for meaning, and meaning emerges from shared experiences that affirm our beliefs, values, and principles. Healthcare in the twenty-first century offers abundant opportunities for everyone to become a part of creating meaningful experiences that promote healing and create a higher quality of life and a greater sense of the unity that strengthens our communities. This is meaningful experience design in American healthcare.

Chapter 18

Meaningful Healthcare Experiences and the Ethics Committee

As organizations implement meaningful experience design, the potential for conflict between the beliefs, values, and principles inherent in the three value streams is always present and should be anticipated. When a conflict identified, it is an indication that the previous alignment has changed or the alignment identified in the design phase of the value streams mapping was not correct. The organizational ethics committee or ethics consultation service offers organizational support to respond to conflicts in value streams by identifying the nature of the misalignment and assisting to resolve the conflict to promote meaningful healthcare experiences.

Mark P. Aulisio stated in a 2016 article in *AMA Journal of Ethics* that "ethics committees are the primary mechanism for dealing with ethical issues in hospitals in the United States today" (p. 546). In his article "Why Did Hospital Ethics Committees Emerge in the US?", he indicates that the development of hemodialysis at University Hospital in Seattle, Washington in the 1960s was the motivation. He describes the origins of hemodialysis as initially developed through the work of a Dutch physician, Willem Kolff, in the 1940s who used an automobile fuel pump to circulate blood outside the body to be filtered and then returned to the body (p. 546). Building on the initial work by Kolff, Belding Scribner, MD, used a Teflon catheter with a shut off valve as a shunt for hemodialysis and developed a permanent indwelling shunts for renal failure patients (p. 546). With the availability of the new Scribner shunts, patients' lives could be extended indefinitely through dialysis, The Swedish Hospital in Seattle, WA, where the shunt was first used created a dialysis center to treat patients with the new shunts, but the demand quickly exceeded the capacity of the center. According to Aulisio, the success of the center created the ethical dilemma of how to determine which patients to choose to receive the treatment since regular dialysis is required to keep renal failure patients alive (Aulisio, 2016, p. 546). Scribner appointed an Admission and Policy Committee consisting of lay people from the community to develop nonmedical criteria for the selection of dialysis candidates.

Aulisio makes the point that the committee appointed to develop criteria for the selection of hemodialysis patients was tasked not with a medical or scientific question. They initially used demographic characteristics such as "age, sex, occupation, marital status, education, dependents, income and net worth" to determine who was most appropriate for the treatment (p. 547). The decision ultimately was a value decision in which individuals would be chosen. Aulisio points out that the reasons for the creation of this committee are the same as for later ethics committees in "technology creating options that formerly seemed unthinkable, value-laden questions that go well beyond what medical science can address, a pluralistic context in which not all involved share the same values, and the need for decisions to be made in a relatively short timeframe" (p. 547).

In addition to the dialysis situation, the Karen Ann Quinlan case in New Jersey in 1976 involving the right to refuse treatment even when it meant the death of the patient added additional emphasis on ethics committees. As noted in an article in the May 2016 *AMA Journal of Ethics*, the New Jersey Supreme Court, in an effort to offer physicians reassurance against legal action if they removed the patient from a ventilator, "ruled that if a hospital ethics committee agreed with their (physicians) prognosis, the physicians would be immune from any legal liability from removing her ventilator at her parents' request" (George Annas, JD, MPH, Michel Grodin, MD, p. 554). Now present in nearly every US hospital, Aulisio points out that ethics committees were virtually nonexistent in the 1960s and 1970s and, as recently as the early 1980s, were present in only 1% of US hospitals (p. 547). By the late 1990s, ethics consultation services (a standard function of ethics committees) were present in all US hospitals with 400 beds or more, federal hospitals, and hospitals that are members of the Council of Teaching Hospitals (p. 547) The final push in the emergence of ethics committees in the US came in 1992, when the Joint Commission on the Accreditation of

Healthcare Organizations (JCAHO) changed its *recommendation* that hospitals have some "mechanism" for dealing with ethical issues in clinical care to a *requirement*. In the 1990s, ethics committees in US hospitals jumped from 60% to over 90% by the end of the decade (p. 550).

Based on Aulisio's observations, ethics committees emerged to address healthcare situations in which "value-laden questions" and "clashes between values in a pluralistic context" occur in an environment in which there is "a relative time-pressure for decision-making" (p. 550). Given these criteria, the association between ethics committees and ethics consultation services with meaningful experience design seems very appropriate. However, the role of the ethics committee in assisting with meaningful experience design represents an expansion beyond the typical parameters for these committees. They tend to be narrowly defined as providing ethical consultation services to clinicians, patients, and families in resolving ethical issues related to patient care such as end of life care.

Expanding the range of consultations for the ethics committee to include conflicts between beliefs, values, and principles in the three value streams of meaningful healthcare experiences is consistent with recent work by Nancy Berlinger and others on the need for leaders in healthcare organizations to "acknowledge explicitly how the system's own conditions create pressures on professionals and staff to improvise solutions" (Berlinger, 2016, p. 166). Using the organization's structure to address ethical challenges in complex adaptive systems would provide benefits to the organization, healthcare workers and people receiving care. It would also provide more engagement with ethical issues for the committee. The ethics consultation provided by the ethics committee assists in clarifying the issue that is creating the conflict and identifies who is designated or most qualified to speak for the patient. This person serves as the voice of the patient who is not able to communicate and offers guidance on the beliefs or values the patient may have expressed about their care. If there is conflict in the family about the care or a concern that the care is not meeting the wishes of the patient, the ethics consultation service can interview the various parties involved and help them to express their views.

According to Nancy Berlinger, M.Div., PhD, "When the sources and consequences of ethical challenges in a complex system are foreseeable, the system's leaders should acknowledge explicitly the systems own conditions create pressures on professionals and staff to improvise solutions to foreseeable problems" (p. 166). Berlinger cites Alan Cribb, Professor of Bioethics & Education at King's College in London, as describing ethical challenges as "basic and pervasive in healthcare work" (p. 5). Berlinger indicates that Cribb sees the source of routine moral stress as arising from the "healthcare worker's own sense of self as a moral agent in relation to three sources of moral authority: official codes and standards; habits and unofficial rules for getting work done; and the assumption that something broadly ethically acceptable or event positively good is going on because this work concerns the care of the sick, the treatment of disease and the restoration of health all of which are recognizable ways to do good" (Berlinger, 2016, p. 4).

Based on the views of Berlinger and Cribb, meaningful experience design is addressing an area that is not addressed in routine performance improvement because it is viewed as different from the steps of a process of the quantification of the time, motion, and activities associated with the delivery of a service. However, in even the simplest of processes, once we recognize that there are three value streams converging and that these value streams are each influenced by the beliefs, values, and principles of the people and organization involved. It is not difficult, then, to see that conflicts between these three sets of beliefs, values, and principles could contribute to the routine moral burden of the worker or the patient. Through this moral stress, patients and healthcare workers may conclude that they do not want to experience this stress repeatedly as they participate in the process. It is at this point that either patient or worker withdraws or develops workarounds or other coping mechanisms to avoid the stress. Berlinger makes the point that "...organizations in which people do healthcare work have an ethical duty to recognize and support workers grappling with the built-in stresses of their roles, include moral stress about what one ought to do for patients given constraints of time and resources (p. 5). Focusing on health care work and the people who do it opens health care ethics to nurses, physician assistants, other clinical professionals, aides, and administrators who, compared with physicians, are less likely to be offered regular opportunities to reflect on the ethical challenges they face" (p. 6).

Based on the perspective that Berlinger and Cribb bring to healthcare work and workers, it seems not only appropriate but important that healthcare organizations approach the work within the context of meaningful experiences and that they utilize the resources of the ethics committee to help in the design and in finding ways to reduce stress that arises from the conflicts between beliefs, values, and principles. An important part of this overall perspective of the moral aspects of healthcare work and the stress associated with it, the potential for moral distress and moral residue are aspects of the work that are often overlooked when the ethics committee is not engaged.

Moral distress was identified in 1984 by Andrew Jameton. He described it occurring "When one knows the right thing to do, but institutional constraints make it nearly impossible to pursue the right course" (Jameton, 1984, p. 6). He described the initial response as the distress that occurs in the moment, as a situation unfolds. This may be followed by reactive distress or moral residue after the situation that elicited moral distress ends After a patient crisis causing moral distress ends, the initial distress may end but some moral residue remains serving as a new baseline for moral distress. Over time, as repeated crescendos of moral distress are experienced, moral residue increases gradually (Epstein & Delgado, 2010). This may be exacerbated by continued unit, team, or institutional dynamics that go unaddressed. Moral residue can be described as distressing feelings that linger long after the situation if the caregiver feels regret or believes that she behaved unethically or betrayed important values. Moral residue can influence both a clinician's practice and life (2010).

It is sometimes the case that the staff has concerns about the care of patients when the family has expressed a desire for patients to have curative care and resuscitation when the hospital staff believes the patient is actively dying. In cases like these, the staff can actually experience moral stress as they care for dying patients because they believe the care is painful to the patient and is unnecessary but they are unable to stop the care due to the family or practitioner preferences. The ethics committee can provide a forum for raising these issues and promoting a consensus around the status of the patient and the ability of the practitioners to provide healing. In this way, the moral stress on the staff can be resolved and their ability to speak up about care can be affirmed. Promoting moral courage is a potential outcome of an organizational culture that is prepared to address moral distress. A potential role for the ethics committee would be to help create an organizational environment to promote moral courage to relieve moral distress by addressing the ethical concerns of staff who may be subject to moral distress.

Moral distress and the accompanying moral residue are viewed as situations in which there is a powerful struggle between the views and values of the staff member and the care that is being delivered to the patient. When the staff members are not able to express those views and values and the situation with the patient deteriorates, the moral distress can become debilitating and lead to the moral residue. When there is a sense on the part of the staff that it is hopeless to try to intervene because of the power of those in charge of the patient or the unwillingness of others to even consider the staff member's view, then the result can be a residual effect in which the staff members have lost the moral courage to speak up or to even participate in efforts to improve care for patients in general because of the effect of the moral distress. In this way, the moral distress can compromise the staff member's ability to practice as a professional or to find fulfillment in their profession.

Meaningful experience design promotes the recognition of the routine moral burden that staff may experience as well as the moral distress that can arise when serious value conflicts affect patient care. By making beliefs, values, and principles an intrinsic part of the analysis of processes and by enlisting the help of the ethics committee and other resources to affirm the importance of these less visible aspects of the value streams, organizations are able to work to develop meaningful experiences. It is in these experiences that staff feel that they are able to work and contribute on a daily basis because their beliefs, values, and principles are respected. For patients, meaningful experiences bring them back to the organization with the sense that they will also find the sense of connection between their beliefs and values and those of the organization.

Within the organization, the importance of creating a structure to specifically respond to conflicts within value streams is part of the commitment to designing meaningful healthcare experience. It is in responding to these conflicts that the organization demonstrates to patients and employees an awareness of their beliefs, values, and principles and the determination by the organization to respect those influences and to address conflicts that may occur. In the design of the organization's value stream, the belief that conflicts will occur and need to be addressed is demonstrated by bringing people receiving services and people delivering services into the design of the healthcare encounter.

For organizations working to implement meaningful experience design, the members of the ethics committee represent an important resource for obtaining ethics consultations when conflicts in beliefs, values, and principles occur in the value streams. Within the context of both the design of meaningful experiences and the resolution of conflicts that occur as value streams meet, the ethics committee offers a valuable resource to the organization, staff, and patients. Realistically, it should be assumed that conflicts may appear in the original design as the three value streams are mapped and the beliefs, values, and principles are assessed for the value streams and their compatibility determined. Conflicts may also occur in the delivery of healthcare services as the people receiving care and the people delivering care interact, and it becomes apparent that there is a misalignment of the influences in the value streams. Finally, the data collected from people receiving care and people delivering care who have documented their emotions and comments as they progressed through their healthcare experience may identify conflicts or patterns in which the meaningfulness of the experience was diminished by a lack of alignment of the value streams.

Using the experience map and identifying beliefs, values, and principles, the organization can engage with the ethics committee to evaluate the lack of alignment within value streams and offer consultations on ways to move toward a consensus. These types of consultations are very reminiscent of the consultations currently offered to staff and patients with ethical concerns. In addition, if healthcare workers should find that their value stream influences are not aligning with those of the patients or organization, then rather than possible suffering moral stress by implementing workarounds, the ethics committee can offer a means for defining the beliefs or values that are affected and work toward a way to resolve the issues (Figure 18.1).

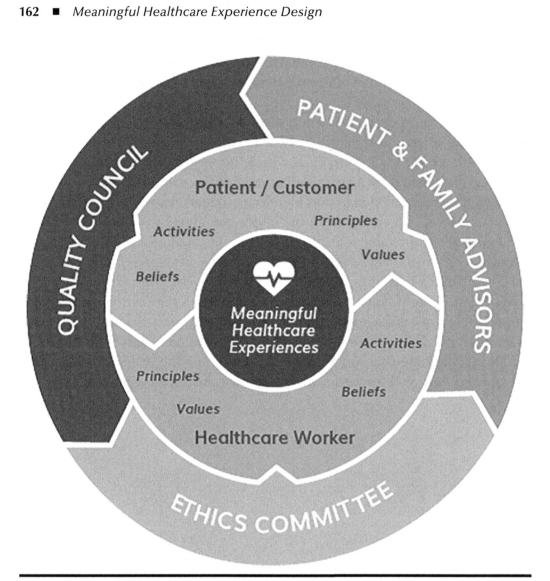

Figure 18.1 The healthcare worker and the patient/customer meet within the context of the organization's processes. Their interactions create the experience that they share. If it is a meaningful healthcare experience, the design of the experience will enable their beliefs, values, and principles to align, and it will contribute to their individual pursuits of meaning in their lives. The organization's structures – Quality Council, Ethics Committee and Patient and Family Advisors – contribute to the design of the processes and provide support for the creation of a meaningful healthcare experience.

INSIGHTS INTO AMERICAN HEALTHCARE HISTORY

4

Chapter 19

The Historical Epochs of American Healthcare

American healthcare has always been a local phenomenon. This does not mean that the way healthcare developed and operated at the local level was unaffected by events involving the country and the world. It is possible to identify periods within the nineteenth and twentieth centuries in which particular aspects of national life were dominant in influencing healthcare. Since healthcare is so much a part of life, identifying these larger national influences provides additional information that serves as context within which to better understand the experiences of people receiving care and healthcare workers during these periods.

It may be helpful to view the national changes that shaped healthcare as epochs. Epochs for our purposes represent periods of time in American history that are characterized by new developments and changes. During each epoch, a dominant influence that is at work in the country and in healthcare is identified. The timeframe for each epoch is ~20–30 years depending on the lasting influence of the change that occurred during the period. Though the use of epochs may seem simplistic given all of the complexities associated with healthcare and the country in general, it is helpful to recognize some significant changes as contributing to the way in which people access and experience healthcare. There may be additional ways to subdivide the periods, but the six that are used offer a preliminary basis for recognizing the way in which national events affect local healthcare experiences.

It is important to recognize national changes and their influences on local healthcare because the lack of a national plan for healthcare delivery makes it seem as though healthcare was only shaped by factors at work in local communities. This can tend to minimize the apparent effects of changes originating outside of the local environment. In addition to identifying the dominant national influences during an epoch, it will be useful to identify the way in which these were perceived in the local communities and the effects on healthcare organizations and access to healthcare services during the period. It is important to keep in mind influences from the national level to the local level affect individuals as well as communities differently. Healthcare reflects the environment in which it exists and the perceptions of the people that work in it and receive care through it and the influences of national changes. Working to understand these epochs will provide useful insights to our own time because much of what occurred early on in American healthcare continue to resonate today.

Healthcare Free Trade Epoch: Prior to 1890s

The period prior to 1890 represents a period in America in which much of the governmental, industrial, and social infrastructure developed. The Revolutionary War had ended, and the Constitution and basic structures of a national government had been put into place, but there was little real governmental involvement in the local communities. Much of the country was rapidly changing at the local level, but communications were relatively limited, so this created an environment in which healthcare among other endeavors was free to develop in a variety of ways. This provides the basis for describing the nineteenth century as the Free Trade Epoch. It highlights the ease of entry and the lack of regulations in the new country that fed the entrepreneurial spirit of healthcare. For the purpose of this discussion, free trade is defined as the freedom to make a product or deliver a service and charge for it in a competitive system without interference by the government.

Hospitals emerged as the foundation for the delivery of healthcare services in America based on the historic precedent set in England. The English who settled in America had a history of hospitals dating back to 937 when the grandson of Alfred the Great established a hospital at York dedicated to the St. Peter (Rosen, 1963, p. 8). However, since there were no clear records until the time of the Norman Invasion in 1066, St. John's Hospital built in York in 1084 is considered by some as the first English hospital (MacEachern, 1957, p. 7). By the middle of the fourteenth century, there were more than 600 hospitals of varying sizes and sponsorships in England (Rosen, p. 9). During the period from 1714 to 1760 in England, general hospitals and hospitals of special groups were created through "private initiative and contributions and some governmental assistance" (p. 20). As the hospitals were being established, there was a need to provide care outside of the hospital and the idea for the dispensary developed with the first dispensary opening in 1769 (p. 21).

The concepts, then, of dispensaries and hospitals were a part of the traditions that the English brought with them. George Rosen comments that the "colonies in America followed the general pattern set by the mother country, but with a considerable lag" (p. 23). Almshouses preceded hospitals with the first opening in Boston in the 1680s (Shryock, p. 104). He notes that the first hospital in the colonies was the Pennsylvania Hospital which opened in 1751 (Rosen, p. 23).

William Pencak in his article, "Free health care for the poor: the Philadelphia Dispensary," contends that the Philadelphia Hospital, "founded in 1731 in tandem with the Philadelphia Almshouse, came first" (Pencak, 2012, p. 26). For the poor who required custodial care, the almshouses and the early hospitals served to provide a place to stay. Pencak notes that the almshouses and hospitals were placed outside of the populated areas as a way of moving less desirable members of the population out of the city. He quotes a Presbyterian minister who described New York's hospital in 1810 the place where the "depraved and miserable of our race" wait to die, specifically calling attention to diseased prostitutes and beggars (Pencak, 2012, p. 27).

Charles Rosenberg (1974) indicates that "the dispensary was invented in late-eighteenth century England; it was an autonomous, free-standing institution, created in the hope of providing an alternative to the hospital in providing medical care for the urban poor" (p. 32). Pencak points out that dispensaries were located in the city and dispensed medicines to those who were able to come for services but would also provide care for patients too sick to come to the dispensary (p. 26). The benefit was two-fold in that it was less costly to care for acutely ill patient in their dwelling rather than to provide care in the hospital, but it was also socially beneficial for the "virtuous poor" not to be exposed to the hardships associated with hospital care and the moral stigma attached to the hospital or almshouse as the place of "last resort for the poor and dying" (p. 26).

The Philadelphia Dispensary was the first in America and was founded in 1786. American dispensaries grew in number and importance throughout the nineteenth century and remained significant providers of healthcare into the twentieth century, according to Rosenberg. Dispensaries opened in New York in 1791, and in Boston and Baltimore in 1800. By 1874, New York had twenty-nine dispensaries, and by 1877, Philadelphia had thirty-three (Rosenberg, p. 33). By the 1920s, however, "the dispensaries were on the road to extinction, increasingly submerged in the outpatient departments of urban hospitals" (p. 32).

The dispensary, according to Rosenberg, was made possible because of the support of the physicians who "formed the core group...in almost every American dispensary" (p. 43). The dispensary provided the benefit of patients necessary for the physicians to advance their education and to build their reputation. This mutual benefit to the patients and the physicians was the basis for the success of the dispensary and, according to Rosenberg, offers important insights into the way in which American medicine and its institutions developed because "without the initiative and voluntary support of the medical profession dispensaries would not have been created nor could they have survived" (p. 43).

Rosenberg contends that the dispensaries appeared because "they were entirely consistent with the assumptions of most Americans in regard to the responsibilities of government and appropriate forms of the public institutions which embodied such responsibilities" (p. 43). The "the prostitute, the drunkard, the lunatic and cripple," Rosenberg states, were viewed as the responsibility of the city and, therefore, provided for in the almshouse or by the city physician. For the virtuous poor, however, "the dispensary... represented an appropriate response of humane and thoughtful Americans to the needs of hard-working fellow citizens, a response demanded both by Christian benevolence and community oriented prudence; it was a form of social intervention limited, conservative and spiritually rewarding" (p. 43).

With hospitals and dispensaries appearing in the cities in the eighteenth century in America, the frontier settlements of the new country were giving birth to a new spirit of freedom and celebration of the individual. This found its most persuasive expression in the emergence of Andrew Jackson and his election to two terms as president. So influential was Jackson's influence on the country that the period was identified as "Jacksonian democracy."

In *The Birth of Modern Politics*, Lynn Hudson Parsons offers colorful insights and commentary on a presidential election that shaped the nineteenth century as a period of transition from an older establishment to a new American perspective that was shaped by frontiers and wilderness and war. The election of 1828 was between John Quincy Adams and Andrew Jackson. They had previously competed in the 1824 election in which there was neither achieved sufficient majority and Adams was chosen through a contingent election by the House of Representatives.

In the 1824 election, "only five states still required property ownership in order for an adult white male to cast a ballot" (p. 45). Parsons comments that "As a result, in more and more cases candidates for public office had to appeal to a broader constituency than had those of the previous generation, and voter participation for state and local elections increased dramatically, even in those states that still restricted the franchise" (p. 45). During this same period, many states dropped the requirement that presidential electors were decided by the legislature (p. 45).

In the election of 1828, Andrew Jackson won the election and was re-elected in 1832 (Parsons, 2009). The well-educated and experienced Adams lost in the election to Jackson who was the military hero of the Battle for New Orleans in 1815 and a duelist. With his election, Jacksonian democracy came to characterize the second quarter of the nineteenth century in America. Jackson's personal history of being a prisoner during the Revolutionary War and growing up in South and North Carolina and Tennessee shaped his frontier mentality far from the Virginia planter and New England establishment that shaped previous presidents including Adams (Parsons, 2009).

In her analysis of the 1828 election, she describes themes that would continue to resonate through the nineteenth century and indeed through the twentieth century as well. As she states, "The two parties whose outlines began to form around Adams and Jackson in 1828 began a dialogue that in many respects continues today" (Parson, p. 179). What was this dialogue? Parsons describes it as the struggle between democratic values expressed within the community as the best way to achieve the common good and democratic values expressed by individuals. "Those whose cultural, social and economic values reflect community-based decisions, in which democracy is converted into power on behalf of the common good, were arrayed against those whose democratic values relied less on the community and more on the individual. In the latter view, the good is best promoted by leaving individuals as much freedom as possible to promote their own interests, from which the common good will emerge" (Parsons, p. 179).

With the freedom of Jacksonian democracy setting the tone for the century, Nancy Tomes (2016) describes healthcare in the first half of the 1800s as the "closest approximation of free market medical care to ever exist. For both practical and ideological reasons, nineteenth century Americans embraced a freewheeling approach to healthcare, characterized by enthusiastic self-medication and unapologetic questioning of medical authority" (p. 20). Consistent with a country expanding into a western wilderness, the recently won freedom from England as well as the need for individuals and families to survive with few resources led to a view that by using common sense and native intelligence, people could take care of themselves. "Every man his own doctor," the title of a colonial healthcare self-help book or domestic medicine developed and passed down from moms to daughters and sons were viewed as the best source of healthcare.

Paul Starr (1982) points out that "By the nineteenth century, in America, popular belief reflected an extreme form of rationalism that demanded science be democratic" (p. 56). For many people, there was no basis for assuming that laws or regulations offered any guarantees of safety or effectiveness. "It had become an article of faith in America that every sphere of social life – law, government, religion, science, industry – obeyed principles that were intelligible to ordinary men of common sense. Insofar as medicine was valid and useful, it also ought to be plain and simple" (p. 56).

Professions were viewed as creating complexities and structures simply to enrich themselves without offer benefits to the people they are supposedly trying to protect. Starr (1982) noted that "The professions offended Jacksonian ideology primarily because of their attempts to establish exclusive privileges" (p. 57). Attempts to create procedures for licensing physicians had been enacted in a number of states but were overturned and removed as the nineteenth century progressed. "What fundamentally destroyed licensure was the suspicion that it was an expression of favor rather than competence" (p. 58).

Starr (1982) argues that "For a time in the first half of the nineteenth century, the democratic claim of accessibility and universality prevailed in medicine" (p. 59). However, as new developments in the application of science brought new technology and treatments to American medicine, the complexity and specialization would renew the need for ways to assess competence to protect the public from those who were not trained to provide care. "The democratic interregnum of the nineteenth century was a period of transition when the traditional forms of mystification had broken down and the modern fortress of objectivity had not yet been built" (p. 59).

During the first half of the nineteenth century, Charles Rosenberg (1983) describes the essential outlines of healthcare as "an affair of shared concepts and personal relationships" (p. 2). Healthcare during the period was delivered by individuals, many of whom were women, using knowledge about plants and botanic medicine passed down from generation to generation.

Outside of the familial and neighbor relationships, there was a medical marketplace. "There was indeed a medical marketplace with almost all care outside the family being on fee-for-service basis" (p. 4). He describes the marketplace as "a confused and confusing marketplace, more like a Middle Eastern bazaar" (p. 4). Within this marketplace, there were elite physicians who were "urban practitioner-consultants" who had the best available medical training (p. 3). Respectable, rank and file apprentice-trained physicians were next in terms of training and skill. Competing with them was a "varied assortment of practitioners: midwives, apothecaries, bone-setters, and itinerant 'specialists' in eye ailments and secret diseases" (p. 4).

As late as the 1870s, according to Tomes (2016), the American medicine marketplace continued to function with most routine issues addressed in the home with both domestic medicine and self-help guides while physicians were called to manage complicated births and fractures and more serious conditions. She notes that in terms of regulations, states allowed medical societies to issue licenses using relatively lenient standards while malpractice cases in which physicians failed to deliver proper care were tried in the courts (p. 25). The poor, immigrants, and others had few options for care beyond the almshouse or charity ward in a hospital. Until the start of the Progressive Era in the 1890s, the healthcare marketplace was essentially unregulated except in the barest terms. Tomes states that "The preference for do-it-yourself care, the desire to mix and match healing services and the general distrust of authority meant that patients preferred to pick their physicians and direct their care" (p. 26).

Starr (1982) points out that the freedom of the medical marketplace created an environment in which sectarianism proliferated. "Of all the divisions that rent the profession, sectarianism was the most virulent" (p. 94). Sectarianism was the term for the competition in the marketplace that developed between various perspectives or sects in American healthcare. In addition to the regular physicians, "medical sects grew in the nineteenth century because of the inadequacy of the contemporary medicine, particularly the disastrous 'heroic therapy' which emphasized bleeding, heavy doses of mercury, and other modes of treatment believed to range from ineffective to lethal" (p. 94).

An example of a medical sect appearing early in the nineteenth century was Thomsonianism. Founded by Samuel Thomson (1769–1843), it exemplified the "populism and egalitarianism that characterized the Jacksonian ear" in America as a "grassroots medical movement reflecting the large social and political environment" of the time (Flannery, 2002, p. 442). Thomsonianism rejected the training and practices of regular physicians using techniques such as bleeding, purging, and mercury and promoted instead a "uniquely American form of self-healthcare" (p. 442). It was based on "system of herbal remedies" that Thomson developed and he sold family rights to practice it (p. 446).

Starr (1982) notes that though Thomsonianism declined, other sects such as homeopaths and Eclectics competed with the regular physicians in the second half of the nineteenth century (p. 96). The Eclectics were botanic doctors and absorbed most of the Thomsonian movement and professed to have acquire the best of the various schools (p. 95). Homeopaths were followers of Christian Frederick Samuel Hahnemann, who was born in Germany in 1755, and advocated the concept of "similia" or "simile" (similarity), which is interpreted as "let likes be cured by likes" (Bellavite, Conforti, Piasere, & Ortolani, 2005, p. 441). This form of treatment involved using a substance that can induce a series of symptoms in a healthy living system in low doses to cure these symptoms (p. 441). Homeopaths would use dilutions of herbs with only minute quantities of herb present for their treatments. All of these various groups had their own medical schools, professional societies, and journals (Tomes, 2016, p. 22).

The state of American healthcare by the 1870s was a "medical marketplace" that Tomes describes as having "remarkably light limits" (Tomes, p. 25). The state medical societies were issuing licenses to practitioners with minimal qualifications, but patients did have the ability to sue for medical malpractice and manufacturers were not permitted to sell poisons as harmless medicines. "Within these bounds, American patients could choose from among a wide variety of medical advice givers and self-treatment regimens" (p. 25).

By the start of the next epoch of American healthcare, the "freewheeling medical marketplace" of the nineteenth century would change not because of discontent of the public, but because of the "determined minority of physicians and laypeople who convinced state and federal legislatures that some bad choices needed to be eliminated" (Tomes, p. 25). The changes would take two forms: the strengthening of medical education and licensure which gave the regular physicians a competitive edge and the emergence of stronger drug regulation to protect consumers from excesses of the proprietary medicine industry (p. 26).

According to Starr (1982), changes occurred toward the end of the nineteenth century that expanded the market for physicians. More people began to live in towns and cities which expanded the potential patient population.

At the same time, the development of the automobile and telephone offered the means for contacting physicians and reduced the cost to the physician and family for the travel to take care of the patient. The reduction in indirect costs and the rise of cities put medical care within the income range of more people. The improved local transportation also decreased the response time for physicians responding to patient calls (Starr, p. 71).

Healthcare Scientific Epoch 1890s–1920s

The period from 1890 through the 1920s, characterized as the Scientific Epoch of American healthcare, serves as an important foundational period for the future and a contrast to the preceding free trade period. E. H. L. Corwin, in his book *The American Hospital*, indicates that the earliest listing of hospitals in the country was compiled in 1873 by Dr. J. M. Toner and published by the American Medical Association (p. 1). At that time, there were 178 hospitals in the country and most of these were in the states of New York, Pennsylvania, Illinois, and Massachusetts. It is interesting to note that by 1927, the basic elements of the modern hospital were in place and the number of hospitals had grown to ~6,800 hospitals from 173 in 1873.

Paul Starr (1982) notes that the impulse to start hospitals typically "came from physicians who struck up alliances with wealthy and power-ful sponsors" (p. 153). This resulted in the organization of hospitals falling under lay leadership who provided the legitimacy in the community and the financial support as the physicians provided the clinical services. The benefit to the benefactors was the enhancement of their reputations in the com-munity as the hospitals provided a place for the diseased, destitute, and deranged away from the population and improved the general environment of the city. "The sponsorship of hospitals gave legitimacy to the wealth and position of the donors just as the association with prominent citizens gave legitimacy to the hospital and its physicians" (p. 153).

Starr views the transition to the modern hospital as beginning with the Florence Nightingale influence that appeared during the Civil War. Nightingale's advocacy for "cleanliness and ventilation" was taken to heart as the Union Army operated 130,000 beds in the last year of the war and treated a million soldiers "with a mortality rate of eight percent" (p. 154). In the years after the war, the "professionalization of nursing" beginning in 1873 and the "spectacular rise in surgery" in the late 1800s were major contributors to the development of hospitals (p. 154). Nursing schools provided hospitals with the labor of unpaid student nurses "who became the mainstays of the hospital labor force" (p. 156).

In the last decade of the nineteenth century, surgeons began to transition their paying patients from "kitchen surgery" to small hospitals specifically for surgery and finally, after 1900, to the hospital (p. 157). The components of surgery such as ether (1846), aseptic surgery (1886), heat sterilization of instruments (1891), and rubber surgical gloves (1889) became part of the surgical process and improved outcomes. Malcolm T. MacEachern (1957) points out that the discovery of the X-ray in 1895 represented an important diagnostic advance that required significant investment in equipment and facilities. Most individual physicians were not able to afford the cost and served as an incentive for the placement of equipment in a community hospital for use by a group of physicians (p. 20). With the advent of testing for a variety of illnesses, laboratories and isolation facilities were also important to the growth of hospitals.

Starr comments that as the cost of operating hospitals increased, hospitals began to seek greater payments by patients and began to design facilities for paying patients. Surgery was the basis for expansion and profit in hospital care (p. 157). MacEachern identifies a number of late nineteenth-century changes that contributed to the development of hospitals. Hospital construction shifted from "25–50 beds in a ward with little provision for segregation of patients" to a new style of architecture with smaller wards and better ventilation that became known as the American plan (p. 19). Starr indicates that "in 1908 large wards declined to only 28 percent of beds designed that year while single rooms accounted for nearly forty percent" (p. 159).

Hospitals at the time provided services based on the ability of patients to pay. For the wealthy, hospitals offered suites and expensive furnishings to create a setting similar to their homes. Their personal physicians and private nurses attended to their needs during their hospital stay. For the middle class who could afford to pay for their care, hospitals provided semi-private rooms with minimum furnishings. The hospital nurses would provide care under the direction of the physician who admitted the patient. Finally, for the poor, the hospitals continued to operate wards or large rooms with a number of patients in the same room. These patients received charity care delivered by physicians who agreed to volunteer time to care for the poor as part of their hospital medical staff membership.

Joel D. Howell comments in his book, *Technology in the Hospital: Transforming Patient Care in the Early Twentieth Century*, "medical care changed between 1900 and 1925 to a form dominated by machines and science" (p. 2). Howell examines changes in two large hospitals during this period and summarizes his findings as reflecting "widespread changes in how healthcare was provided in US hospitals between 1900 and 1925" (p. 2). He observed that "In 1900, physicians rarely used laboratory tests to guide their clinical decisions, patients rarely thought that science could be relevant for their day-to-day care. In 1900, few specialized tests were being done in the hospital. Few medical tests were being done at all" (p. 3).

In contrast, he found that "By 1925, the hospital world...had changed considerably. Blood tests played an important role in assigning a diagnosis to many patients' ailments. Ward laboratories near the patients' beds made it easier for house officers to do numerous tests on almost all patients; clinical laboratories run by people who based their careers on administering laboratories were active day and night. X-ray examinations had become routine for essentially all persons suspected of having broken bones as well as for patients with a variety of other conditions" (p. 3).

Howell explains that "...early in the twentieth century science seemed to mean more than merely a body of knowledge, it was a 'method and a spirit,' one that was believed to be compatible with and beneficial for just about any aspect of society" (p. 30). He points out that because of the advances in scientific medicine and medical education, it is not surprising that healthcare delivery in America would be an area in which this thinking would be prevalent (p. 31).

In America, confidence in science and scientific methods of observation and rationalization became a defining aspect of the Scientific Epoch. This modern perspective permeated all aspects of society including healthcare as scientific discoveries led to innovations and the creation of new technology that improved life. The railroads, telegraph and telephone, and electricity expanded throughout the country in the late nineteenth century. These provided a clear illustration to people of the important changes in everyday life resulting from the application of scientific discoveries.

The scientific discoveries related to pain management and sterility found their most profound application in the development of the operating room in the hospital. Internist was quite capable of providing care for their patients in the traditional setting of homes, but the new science associated with surgery made it much more difficult to create the appropriate environment with the appropriate staff in a patient's home. Sterility had become an important aspect of surgical procedures, and it was much easier to establish this level of care in an operating room.

Howell emphasized that the critical importance of lighting to surgery, particularly in deep wounds and incisions made the hospital operating room the preferred site over homes. Although surgery could be performed using sunlight, electrical lighting provided a more dependable illumination and could be specifically designed for the type of lighting required for the surgery. In addition to improved illumination, the hospital operating room could provide the new instruments that were designed to be sterilized in the autoclave. Not all surgeons possessed this type of instruments and it was much more convenient for the hospital to provide them (Howell, p. 59).

Howell identifies another important factor that contributed to the use of hospital operating rooms. As the number of surgeries dramatically increased in the 1920s, the ability of the hospital to coordinate and facilitate the flow of the surgical patients into the operating room and out again represented a significant technological advancement for the surgeons and the patients. According to Howell, there was a significant increase in the number of surgeries at Pennsylvania Hospital from 870 in 1900 to 4,180 in 1925 (Howell, p. 65).

Corwin (1946) notes in a study of 8,758 families in 130 localities in 18 states between 1928 and 1931, of the total number of hospital cases in these families, 62% were surgical. Tonsils and adenoids accounted for nearly a third of the cases. Among the families studied, 78% of the surgical cases were hospitalized while 6% of the non-surgical cases were hospitalized (Corwin, p. 91). Howell emphasized that the large number of surgical cases affected housekeeping, nursing, cooking, accounting and essentially required a transformation of hospitals to handle the volume of cases as well as the volume of paperwork associated with the cases (Howell, p. 65).

As industry and medicine displayed the advances of science, concepts associated with scientific management and efficiency influenced the views of businesses and other organizations. Scientific management was the means for promoting efficiency. Efficiency during this period was associated with four principles (Haber, 1964, p. ix): (1) Personal attribute – "an efficient person was an effective person" which encompassed hard work and discipline (p. ix); (2) Machine – "the word signified the energy output-input of a machine" (p. ix); (3) Commercial efficiency – "the output-input ratio of dollars" associated with business enterprise (p. x); and (4) Relationships or social efficiency – "efficiency meant social harmony and the leadership of the "competent" (p. x).

Frederick W. Taylor's program of industrial management or "scientific management" sought to uncover the laws of management which could be universally applied. He was an important contributor to the promotion of efficiency (Haber, pp. ix–xi). The concepts promoted by Taylor and others of the universally desirable effects of scientific management and the associated efficiency influenced the organizational restructuring of businesses beginning with the railroads. "U.S. entrepreneurs came to believe that the road to growth, success, and increased profits was paved by the precise application of scientific methods to their business management" (Howell, p. 31). Railroads used healthcare services in the treatment of worker injuries and the success of the efficiency movement in the railroads proved influential in the operation of hospitals as well. As hospitals performed more surgeries, the need for efficient movement of patients through the care process required better coordination between a number of departments (Howell, p. 59).

With the increasing numbers of paying patients receiving surgeries in the hospital, the ability to accurately track the expenses and the revenue associated with these patients became a major concern for hospital benefactors who were familiar with similar issues in business and the value of efficiency. "There was a widespread belief that careful, systematic, scientific attention to finances would enable the hospital to operate in a more efficient manner to use its limited funds better in serving the needs of whatever community relied on it for care" (Howell, p. 33).

According to Howell, by 1925, the identification of hospitals with science was well advanced, and the efficiency movement was a significant influence in the administrative structure of the hospital and in the design of the financial and accounting system that were shaping hospital operations more and more (Howell, p. 3). In many communities, the hospital became the clearest expression of the link between the community and the progress that was being made in scientific research and the innovations resulting from that research. The distinctive architecture of the local hospital often sets it apart from other buildings. As facilities that were required to operate 24 hours a day, hospitals had electricity, plumbing, heating and ventilation systems, and other support systems that were often unique in the community.

Early in the twentieth century, the evolution of hospitals across the country moved toward the dual structure of an administration to oversee the general operation of the hospital and a medical staff to organize the work of the physicians and clinical operations. By the 1920s, the organization of hospitals and the professional status of physicians had become sufficiently defined to be considered relatively consistent across the country as evidenced by the American College of Surgeon efforts to establish and survey hospitals and to rate their compliance with minimum standards. The first "standard" document for hospital standardization was adopted by the American College of Surgeons Board of Regents on December 20, 1919. The 1918 standard (1) established medical staff organizations in hospitals, (2) restricted membership to licensed practitioners in good standing, (3) mandated that the medical staff work with hospital administration to develop and adopt regulations and policies governing their professional work, (4) required standardized, accessible medical records, and (5) required availability of diagnostic and therapeutic facilities (Wright, 2017).

Professional status of physicians evolved during the late nineteenth and early twentieth centuries into the form that exists today. The American Medical Association (AMA) led the effort for the professionalization of physicians in a variety of structures. Three key elements of physician professional status are the licensure granted by the states, privileges granted by local healthcare organizations, and Drug Enforcement Administration (DEA) registration permitted the prescribing of medications.

The State Boards of Medicine established the standards for issuing licensure to practice medicine in the states. Since the early twentieth century, graduation from accredited universities and medical schools became the standard for licensure. Physicians who had acquired licenses were able to apply for privileges at local hospitals. The hospitals approve which privileges they may exercise at the local hospital. Finally, the DEA authorizes physicians to prescribe medications.

Based on this structure, physicians can work as independent practitioners with only minimal oversight by local hospitals and local hospital administration. Eliot Freidson described physicians as the "preeminent professionals" in America primarily due to their autonomy in the technical and clinical aspects of American healthcare. It is in the autonomy of physicians based on licensure and their role in defining health, illness, and treatment that the profession exercises its dominant influence. The federal government and states have permitted the profession via the AMA and the State Medical Societies to establish the standards for both education and licensure to practice.

Hospital organizational structures promoted by the American College of Surgeons through its surveys have proven resilient and continue today. Under the governing body, the administrative structure and medical staff structure coexist within the organization. These two structures operate differently from each other. The administrative structure is bureaucratic and incorporates all the elements of bureaucracy: hierarchical accountability with both discipline and pay included in the evaluation by the superiors; job titles and descriptions, and specific policies and procedures that require compliance in departmental functions and responsibilities; and deference to and support for organizational values and strategic initiatives. The medical staff on the other hand is a fraternal organization in which membership is determined by vote of the officers and approval by the board. Officers are elected by the members of the medical staff. The medical staff members agree to abide by the Bylaws and Rules and Regulations of the Medical Staff. Medical staff members that are independent practitioners may be asked to abide by organizational policies and procedures, but decision related to the care of the patient is ultimately the decision of the independent practitioner. Removal from the medical staff is by vote of the officers of the medical staff and approval by the board.

By the 1920s, the two universally recognized icons of American healthcare had been established: the hospital and the physician. These two elements of healthcare formed the foundation upon which twentieth-century American healthcare was based and all that followed through the remainder of the century grew out of this foundation. The hospital served as the symbol in almost every community of the quality of life and the aspirations of the citizens. As hospitals expanded their range of services to include 24-hour emergency rooms, maternity services, intensive care units, highly sophisticated diagnostic and laboratory capabilities, and surgical suites with highly trained operating teams, communities took great pride and comfort from the presence of these facilities.

Often hospitals became one of the largest employers in the area and attracted highly skilled and educated employees to the community. Industries looking to expand favored communities that had hospitals as improving their ability to recruit workers and to maintain the health of their workforce. Other healthcare services in the community such as drug stores, medical equipment suppliers, nursing homes and ambulance services became closely associated with the hospital and depended on the organization for referrals and clinical services.

Community hospitals drew significant support from residents in the form of philanthropy in the early decades of the century. For many members of the community, supporting the local hospital was a source of pride and a meaningful commitment to improve the health and the quality of life community supporting the local hospital in its efforts to grow and expand services. Granted its own signage of the white "H" against a blue background, hospitals since the early twentieth century epitomizes American healthcare.

In many communities, the local hospital became a symbol of progress and quality of life in the community.

A key issue throughout the twentieth century for physicians and hospitals was the ability of patients to pay for services. As hospitals acquired more equipment and expanded services, philanthropy to provide care for charity patients was no longer sufficient for meeting the costs of operating the hospital. The paying patients admitted by physicians on the medical staff became an important source of revenue for the hospitals. Hospitals turned their attention to designing services specifically for paying patients, particularly in terms of hotel-type services and room arrangements. At the same time, physicians became more dependent on the local hospital to care for their patients as medical education for physicians occurred in hospitals associated with medical schools and universities. Having been trained to depend on hospital services, physicians turned to hospitals to provide the services for their patients. With the increasing cost of care, many patients found it difficult to pay both the physician and the hospital. The physicians and hospital also found that the rising costs decreased the number of local residents who were able to afford hospital care. This became especially acute in the 1930s as the country struggled through the effects of the Great Depression and hospitals found they had empty beds with fewer patients.

Healthcare Scarcity Epoch 1930s–1940s

The Scarcity Epoch marks the period during the 1930s and 1940s when the Great Depression upended the economy of the entire country and the World War II shifted resources, particularly the labor force, in a variety of ways to support the war effort. Healthcare struggled along with the rest of the country during this period as the move to hospital-based care delivered by licensed physicians and nurses had accelerated during the Scientific Epoch and now found fewer patients with the means to obtain the more expensive care.

Rosemary Stevens (1999) states, "The failure of the stock market led, in rapid succession, to widespread unemployment, huge increases in the welfare rolls, and a sharp drop in savings and charitable donations" (p. 141). The implications for hospitals were severe as "patients flocked to hospitals as ward rather than private patients and to government hospitals rather than nongovernmental institutions" (p. 141). Stevens indicates that "no major hospital closed its doors during the Depression (p. 142), but while governmental hospitals saw a tremendous increase in patients, private nonprofit hospitals had whole floors that were empty of patients" (p. 143). In 1933, the overall occupancy rate for government hospitals of all types was over 90%, compared with only 55% for nongovernmental hospitals as a whole. In response to the decline in paying patients and sources of charitable contributions, hospitals responded by cutting salaries and wages, reduced working hours and delayed building maintenance. Nurses and young doctors continued to work for less pay or even no pay but with food and lodging (p. 143).

Hospitals offered credit and worked hard to collect on bad debts from sources who could pay, but a number of hospitals closed between 1928 and 1936. "A survey in 1936 found that more than two out of every five or 400 hospitals owned by individuals and partnerships closed between 1928 and 1936" (Stevens, p. 147). Almost one out of every five government hospitals closed during the period, one out of six hospitals run by corporations and more than one out of ten of the hospitals owned by churches and fraternities (p. 147).

Interestingly, as smaller hospitals and specialty hospitals failed during the period, large community hospitals expanded and increased their number of beds. "The average general hospital grew from 84 beds in 1929 to 104 beds in 1940" (Stevens, p. 148). The loss of small and underperforming hospitals created a climate for consolidation in the larger hospitals that were able to absorb the costs associated with radiology, pathology, and other technical services (p. 148). These larger hospitals actively solicited funds from local governments to cover the charity care costs for patients who could not pay (p. 149).

World War II ultimately brought the Great Depression to an end, but it created additional difficulties for American healthcare due to the demands for personnel for the war effort and the need to respond to changes resulting from the movement of people around the country. "From the end of 1941…existing hospitals were hard pressed even in major cities because of the staff losses to the war effort" (Stevens, p. 208). In cities with existing hospitals, the influx of additional workers to produce war materials added demands to hospitals that were already closing beds due to lack of staff. "An estimated 1.5 million civilians were expected to move into encampments adjacent to military bases and into newly developed industrial areas…" (p. 208). As many as 6,300 new hospitals beds were needed at a time when staffing existing beds was very difficult.

Stevens graphically illustrates the problems faced by people seeking healthcare during the war in the lack of adequate hospital insurance for young servicemen and their wives. "By late 1941, areas around military camps and installations were badly congested. Babies were born in substandard conditions because of inadequate family funds to pay the hospitals and physician" (p. 210). She notes that the issue was particularly associated with obstetrics because it was "a population of young families and the proportion of births in hospitals was rapidly increasing (to almost 80 percent by the end of the war)" (p. 210). The federal government initiated a program to provide obstetrics, hospitals, and pediatric care around military camps and installation which ultimately covered over one million maternity cases.

Costs for hospital services began to rise with the success of surgery in the Scientific Epoch. It is estimated that by 1929, ~14% of a family's total healthcare bill was hospital services. By 1934, that percentage had increased to 40% of a family's medical bill (Thomasson, 2003). For insurance companies in the 1920s, coverage for healthcare services represented a dilemma. Sickness insurance was available to provide income if someone was sick or injured and could not work, but insurance for healthcare services was not viewed as an insurable commodity because of the inability to predict either the overall cost of care if someone became sick or how many people would end up sick in a group of insured individuals (2003).

Interestingly, the issue was initially resolved by an administrator who faced a problem of empty beds and rising costs with falling charitable contributions at Baylor University Hospital in Dallas, Texas (Cunningham III & Cunningham Jr., 1997, p. 3). Costs had been rising at University Hospital as it went through the transition from almshouse to a "gleaming palace of technology" (p. 4). In 1929, more than a third of all general hospitals' beds in the United States were empty, and University Hospital was behind in its bills and overdue on its debts (p. 4). The administrator had previously created an insurance fund where teachers paid $1 per month for a plan that paid $5 per day in income replacement after the first week of illness. This idea was blended with the concept of "contract medicine" or "company doctor" that was used by railroads and other companies to provide care for workers. The administrator contacted the school administrators to ask if teachers would be interested in a way to plan to pay 50 cents per month for 21 days a year of hospital care (pp. 6–7). This was an early form of prepayment that helped to create a concept for healthcare insurance that would become a fundamental element of American healthcare through the rest of the century and into the twenty-first century.

While hospitals were originally able to cover their costs with endowments and charitable contributions when only charity care was provided, the emergence of medicine as science and the hospital as the delivery system led to increased costs and the need for new payment method. As paying patients became the life's blood of hospitals, pre-payment plans created a way to enable patients to manage the cost of hospitalization. The Great Depression reduced incomes and decreased the number of people who could afford hospital care. Though the plans were promoted as helping the patients, it is clear that hospitals needed enrollment in the pre-payment plans to ensure an adequate number of patients. The American Hospital Association encouraged hospitals to embrace these new payment plans. Though the original model involved one hospital subscribing potential patients to use that particular hospital, the proliferation of plans resulted in increased competition between hospitals to sign up employers to use their hospital (Thomasson). The need for a cooperative arrangement became apparent in the 1930s when tax-supported hospitals care for the poor and veterans were full, while voluntary hospitals nationwide had fallen to 50% occupancy and by the end of the decade hundreds of voluntary hospitals went out of business (Cunningham III & Cunningham Jr., 1997, p. 10).

In 1932, two hospitals in Sacramento, California, set up the first joint pre-payment plan and pooled their resources to underwrite cost. The joint plan actually began with the hospitals seeking to provide hospitalization insurance for their own employees and then broadened out to include the general public. By 1935, the association had grown to involve seven hospitals and almost 6,000 members (p. 11). The first multihospital plan that would ultimately become the Blue Cross system involved the Essex County Hospital Council which included seventeen-member hospitals. The executive director traveled to Dallas and researched the Baylor Plan. Returning to New Jersey, he started the Newark Plan in 1933 which had 6,000 members and thirty hospitals participating with a year (p. 12).

As plans developed, the American Hospital Association began to provide the structure to prevent price competition between hospitals and plans. A basic requirement for the Blue Cross designation included subscribers having free choice of physician and hospital which eliminated single-hospital plans. Blue Cross plans were given special consideration at the state level that proved very beneficial. They were designated as non-profit and granted tax-exempt status. They were permitted to operate outside of the usual insurance regulations, specifically regarding financial reserves. Blue Cross plans were viewed as underwritten by the hospitals in the plan and, therefore, did not need to maintain the reserves required of other insurance plans (Thomasson, 2003).

Physicians viewed any form of healthcare insurance as potentially affecting their ability to set their own fees. The AMA vigorously opposed all efforts at national healthcare insurance throughout the twentieth century. The success of the Blue Cross plans implemented by the hospitals raised serious concerns for the physicians and the AMA that they might eventually seek to include physicians service fees in the plans. Social Security was created in 1935, and there was concern at the time that healthcare benefits could be incorporated into Social Security. Rather than permit hospitals or the government to initiate efforts to cover physician fees and services, the AMA in 1934 passed a set of ten principles including provisions for physicians to set their own fees as guidelines for health plans. Blue Shield plans, as the physician services plans were designated, first appeared in California in 1939. Most Blue Shield plans permitted physicians to charge patients who were in the plans the difference between what the Blue Shield plan paid and the physician's actual charges. This enables physicians to continue to set their own prices and to discriminate between the ability of patients to pay (Thomasson, 2003).

Commercial insurance companies had been reluctant to enter the healthcare insurance market due to the problem of determining the potential financial risks associated with insuring a population. Without some means of estimating the costs of illnesses and the number of individuals who may become ill and require services, the commercial insurers were afraid of incurring significant financial risks. According to Thomasson (2003), the commercial insurers noticed the success of the Blue Cross plans in overcoming the issue of adverse selection by providing health insurance only to groups of employed workers. "This would allow commercial insurance companies to avoid adverse selection because they would insure relatively young, healthy people who did not individually seek health insurance" (Thomasson, 2003). This led to rapid increase in the number of commercial companies offering health insurance beginning in 1940. Thomasson points out that two factors worked in favor of the commercial insurers. The Blue Cross plans, as non-profits, had to community rate their policies in which sicker people are charged the same premium as healthy people. Commercial plans were permitted to rate their policies based on experience and charge higher prices for sicker people and lower premiums for healthy people. For healthy populations, the commercial insurers could lower than prices and successfully compete with the Blue Cross plans. By the early 1950s, the commercial insurers had more subscribers than Blue Cross and Blue Shield (Thomasson, 2003).

The association of health insurance with employment began with the Blue Cross program and grew as commercial insurers entered the market. However, it was during World War II and afterward that the foundation for employer-sponsored health insurance was established. During World War II when wage and price controls were in place, employers competing for labor were permitted to add employee insurance plans to their benefit packages. After the war, pension and insurance benefits were included in wages and unions were allowed to negotiate benefit packages.

Perhaps the biggest boost to the association between employment and health insurance was the tax provisions established in 1943 in which employers did not have to pay payroll taxes on their contributions to employee health plans, and under certain conditions, employees did not have to pay income tax on their employer's contributions to their health plans. These provisions led to a significant increase in the demand for health insurance in the 1950s (Thomasson, 2003).

When a hospital or other entity sets up a pre-payment plan, there is a risk of adverse selection in which patients who are included in the plan use more services than expected, and the amount of money collected in advance if the plan does not price the pre-payment correctly to cover the potential usage. For the early pre-payment plans, working with employers to cover their employees provided a reasonable basis for assuming that the potential patients were healthy enough to work and so would probably not all need care in any given time period. Built into these pre-payment plans is a potential for managing care in such a way as to improve the likelihood that the costs for any individual will be less than expected if that person is assisted in taking care of their health or using healthcare services wisely. Following the initial success of pre-payment plans in Blue Shield, other major pre-paid group practice plans were initiated between 1930 and 1960, including the Group Health Association in Washington, DC, in 1937, the Kaiser-Permanente Medical Program in 1942, the Health Cooperative of Puget Sound in Seattle in 1947, the Health Insurance Plan of Greater New York in New York City in 1947, and the Group Health Plan of Minneapolis in 1957.

Hospitals assumed a growing role in the healthcare delivery system as more and more people were given access to this care through their employers and the insurance programs. Also, at the end of World War II, many more people who served in the armed forces were eligible for Veteran Administration (VA) benefits and were able to have access to VA hospitals. At the same time, physicians were locating in areas with hospitals and this was leaving many rural areas outside of cities with too few physicians to meet the need. To respond to the need for more hospitals to care for a growing population and to encourage physicians to relocate to areas in need of doctors, Congress passed the Hill-Burton Act in 1946 to share the cost of hospital construction between the states and the federal government. This resulted in a boom in hospitals construction that expanded the role of hospitals as the centers of healthcare delivery in areas that previously did not have hospitals.

Healthcare Prosperity Epoch 1950s–1970s

The Scarcity Epoch was followed by the Prosperity Epoch from the 1950s to the 1970s when all the world seemed to belong to American industry and American workers were benefiting from high-paying jobs and lots of benefits. This was the period in which the government promoted the expansion of healthcare. Hospital construction and Medicare and Medicaid programs expanded access to care, and new pharmaceuticals and technology appeared as American industry turned its attention from war to healthcare. The funds to support the growth seemed endless, and more people than ever were able to use the services.

Hospital-based healthcare is expensive. It brings together the skilled surgeons and physicians, nurses, technicians, therapists, and support staff along with very sophisticated technology to deliver care that incorporates the latest developments in medical science. When American policy makers determined that healthcare should be delivered through hospitals, they essentially made the decisions that the costs of this type of care were acceptable. Unfortunately, for people throughout America for most of the twentieth century, the mechanism for managing the costs for these services was not provided. Being unable to afford hospital care in a system that is based on hospital care means running the risk of incurring significant debt simply by trying to manage a healthcare problem at the lowest possible costs. The system is designed around the hospital, and it is very difficult to obtain even minimal care without encountering the expense of hospital care.

Following the development in the 1930s of the employer-based healthcare insurance through Blue Cross and commercial insurers, individuals working for companies either pre-paid for hospital care prior to using it or had their healthcare insurance paid by their employer. This method of paying for healthcare expanded significantly during World War II when government provisions for tax benefits enabled employers to expand healthcare coverage as a way to recruit employees. At the same time, unions were permitted to include healthcare as part of contract negotiations with employers. Finally, employees were not taxed on the healthcare benefits they received from their employers. According to Melissa Thomasson (2003), these inducements made healthcare insurance a valuable part of employment throughout latter half of the twentieth century in which 75% of Americans in 1958 had some form of private health insurance.

With the high employment rate during World War II and with the soldiers returning from the war with military benefits, the demand for healthcare services increased significantly. In addition to the increased demand for services, the country faced a problem with the distribution of physicians to provide care. As part of the expanded requirements for medical training for physicians that grew out of the changes in the early part of the century, physicians were required to train at medical schools associated with universities, and practical experience in hospitals was an important part of the training. As a result of the requirement for hospital-based experience, physicians completing their training and qualifying for licensure sought to live in places where they had access to the services provided by hospitals.

Most communities in rural areas did not have hospitals and were unable to attract physicians out of the large towns and cities to come and work in their communities. In recognition of the demand for hospital services, the importance of hospitals to the delivery of care and the need for communities in rural areas to construct hospitals to attract physicians, Congress passed the Hill-Burton Act in 1947. The Plan provided for federal funds to be used to augment state funding to construct hospitals. In the years following the passage of Hill-Burton, the number of hospitals and the distribution of hospitals to more rural areas increased.

John Henning Schumann (2016), a doctor in Tulsa, Oklahoma and a president of the University of Oklahoma-Tulsa, comments that Hill-Burton, known formally as the Hospital Survey and Construction Act, was the most significant health legislation in the twentieth century besides Medicare and Medicaid. It provided construction grants and loans to communities based on their population and per capita income to assist in constructing healthcare facilities. New facilities were constructed including many in the 40% of US counties that lacked hospitals in 1945. According to Schumann (2016), by 1975, Hill-Burton assisted in the construction of nearly one-third of US hospitals. By the end of the century, 6,800 facilities in 4,000 communities had received financing (2016).

The Hill-Burton Act that supported federal assistance to states for the construction of hospitals to expand access to healthcare was "the first and only federal program to incorporate a guarantee of racial parity within segregated facilities" (Thomas, 2006, p. 839). Hill-Burton included a clause that required "racial parity in areas where segregation was required by law" (p. 825). Thomas states that this "…was the only federal program to include such a clause, which resulted in the proliferation of modern, well-equipped hospitals that admitted black and white patients but internally segregated them by ward or floor" (p. 825). The "biracial hospitals" built with funds from the Act "included blacks in the dramatic postwar expansion, modernization and geographic redistribution of southern hospital facilities, without which the federal program would have remained racially separate and grossly inadequate for patients of all races" (p. 826). Thomas contends that Hill-Burton was applied most successfully in North Carolina. Hospital facilities were built in "areas where the majority of the state's ~1 million African Americans were concentrated and significantly increased the amount of care available to black and indigent patients" (p. 826).

According to Thomasson (2003), critics of national health insurance pointed out that most Americans should be able to afford health insurance on their own or through their employers. They also made the case that national health insurance was costly and was not needed by average Americans who enjoyed reasonably good health. By focusing attention on the plight of the elderly, the supporters of national health insurance were able to overcome these objections. The elderly were not assisted by employers in obtaining health insurance, and their incomes were modest due to living off of savings or Social Security. At the same time, this population had the greatest need for healthcare services, and their quality of life was negatively affected by their inability to pay for these services. The supporters also limited the opposition by recommending that only hospital services should be covered by the nationalized health insurance. This helped to turn back the argument that nationalized health insurance would finance unnecessary healthcare services (Thomasson, 2003).

With the election of John F. Kennedy in 1960 and with Lyndon Johnson's election in 1964 along with the Democrats winning a majority in Congress, the way was open for another attempt at national health insurance. Medicare became law in 1965 and consisted of two parts. In Part A, the elderly were automatically enrolled when they turned 65 years old. Part B of Medicare provided supplemental medical insurance to subsidize physician services. To assuage the concerns of physicians and to prevent them from refusing to serve Medicare patients, Part B reimburses physicians for "usual, customary and reasonable" and permits physicians to continue to price discriminate by charging patients more than what the program paid and forces patients to pay the difference. Like Social Security, Medicare is funded through payroll taxes, income taxes, trust fund interest, and enrollee premiums for Part B (Thomasson, 2003).

As part of the national health insurance plan, Medicaid was passed to provide care for the poor. Unlike Medicare, Medicaid is funded through federal-state program that requires recipients to meet certain requirements. The federal contribution is based on each state's per capita income relative to the national per capita income. Much of the Medicaid program is handled by the states with the federal government establishing minimum standards, and so the benefit provided by the states varies considerably within the broader federal guidelines. Prior to Medicaid, unemployed and disabled individuals were not able to obtain insurance or could not afford to purchase healthcare insurance on their own. The disabled tend to require more healthcare, but they were effectively excluded from accessing the healthcare services in hospitals and physician services while healthier working individuals were able to take advantage of these services. The disparity between these groups and the working population ultimately proved to be the motivation for Congress to create a way for these groups to obtain care. However, largely due to the opposition of the AMA, no national health insurance program succeeded in gaining sufficient political support to pass (Thomasson, 2003).

After the passage of Medicare in 1965, the cost of healthcare paid for by the federal government increased to cover the millions of newly eligible Medicare recipients as they began to use services they could not access in the past. In the effort to gain support for the Medicare program, the provisions for reimbursement for services delivered to Medicare recipients were very generous. As expected with automatic enrollment, the number of enrollees would grow quickly and the costs associated with the program would grow along with the enrollees. As a cost-based reimbursement program, Medicare compensated hospitals not only for the specific costs of caring for the patients but also funding for other services and expenses that the hospital found necessary in order to care for Medicare patients.

Within only a short period, concerns began to be raised that the federal budget was at risk due to the rising costs of healthcare services under Medicare. This led to exploration of ways to control costs. The federal government began to search for ways to reduce cost and to ensure that the funds were being spent for necessary care. Medicare Part A was paid based on the costs of the hospital to deliver care and provide services. With cost as the basis for reimbursement for care delivered to Medicare patients and with additional Medicare support for services associate with elderly patients, hospitals had little incentive to reduce costs. As a matter of fact, it made perfect sense to increase costs by adding additional services whenever it was deemed appropriate for patients because the federal government would reimburse the costs.

From 1967 to 1985, the number of enrollees in Medicare increased from 19.5 to 31.1 million and the expenditures rose from $4.7 to $72.3 billion (HHS Office of Inspector General, 2001, p. 2). Two factors were identified as the sources of the rapid growth in expenditures: (1) payment methodologies that paid providers based on their charges for providing services and consequently created an incentive to provide more services and (2) increases in costly medical technology (2001).

As access to care increased in the Prosperity Epoch, costs increased. Toward the end of the epoch, the political sentiment shifted, and the federal government took steps to address the increasing costs. In 1973, the Health Maintenance Organization (HMO) Act of 1973 (P. L. 93–222) provided a major impetus to the expansion of managed healthcare with $375 million authorized to establish and expand HMOs (National Council on Disability, n.d.). Employers with more than twenty-five employees were required to offer an HMO option and restrictions of HMOs at the state level were overridden. With this legislation, the federal government introduced the concept of for-profit HMO corporation operating in healthcare. The reason for promoting the HMO approach was to facilitate the movement of care out of hospitals as the highest priced setting and to move it to the outpatient facilities (National Council on Disability, n.d.). From 1970 to 1980, Medicare hospital payments increased by 88% (HHS Inspector General, 2001, p. 3). In response to payment growth, Congress adopted a prospective payment system (PPS) to curtail the amount of resources the federal government spent on medical care for the elderly and disabled.

Healthcare Globalization Epoch 1980s–2000s

The Globalization Epoch of American healthcare, spanning the decades from the 1980s to the 2000s, represents a unique time at the end of the twentieth century in which influences from outside of the country as well as within shaped the perspective on healthcare. Following World War II and America's increased engagement with the world, the competition between countries expanded commercially and comparisons of quality of life and provision of basic services between countries became more common. Many countries set up or developed national health systems following the war and provided universal coverage to their populations. Information for comparison on various aspects of the quality of healthcare became available and began to influence American perspectives of their healthcare.

Though America did not set up a national health system after various attempts throughout the twentieth century, it did expand coverage. The last decades of the century, which included the expansion of hospitals and the passage of Medicare, were a time in which the rising cost of healthcare moved from a family concern discussed around the kitchen table to a national concern debated in Congress. Tomes (2016) observed that "In essence the 1980s represented the end of the generous postwar funding for both hospitals and physicians that helped to finance the dramatic expansion of the medical-industrial complex" (p. 329). The federal government, insurers, and businesses sought to slow the increase in healthcare costs through a variety of methods shaped by the prevailing views of the times while individuals and families worked to keep whatever healthcare insurance coverage they had as it was rapidly being undermined in the name of healthcare reform.

In the 1970s, as the government struggled to resolve Vietnam and to recover from Watergate, it also had to deal with high rates of inflation with limited growth. During this period, cost-based reimbursement to Medicare and increasing business costs for employer-sponsored healthcare insurance took larger portions of the federal budget and hit business bottom lines. At the same time, a growing reaction to the 50 years of Roosevelt-inspired expansion of federal involvement in the social welfare of Americans joined with the stagflation of the 1970s to open the way for a new type of liberalism – neoliberalism – to appear as Ronald Reagan in America and Margaret Thatcher in Britain in the 1980s began to implement this new perspective.

Neoliberalism brought a radical new view of individuals and the role of governments. It reconceived the original concept of liberalism, which promoted the freedom of individual human beings to live life with limited governmental interference, into a new vision of individual human beings defined not by their humanity but their success as consumers and equating their freedom as human beings with the freedom of exchange in a marketplace. Neoliberalism re-imagined the government's role as expanding opportunities for businesses through the privatization of public services and deregulation of the commercial environment to facilitate the ability of consumers and businesses to buy and sell without interference. In this neoliberal environment, the government would step back from providing a comprehensive safety net to protect its people and focus instead on expanding their ability to function as consumers to choose the services they desire and that met their needs. Individuals as consumers and businesses would be participants in a global market of products and services with minimal government involvement. According to David Harvey, "Neoliberalization has meant, in short, the financialization of everything" (Harvey, 2005, p. 33).

As neoliberalism shaped the views of government, business, and individuals, globalization as a form of capitalism that views the world as an integrated and minimally regulated market was a natural fit. By the 1970s, the dynamic of the post-war boom that favored America was fading. America was dealing with high rates of inflation exacerbated by oil embargoes and geopolitical issues and lack of continued economic growth. By the 1980s, the focus was on expanding the flow of financial resources globally to fund the expansion of business in developing countries as a defense against communism. Governments would promote and support industrial and business development and the role of individuals as consumers.

One example of the way in which globalization works is Walmart. Beginning as a single store in Arkansas in the 1960s, Walmart expanded across America by creating the most efficient system for supplying its stores that the country had seen. This required a sophisticated information system and delivery system and relationships with suppliers around the world to enable the stores to replace products as quickly as they were sold. Its global system of suppliers enables it to receive products from around the world and works closely with the suppliers to reduce costs and to ensure uninterrupted stream of products. Walmart was so successful that by 2019 it weekly served over 275 million customers and members from their more than 11,300 stores in 27 countries and eCommerce websites. With the fiscal year 2019 revenue of $514.4 bill, it is considered the world's largest retailer (Walmart-Our Story, 2019).

As Walmart and other businesses searched for suppliers who could meet their requirements for quality and price, the ability of foreign suppliers to sell to retailers like Walmart at lower prices due to lower production costs put American manufacturers at a disadvantage. As the quality of foreign products improved in the 1980s and American production costs increased due to the costs of labor, which included rising costs associated with employer-sponsored healthcare insurance, American companies began to move their production facilities to Mexico and other countries with lower labor costs. As trade agreements increased the flow of foreign goods and American goods produced in foreign countries, the outmigration of American jobs to foreign countries increased. This led to the loss of higher paying manufacturing jobs in a number of major industries such as auto manufacturing and textiles and the loss of healthcare insurance for many workers whose job went away.

Healthcare costs continued to rise until they reached 10.8% of Gross National Product by 1983. The Social Security Amendments of 1983 mandated the PPS for hospitals, effective in October of fiscal year 1983 (HHS Office of Inspector General, 2001). Congress in 1983 capped hospital reimbursement rates under the Medicare program and the secretary of Health and Human Services developed a methodology for reimbursing hospitals based on diagnosis-related groups (DRGs). Following negotiations involving federal officials and representatives of the hospital industry, a Medicare PPS was developed with 468 DRGs, with a fixed hospital payment rate assigned to each group. The DRGs "bundle" services (labor and non-labor resources) that are needed to treat a patient with a particular disease. For fiscal year 2002, there were 499 DRGs with a prospective price based on average resources used in treating patients (2001).

Medicare inpatient payments to hospitals stabilized with the DRG system (HHS Office of Inspector General, 2001). Reducing the growth in healthcare costs was consistent with the neoliberal view of healthcare as part of a marketplace in which the government's role was to promote conditions favorable to the market dynamics of supply and demand and competition. Whenever possible, the government would provide opportunities for private enterprises to take on a larger role in what had previously been viewed as governmental services. Commercial healthcare insurance delivered via managed care was consistent with the view.

Since DRGs were applied exclusively to Medicare payments, hospitals also began to shift unreimbursed costs to private health insurance plans. As a result, average per employee health plan premiums doubled between 1984 and 1991, rising from $1,645 to $3,605. With health insurance costs eroding profits, many employers took aggressive steps to control healthcare expenditures. Plan benefits were reduced. Employees were required to pay a larger share of healthcare costs through higher insurance premiums (National Council on Disability Appendix B, n.d.).

More and more employers – especially large corporations – decided to pay employee health costs directly rather than purchasing health insurance.

A steadily increasing number of businesses turned to managed healthcare plans to rein in spiraling healthcare outlays. During the late 1980s and early 1990s, managed care plans sought to eliminate unnecessary hospitalizations and negotiated with participating physicians and other healthcare providers to provide services at reduced rates. Through these efforts, the costs of care began to decline. By 1993, a majority (51%) of Americans receiving health insurance through their employers were enrolled in managed healthcare plans (NCD).

In working to reduce costs, however, the managed care plans created an adversarial relationship with their members and the complaints began to reach state lawmakers. In response, many states imposed requirements on managed care companies to address the complaints of patients. Though the reality may have been different from the perception in that only a small percentage of patients were denied services and the medical outcomes of managed care compared to fee-for-service health plans were similar, the denials were sufficient to create a sense of distrust between the managed care plans and their patients. Healthcare, whether its services or payment, requires a sense of trust due to the potential for affecting an individual's health. In failing to address these concerns, the managed care companies were viewed as overly concerned with costs compared to patient well-being and only interested in mass marketing their services for profit (NCD Appendix B, n.d.).

Hospitals also discovered an opportunity for recovering revenue loss to DRGs through outpatient departments. Many hospitals expanded their outpatient services in order to offset revenues lost as a result of shorter hospital stays. Between 1983 and 1991, the percentage of hospitals with outpatient care departments grew from 50% to 87%. Hospital revenues derived from outpatient services doubled over the period, reaching 25% of all revenues by 1992.

As American healthcare absorbed the changes associated with reduced payments through Medicare prospective payment and managed care in the 1990s, increasing globalization began to influence American healthcare in an unexpected way. American industries were competing with foreign producers, and they were challenged by the developments in Japan in electronics and automobile manufacturing. In the 1970s and 1980, Toyota made its presence felt in the American car market by producing high-quality automobiles while maintaining low production costs. Motorola was struggling with poor-quality electronics products competing with much higher-quality Japanese products that sold at competitive prices. American industry slowly realized that the Japanese had developed new methods of production that gave them a significant advantage.

Toyota management and Taiichi Ohno, in particular, expanded on the ideas promoted by American quality experts Edwards Deming, Joseph Juran, and others. Ohno developed the Toyota Production System which successfully competed with American car manufacturers in the 1980s and 1990s with less waste and higher quality supporting larger profits on cars. In 1990, the book *The Machine that Changed the World* introduced the Toyota Production System that was later identified as "Lean" in America (Womack, Jones, Roos, 2007). In order to compete in a global market, American companies needed to change the way they produced their products and this led to the development of Toyota-style Lean manufacturing techniques in car manufacturing. Motorola responded to the Japanese challenge in electronics by developing techniques to achieve Six Sigma levels of defect-free manufacturing.

An analysis of studies published in an article in 1988 in the MIT Sloan Management Review by Michael Cusumano offered a simple explanation for the way Toyota had been so successful in creating high-quality cars at reasonable prices that produced high margins for the company. "To a large degree Toyota and Taiichi Ohno built upon Taylor's work in process analysis and Ford's efforts to create an integrated, smoothly running mass-production system. But Toyota and other Japanese companies introduced a fundamental concept: continual rather than one-time improvement, achieved through successive process refinements and a greater integration of workers and suppliers into the production system" (Cusumano, 1988).

The "Taylor" referred to by Cusumano (1988) in the quote above is Frederick Taylor who early in the twentieth century promoted the concept of scientific management as the means to create efficiency in work processes (Taylor, 1911). The Ford is Henry Ford who designed the famous Ford assembly line. Taiichi Ohno who worked at Toyota was responsible for moving the Toyota Production System or Lean in America to its full development. Even as Henry Ford had sought to incorporate every part of the production of a car into an integrated whole, so Toyota built a system in which their suppliers and their employees were integrated into the production process. Toyota Production System focused on the flow of the production process and the pursuit of perfection. This essentially meant that every step in the process had to fit neatly into the step that followed and the effort to improve was continuous. The value stream of production required the elimination of as much waste as possible to ensure the lowest possible cost and the fastest possible production.

During this period, Motorola, an American electronics manufacturer, was struggling with the same problem that had afflicted the American automotive industry. Japanese electronics manufacturers were producing equipment with higher quality and fewer defects and doing it at lower costs than American manufacturers. Searching through all the available resources on quality improvement and cost reduction, quality staff at Motorola formulated Measure, Analyze, Improve, and Control and incorporated a variety of quality tools into this structure. The key aspect of the program that they developed was reducing defects in products to 3.4 defects per 1 million opportunities/products. This rate of defects equates to Six Sigma variation in products. This is so that even variation out to six standard deviations in a control chart are still within the specifications required by the customer. As a result of its success with the Six Sigma program, Motorola was awarded the first Malcolm Baldrige Award. As a recipient of the award, Motorola was required to share its program in order to improve American manufacturing as a whole. General Electric and Allied Signal began to use the concepts and techniques developed by Motorola in the Six Sigma program, and they further developed it to its final structure as DMAIC – Define, Measure, Analyze, Improve, Control.

Charles Kenney (2008) describes the way in which Paul Batalden, MD, and Don Berwick, MD, encountered W. Edwards Deming and ultimately introduced industrial quality improvement into healthcare. Paul Batalden, MD, pediatrician worked at the National Institutes of Health and as a quality assurance director for a health policy group. He published *Quality Assurance in Ambulatory Care.* After reading an article about Edwards Deming in 1981 and called him and went to a seminar taught by Deming in December 7–10, 1981. Deming won him over and he wrote a section in Deming's book, *Out of the Crisis* on the 14 points for healthcare. Batalden contacted Tommy Frist, CEO of Hospital Corporation of America, to fund a quality resource group within Hospital Consumer Assessment (HCA) which owned or managed 390 hospitals. Quality Resource Group taught thousands of HCA employees Deming's Profound Knowledge.

Don Berwick, MD, pediatrician, joined Harvard Community Health Plan to work on quality assurance in 1982. Berwick visited industries to learn about quality, including NASA and Bell Labs and met Batalden at a conference in the mid-1980s. Batalden convinced Berwick to attend a Deming seminar in 1986. After an odd meeting with Deming, Berwick was won over (Kenney, 2008). In 1987, Berwick and others held the National Demonstration Project on Quality Improvement in Healthcare with twenty-one healthcare organizations and quality experts meeting in Boston to answer the question: "Can the tools of modern quality improvement with which other industries have achieved breakthroughs in performance help in healthcare as well?" Is quality in healthcare a simple matter of people – doctors usually – just doing their jobs right? Berwick and Batalden continued to explore quality in healthcare and were joined by Gene Nelson, an early expert in quality measurement. Nelson suggested that they form a group, which became the Birthday Club, to explore quality in healthcare. In 1991, the group created the Institute for Healthcare Improvement (IHI) with Batalden, Berwick, etc. in leadership roles.

The Toyota Production System as designed by Taiichi Ohno operated as a continuous process for reducing waste. Americanized Lean was also focused on reducing waste but operated on a project basis. Lean has a flexible methodology that focuses on basic improvement tools such as flowchart, value stream mapping, and cause and effect diagrams to identify opportunities for reducing any of the famous eight types of waste named by Taiichi Ohno (1988). Improvements are implemented using the Plan-Do-Study-Act cycles (also known as Deming or Shewhart cycles) as tests of changes that might lead to improvement.

Six Sigma in its original form has not been as successful in penetrating the healthcare market primarily due to the intensity of data collection and analysis that is required. Healthcare organizations throughout the Globalization Epoch struggled to collect data. Despite its sophisticated technology, American healthcare has not become comfortable with data analysis specifically from a statistical perspective as required for Six Sigma analysis.

Since Lean had no inherent project structure, Six Sigma offered a structure and a complementary approach to identifying and removing defects that could be used in conjunction with Lean. Over time, quality improvement training combined the two methodologies. Lean offered a philosophy and tools for identifying and eliminating waste. Six Sigma offered the "DMAIC" structure of "Define-Measure-Analyze-Improve-Control" and a statistical approach to identifying defects in products and services. Healthcare organizations began to use Lean, Six Sigma, and Lean Six Sigma to approach quality improvement in the 2000s (Glasgow, Scott-Caziewell, & Kaboli, 2010).

As healthcare organizations explored industrial quality improvement during the Globalization Epoch, the costs of healthcare continued to increase. During the 1990s, managed care slowed the increase in healthcare costs through aggressive reviews of the utilization of services. However, this approach proved unacceptable to patients and healthcare professionals and was reduced or eliminated (National Council on Disabilities).

An interesting perspective has come to light in recent years concerning the costs of healthcare that helps to explain why it has been so difficult for healthcare using quality improvement to control costs. There has been a disconnect between the methodologies of quality improvement and the actual sources of higher costs in American healthcare. As a percentage of Gross Domestic Product, healthcare in America is approaching 20% and is continuing to rise. A recent article in the *Journal of the American Medical Association* reported that spending in other high-income countries ranged from 9.6% (Australia) to 12.4% (Switzerland) with the United States spending 17.8% (Papanicolas, Woskie, & Jha, 2018, p. 1024). Life expectancy in the United States is the lowest of eleven countries in the study (p. 1024).

The article identified three primary drivers of that rise in the United States as compared with other high-income countries: Administrative costs – planning, regulating, and managing health systems accounted for 8% in the United States vs 1%–3% in other countries; pharmaceutical costs – spending per capita of $1443 in the United States vs a range of $66–939 in other countries; salaries of physicians and nurses in the United States were higher compared with other countries, such as generalist physician salaries $218,173 in the United States compared with a range of $86,607–$154,126 in other countries (p. 1024). Utilization rates in the US were comparable to other countries in the study. It was noted in the article that utilization rates in the United States "were largely similar to those in other nations" (p. 1038).

Given the sources of increases in healthcare spending, efforts targeting utilization alone are unlikely to reduce the growth in healthcare spending in the United States (p. 1038). It is interesting to note that the areas identified as contributing to cost increases such as physician salaries, pharmaceuticals and administrative costs have their roots in the way in which American healthcare developed in the early and middle twentieth century when other countries were developing national programs for healthcare. The cost problems in American healthcare could be traced back to the way America trains and compensates its physicians, rewards pharmaceutical companies and other organizations for technological innovation, and pays management in healthcare organizations. Most of these drivers of cost reached grew out of the cost-based reimbursement scheme of the 1970s and 1980s and the tradition of American healthcare's cultural past. Based on this research, industrial methods of improvement will not be enough to reduce costs as was hoped in the 1980s.

Though managed care and industrial quality methods have not been successful in providing a sustained decrease in the rising costs of healthcare, they have contributed to the transformation of American healthcare from a relationship based in a community to the view of healthcare as a commodity that is produced and sold in the marketplace like other commercial products. The implementation of industrial quality methods into American healthcare has resulted in the expansion of neoliberalism into the relationship between organizations delivering healthcare and the people receiving healthcare.

The Globalization Epoch of American healthcare was a period in which comparisons with healthcare around the world and as well as new methods for improvement became important influences. The high costs of healthcare and the quality as compared with the rest of the world became clearer. Lean brought the Toyota Production System into American healthcare as a major change in the way care was to be improved. The combination of a global perspective on healthcare and the views of customers as espoused by Lean brought neoliberal views into American healthcare.

In light of these new influences, healthcare began to develop a new perspective on the partnership of the people receiving care with the people delivering care that comes to the forefront in the Sociotechnical Epoch that follows. As technology becomes an integral part of healthcare delivery, it has finally become possible for the people receiving care to be able to actively participate in the design of care and in the determination of the way in which care is financed. Having passed through a dynamic era of change, healthcare is moving out from the rigid structure of the past to fully express its properties as a complex adaptive system. This enables it to focus on the nature of healthcare as an experience between the people seeking care and the people providing care within the context of the organizations in which it occurs. This is where the greatest opportunities lie for improving healthcare.

Healthcare Sociotechnical Epoch 2010s–Present

Klaus Schwab, Founder and Executive Chairman of the World Economic Forum, set forth the case that the world is entering an unprecedented era that he dubbed "The Fourth Industrial Revolution" in an article in 2016. "We stand on the brink of a technological revolution that will fundamentally alter the way we live, work, and relate to one another. In its scale, scope, and complexity, the transformation will be unlike anything humankind has experienced before. We do not yet know just how it will unfold, but one thing is clear: the response to it must be integrated and comprehensive, involving all stakeholders of the global polity, from the public and private sectors to academia and civil society" (Schwab, 2016).

He places the current world state in the context of the industrial revolutions of the past. "The First Industrial Revolution used water and steam power to mechanize production. The Second used electric power to create mass production. The Third used electronics and information technology to automate production. Now a Fourth Industrial Revolution is building on the Third, the digital revolution that has been occurring since the middle of the last century. It is characterized by a fusion of technologies that is blurring the lines between the physical, digital, and biological spheres" (Schwab, 2016). The difference in the Fourth from preceding revolutions, according to Schwab, is the speed of change, the breadth of the effects in terms of industries and countries, and the nature of the systems of production, management, and governance that are changing.

Perhaps the most intriguing are his remarks that "The Fourth Industrial Revolution, finally, will change not only what we do but also who we are" (Schwab, 2016). He argues that the changes will affect "our identity and all the issues associated with it: our sense of privacy, our notions of ownership, our consumption patterns, the time we devote to work and leisure, and how we develop our careers, cultivate our skills, meet people, and nurture relationships" (2016).

In terms of healthcare, he anticipates that it will lead to a "quantified" self, and an "augmentation" that expands beyond our physical being to create a "symbiosis" with the environment. "This augmentation," he contends, will result as "Engineers, designers, and architects are combining computational design, additive manufacturing, materials engineering, and synthetic biology to pioneer a symbiosis between microorganisms, our bodies, the products we consume, and even the buildings we inhabit" (2016).

Given the profound changes envisioned by Schwab, it seems appropriate to designate the current epoch of American healthcare as the Sociotechnical Epoch and to give it a starting point somewhere around 2010. This epoch focuses on new technology involving electronic information systems and communications that transforms the way in which people and organizations deliver healthcare and the way in which people receive healthcare. Two important changes in American healthcare form the basis for understanding the Sociotechnical Epoch as it is differentiated from the earlier periods on healthcare development in America.

The first is the revolution in the work environment within healthcare organizations that resulted from incorporating electronic information systems into all aspects of the work and the work took on the characteristics of a sociotechnical system. Secondly, the emergence of the experiences of people receiving care as an important consideration in the design of the processes and the quality of care delivered by healthcare organizations. These two perspectives come together in the design of meaningful healthcare experiences during this epoch of American healthcare.

The year 2010 offers a meaningful starting point as the beginning because of the passage of two pieces of legislation by Congress which initiated the change in the information systems in American healthcare. The American Recovery and Reinvestment Act (ARRA) of 2009 included an unprecedented $47 billion federal investment in health information technology (HIT) initiatives. ARRA included electronic health record (EHR) incentive payments of $21.6 billion in Medicaid funding and $23.1 billion in Medicare funding to encourage physicians, hospitals, and other healthcare providers to adopt and "meaningfully use" certified EHRs.

On March 23, 2010, President Barack Obama signed comprehensive health reform, the Patient Protection and Affordable Care Act, into law. To comply with the provisions of the law, healthcare organizations were required to significantly expand their information technology systems. Together, this legislation with ARRA provided significant funding and regulatory incentive to support the development and implementation of electronic information systems in healthcare organizations across the country.

Computers in businesses and organizations can be traced back to the 1950s and electronic information systems appeared in healthcare in the late 1960s. Just as hospitals emerged during the twentieth century based on community's needs, so hospitals and healthcare organizations initially acquired healthcare information technology based on the internal needs and dynamics of the local hospitals. However, these systems began to permeate and revolutionize healthcare only in the late 2000s when the federal government funding and regulatory incentives required and promoted implementation.

There were no standards initially in the type of systems that hospitals should have. There were a variety of vendors and types of systems designed for individual departments such as laboratory or emergency department all the way to enterprise system encompassing all areas. The decisions about the acquisition of information technology reflected the way each organization was governed and the resources available to purchase, equip, and operate the system. For individual hospitals as well as healthcare systems, the selection and implementation of healthcare information technology represented a commitment to years working with the vendor to purchase millions of dollars in equipment, to hire and train new employees to support the system, to adapt the software to the needs of the organization, and months of implementation to ensure that all areas of the system operate appropriately and that all users of the new technology are able to perform their work using it.

For most healthcare organizations, the physicians were a key stakeholder group to the final decisions concerning these systems because of their involvement in using the technology in their work. Physicians designed hospital processes during the twentieth century to accommodate their work. When the new technology appeared, the goal for many physicians was to take their current work processes and documents and create an electronic expression that would accommodate their current way to performing their work. However, this approach served to create hybrid systems in which the existing paper processes undermined the electronic information systems and produced duplication and customized systems that failed to satisfy the practitioners and actually to bring out the potential benefits inherent in the electronic systems.

The introduction and promotion of electronic information systems in healthcare organizations was a result of governmental actions to respond to an economic crisis in the country as well as to bring healthcare into the twenty-first century. The second element of the change in information systems arose from the adoption of personal communication devices by the individuals. It was on January 9, 2007, that Steve Jobs, the founder of Apple, introduced the iPhone and the pocket computer smart phone revolution began (Pierce & Goode, 2018). The iPhone was introduced as a new iPod with revolutionary features. The iPod music player appeared on October 23, 2001, with the capacity to store and play thousands of songs in a device the size of a pack of cards (Edwards, 2011). People could listen to their music wherever they went. Steve Jobs was said to have remarked that he knew the iPod was going to do well when he was walking in New York and saw many people with wired earbuds listening to music as they walked. By September of 2007, over a million iPhones had been sold. By 2018, over 1.5 billion iPhones had been sold (Pierce & Goode, 2018).

Using the iPhone, people could make a call by simply touching a name on a screen and they would be connected. Voicemails could be read as text. The iPhone was referred to as a "full-screen iPod." The touchscreen was more sensitive and responsive than any before it and the QWERTY keyboard appeared on the screen to reduce the size of the device from that of the Blackberry devices that were so popular at the time. It also incorporated Apple's Safari web browser to provide an exceptional ability to read emails, use the web as well as making calls. With the arrival of the new iPhone in 2007, people were able to make phone calls, check and send emails, and listen to music wherever they went. And, as signals for use with the phone proliferated with towers and Wifi in stores, homes, and public spaces, the iPhone and other mobile phones became the constant companion of everyone. This transformed electronic communication from something that occurred at specific locations through wire devices to something that was easy to carry and continuously available (Pierce & Goode, 2018).

In healthcare, iPhones have extended the ability to obtain information and to communicate almost anywhere. The websites of major healthcare insurance companies proudly proclaim, "Virtual visits: The doctor will see you now." The websites are accessible as a visit that can be performed through a mobile device, tablet, or computer. It takes 20 minutes or less. You can obtain a prescription if needed. The website indicates that the cost is significantly less than going to a hospital emergency department. Patients can use their smart phones and a credit card and have a physician visit whenever they feel they need it. Rather than supplementing the physical presence of the physician, the technology literally creates the interface between the physician and patient during a virtual visit. It is convenient and less expensive. The meeting via technology creates a new experience for both the patient and physician.

New technology is the critical factor that shapes the processes and experiences of the people delivering care and the people receiving care as their interactions are mediated through the technology. As the Academy of Medicine expressed in the 2018 report *Crossing the Global Quality Chasm*, "Given the multiple interactions that occur and the highly complex environment in which they occur, a healthcare system can be characterized formally as a sociotechnical system" (Crossing Global Quality Chasm, p. 56). The introduction of electronic information systems into American healthcare and the introduction of new personal technology that revolutionized the experience of healthcare created the foundation of the Sociotechnical Epoch of American healthcare.

The term "sociotechnical" was initially used by a group of researchers at the Tavistock Institute in London, England. The Tavistock Institute consisted of therapists, researchers, and consultants who were interested in finding ways to use techniques that they had developed following World War II while assisting soldiers who were traumatized by the war. According to Eric Trist (1981), a founding member at Tavistock, the "socio-technical concept arose in conjunction with the first of several projects undertaken by the Tavistock Institute in 1949 as part of the postwar reconstruction of industry (1981)." The one specific request associated with sociotechnical concept was a project "on the diffusion of innovative work practices and organizational arrangements that did not require major capital expenditures but which gave promise of raising productivity" (1981).

In researching innovative work practices, the Institute discovered a situation in which workers in a coal mine in South Yorkshire England organized themselves to improve their work. According to the men involved in the work in the mines, the introduction of mechanization into the mine had resulted in a change in the way the work was organized (Trist, 1981). When the new machines were brought into the mines, management organized the workers into large groups with the work broken down into "one-man/one-task roles" and "coordination and control were externalized in supervision" (1981).

Prior to the introduction of the machines, the workers had organized themselves into small, autonomous groups and the groups managed their own shifts and roles with minimum supervision. "The men told us that in order to adapt with best advantage to the technical conditions…, they had evolved a form of work organization based on practices common in the unmechanized days when small groups, who took responsibility for the entire cycle, had worked autonomously. These practices had disappeared as the pits became progressively more mechanized…." (Trist, 1981). The workers "found a way, at a higher level of mechanization, of recovering the group cohesion and self-regulation they had lost and of advancing their power to participate in decisions concerning their work arrangements" (1981).

According to Trist, the situation in the mine in South Yorkshire demonstrated that there needed to be a change in the way organizations designed systems in relation to technology. Trist stated that "For several decades the prevailing direction had been to increase bureaucratization with each increase in scale and level of mechanization. The organizational model that fused Weber's description of bureaucracy with Frederick Taylor's concept of scientific management had become pervasive" (1981).

Trist (1981) summarized the new approach as recognizing that people use technology to carry out their work. This requires a new conception in which work organizations are viewed as sociotechnical systems. "The social and the technical systems were the substantive factors – the people and the equipment" (1981). "Their core interface consists in the relations between a nonhuman system and a human system" (1981). Trist commented that hospitals are inherently sociotechnical as well as psycho-social, which accounts for the complexity of some of their dilemmas.

Enid Mumford (2006), a British social and computer scientist and Professor Emerita of Manchester University, was a council member of the Tavistock Institute. In her article, "The story of socio-technical design: reflections on its successes, failures and potential," she traces the history of the Tavistock Institute's work in sociotechnical design emphasizing the values promoted as an essential aspect of this approach to organizing work. Mumford points out that a key element of their work was to emphasize the human or social aspect of the design of work in organizations by giving the workers the ability to participate in the design of the work particularly as it related to introduction and use of new technology. She defines sociotechnical as an approach and methodology in which technology, defined as machines and associated work organization, is not allowed to be the controlling factor when new systems are implemented. Equal attention, according to Mumford, is focused on providing a high-quality and satisfying work environment for employees. Within his context, she points out that sociotechnical design "had an important democratic component: employees who used the systems should be involved in determining the required quality of working-life improvement" (p. 318).

The Tavistock Institute developed specific principles for the sociotechnical design of work in organizations that bring together the technical aspects of the uses of modern technology as well as the social aspects of employee engagement and work. Albert Cherns, an associate of the Tavistock Institute, in a 1976 article in *Human Relations* stated "How, then, do you design a socio-technical system? Can we communicate any principles of socio-technical design?" (p. 3).

Cherns (1976) argued that the phrase sociotechnical system had acquired "the connotation that organizational objectives are best met not by the optimization of the technical system and the adaptation of a social system to it, but by the joint optimization of the technical and the social aspects, thus exploiting the adaptability and innovativeness of people in attaining goals instead of over-determining technically the manner in which these goals should be attained" (1976).

Mumford (2006) described the following nine principles for sociotechnical system design identified by Cherns (pp. 322–323).

Principle 1 – Compatibility – The process of design must be compatible with its objectives. This means that if the aim is to create democratic work structures then democratic processes must be used to create these.

Principle 2 – Minimal Critical Specification – No more should be specified than is absolutely essential. But the essential must be specified. This is often interpreted as giving employee groups clear objectives but leaving them to decide how to achieve these.

Principle 3 – The Sociotechnical Criterion – Variances, defined as deviations from expected norms and standards, if they cannot be eliminated, must be controlled as close to their point of origin as possible. Problems of this kind should be solved by the group that experiences them and not by another group such as a supervisory group.

Principle 4 – Multifunctionality Principle – Work needs a redundancy of functions for adaptability and learning. For groups to be flexible and able to respond to change, they need a variety of skills. These will be more than their day-to-day activities require.

Principle 5 – Boundary Location – Boundaries should facilitate the sharing of knowledge and experience. They should occur where there is a natural discontinuity – time, technology change, etc. – in the work process. Boundaries occur where work activities pass from one group to another and a new set of activities or skills is required. All groups should learn from each other despite the existence of the boundary.

Principle 6 – Information Flow – Must go, in the first instance, to the place where it is needed for action. In bureaucratically run companies, information about efficiency at lower levels is collected and given to management. It is preferable for it to go first to the work group whose efficiency is being monitored.

Principle 7 – Support Congruence – Systems of social support must be designed to reinforce the desired social behavior. If employees are expected to cooperate with each other, management must also show cooperative behavior.

Principle 8 – Design and Human Values – High-quality work requires: jobs to be reasonably demanding, opportunity to learn, an area of decision making, social support, the opportunity to relate work to social life, and a job that leads to a desirable future.

Principle 9 – Incompletion – The recognition that design is an iterative process. The design never stops. New demands and conditions in the work environment mean that continual rethinking of structures and objectives is required.

Understanding the components of HIT as it is employed in healthcare organizations and contributes to the creation of a sociotechnical system is important to gaining insight into the dynamics of the Sociotechnical Epoch of healthcare. Dean F. Sittig, PhD, and Hardeep Singh, MD, MPH, in their article "A new socio-technical model for studying health information technology in complex adaptive healthcare systems" offer an analysis of the dimensions of the sociotechnical aspects that pertain to HIT within complex adaptive systems.

Sittig and Singh (2010) state that "an ongoing challenge to the design, development and implementation and evaluation of health information technology interventions is to operationalize their use within the complex adaptive health care system that consists of high-pressured, fast-paced and distributed settings of care delivery" (p. 2). They developed a "socio-technical model" as a way of approaching the "design, development, use, implementation and evaluation of health information technology" (p. 3).

The following eight dimensions identified by Sittig and Singh (2010) offer a framework for understanding HIT and the considerations associated with its use in healthcare organizations (pp. 4–6).

1. **Hardware and Software Computing Infrastructure** – This dimension of the model focuses solely on the hardware and software required to run the applications. In short, this dimension is purely technical; it is only composed of the physical devices and the software required keeping these devices running. One of the key aspects of this dimension is that, for the most part, the user is not aware that most of this infrastructure exists until it fails.
2. **Clinical Content** – This dimension includes everything on the data-information knowledge continuum that is stored in the system (i.e., structured and unstructured textual or numeric data and images that are either captured directly from imaging devices or scanned from paper-based sources).
3. **Human–Computer Interface** – An interface enables unrelated entities to interact with the system and includes aspects of the system that users can see, touch, or hear. The hardware and software "operationalize" the user interface; provided these are functioning as designed, any problems with using the system are likely due to human–computer interaction (HCI) issues.
4. **People** – This dimension represents the humans (e.g., software developers, system configuration and training personnel, clinicians, and

patients) involved in all aspects of the design, development, implementation, and use of HIT. It also includes the ways that systems help users think and make them feel. In most cases, users will be clinicians or employees of the health system. However, with recent advances in patient-centered care and development of personal health record systems and "home monitoring" devices, patients are increasingly becoming important users of HIT.

5. **Workflow and Communication –** This is the first portion of the model that acknowledges that people often need to work cohesively with others in the healthcare system to accomplish patient care. This collaboration requires significant two-way communication. The workflow dimension accounts for the steps needed to ensure that each patient receives the care they need at the time they need it. Often, the clinical information system does not initially match the actual "clinical" workflow.

6. **Internal Organizational Policies, Procedures, and Culture –** The organization's internal structures, policies, and procedures affect every other dimension in our model.

7. **External Rules, Regulations, and Pressures –** This dimension accounts for the external forces that facilitate or place constraints on the design, development, implementation, use, and evaluation of HIT in the clinical setting. For example, the recent passage of the ARRA of 2009, which includes the Health Information Technology for Economic and Clinical Health (HITECH) Act, makes available over $20 billion for healthcare practitioners who become "meaningful users" of HIT. Thus, ARRA introduces the single largest financial incentive ever to facilitate EHR implementation.

8. **System Measurement and Monitoring –** This dimension has largely been unaccounted for in previous models. We posit that the effects of HIT must be measured and monitored on a regular basis. An effective system measurement and monitoring program must address four key issues related to HIT features and functions: availability, determine how the various features and functions are being used by clinicians, effectiveness of the system on healthcare delivery and patient health, and identify and document unintended consequences that manifest themselves following the use of these systems.

EHRs represent an important intersection in the implementation of HIT and the delivery of healthcare services. As the nature of healthcare organizations as complex adaptive system has become more familiar, the importance of the relationship between the technical and social aspects has also become clearer when HIT is considered and especially in terms of patient safety as it shapes the implementation and use of EHRs.

In their article in the *Journal of American Medical Information Association* "Exploring the sociotechnical intersection of patient safety and electronic health record implementation," Meeks, Takian, and Sittig highlight the way in which patient safety considerations associated with EHRs illustrate the application of sociotechnical designs in healthcare organization. In understanding the patient safety aspects, they recognized initially that the "intersection conceptualized the healthcare system as an evolving complex adaptive system in which safety risks often emerge from users' interactions with the electronic health record that lead to new clinical workflow processes" (p. e28). The complexity of the workflow changes related to the different environmental aspects such as human interaction with physical devices, cultural aspects associated with role changes results from EHR implementation and sociopolitical elements associated with such factors as clinical power structure. Second, the safety risks come from a variety of sources and rarely are identified with a single issue. Third, improving patient safety within a system utilizing an EHR requires addressing the sociotechnical elements and functionalities of the health record evolving over time (pp. e28–e29).

They recommended a three-phase approach to "understand the intersection of electronic healthcare records and patient safety." The three phases "account for the variation in the stages of implementation, levels of complexity, and related patient safety concerns within an EHR-enabled healthcare system" (p. e29). The first phase focuses on safety events related to the technology that may appear early in implementation. The second phase narrows the focus to the overall workflow changes due to the technology change. Finally, the third phase is the use of "technology proactively to identify and monitor potential safety concerns before harm occurs to the patient" (p. 29).

These considerations related to sociotechnical aspects of healthcare organizations in EHRs offer insights into the overall nature of healthcare in the twenty-first century. Technology is a pervasive presence in all aspects of healthcare within organizations and between organizations and the people receiving care. It shapes the experiences of the people delivering care in the design of their work and in the operations associated with their work. It is also important to recognize the sociotechnical nature of healthcare organizations and their operations, the ethical implications of the design of the work, the relationship between the people receiving care and the people delivering care, and the role of the organization in shaping these interactions.

Mumford noted in 2006 that "the most important thing that socio-technical design can contribute is its value system. This tells us that although technology and organizations may change, the rights and needs of employee must be given has high a priority as those of the non-human parts of the system" (p. 338). She identified democracy as an important sociotechnical value. "Employees should be allowed and encouraged to participate in, and influence, decisions that concern them" (p. 338). Mumford related these values to the ethics of system designs in which technology is introduced into organization and to the ethical implications of the associated changes in which the lives of workers are shaped by the technology and by its introduction and the way this shapes their ability to have a meaningful work experience.

It is interesting to note that the views of the Tavistock Institute concerning sociotechnical systems were found by some to be overly utopian in the 1990s as Lean and business re-engineering took precedence in the business world (Ghaffarian, 2011, p. 1502). However, in the sociotechnical epoch of healthcare, the values of the Tavistock Institute concerning worker engagement in the design and improvement of work offer a helpful direction. It is interesting to see how the changes in healthcare technology and work in the 2010s have created an environment that is reminiscent of that which led to the creation of the Tavistock Institute. In the 2019 report, "Taking Action Against Clinician Burnout: A Systems Approach to Professional Well-Being," the National Academies of Sciences, Engineering and Medicine noted that "the changing landscape of the U.S. health care system – how care is provided, documented, and reimbursed – has had profound effects on clinical practice and consequently on the experiences of clinicians, learners, patients, and their families" (p. 2). The report identified "systems pressures" as major contributors to "clinician burnout" in healthcare organizations (p. 2). These pressures include "workload, time pressures, technology challenges, moral and ethical dilemmas, insufficient job resources and support such as adequate job control, alignment of professional and personal values and manageable work-life integration" (p. 2). Burnout, as defined in the report, "is a syndrome characterized by high emotional exhaustion, high depersonalization (i.e. cynicism) and a low sense of personal accomplishment" (p. 1). It is estimated that "between 35 and 54 percent of U.S. nurses and physicians have substantial symptoms of burnout" (p. 1). Similar levels were noted in medical students, and residents and it is likely that "all types of clinicians and learners" are experiencing burnout at a level that is "a growing public health concern" (p. 2).

In response to the need to address burnout in healthcare organizations, the report argues that there must be a "systemic approach that focuses on the structure, organization and culture of healthcare" (p. 3). This "systemic approach" includes a "thorough knowledge of the stakeholders, their goals and activities, the technologies they use and the environment in which they operate" (p. 3). There is recognition that only by addressing all aspects of the issue and working together can progress be made to "prevent, reduce, or mitigate burnout and improve professional well-being" (p. 3).

In line with the National Academies of Sciences research, Nancy Berlinger (2016) and others are discovering that the ethical dilemmas in healthcare organizations associated with the work are affecting the people who deliver care. They are examining the way in which organizations are designing work that is creating ethical dilemmas for workers. Similarly to the National Academies of Sciences, they are finding that workers are experiencing moral stress as they try to accommodate the demands of the new technology and remain consistent with their personal and professional values. When the expectations of organizations based on the implementation of technology are to see improved productivity and quality without recognizing the way in which the technology affects the workers' relationship to their work, then the results are often demoralization and moral stress that compromises the work and the experiences of the worker. It is into this context that the original views of the sociotechnical nature of work design and operation speak to American healthcare in the current epoch. This brings to the forefront the importance of design of the work that incorporates the person delivering care and the person receiving care and the organization to create an experience for all that is meaningful.

Though the design of sociotechnical systems originally developed by Tavistock focused on the workers and their ability to meaningfully integrate the organization of their work with technology, healthcare organizations must confront the challenge of a sociotechnical system that involves the creation of an experience by the worker and the person receiving care. As technology was implemented in a variety of healthcare workflows including documentation in EHRs, the use of smart IV pumps and monitoring devices with alarm systems and clinical decision-making systems, the potential for errors that could harm patients began to be noticed. Though not recognized initially, the relationship between the person delivering care and the person receiving care changed as technology was integrated into the patient care processes. Healthcare workers prioritized the demands of the technology and the information provided by the technology and diminished the value of attention provided to the person receiving care and the information that they provided.

The Joint Commission issued its initial Sentinel Event Policy in 1996, and in 2000, the Institute of Medicine (Academy of Medicine) published the report on healthcare errors in *To Err Is Human: Building a Safer Health System*. Though there was significant push back from healthcare professionals to the initial estimate of up to 100,000 deaths per year due to iatrogenic mortality, the issue of patient harm as a result of healthcare processes reinforced the need to focus on the patient as a participant in care and in the design of care (Kohn, Corrigan, & Donaldson, 2000, p. 1). It did not immediately bring the patient to the table of healthcare redesign, but the patient safety movement increased the pressure on American healthcare to take note of the patients' wishes and their experiences.

The federal government through the Medicare program began to survey the way in which the people receiving care perceived the care provided to them. Medicare added financial incentives for hospitals to report on patient perceptions of care in the form of Hospital Consumer Assessment of Healthcare Providers and Systems (HCAHPS) reporting beginning in 2007. These surveys expanded to cover more and more areas of healthcare delivery and required that all adult patients be included and not just Medicare patients. Initially, hospitals were required to report on the results of the HCAHPS surveys, but by 2010 reporting had been built into the CMS Value-Based Purchasing Program and contributed to the score and reimbursement of hospitals (VBP, 2019).

By the second decade of the twenty-first century, it became clearer that understanding the experiences of people receiving care and the experiences of people delivering care together provided important insights into the overall healthcare experience. Patient experiences as described by the patients offered valuable information that hospitals and other healthcare organizations could use to find ways to improve the quality of care, keep patients safe, and, perhaps, encourage patients to become loyal supporters as the healthcare payment system began to move from the number of patients and procedures to the value of the services provided.

A new addition to the committee structure of many healthcare organizations was a patient and family advisory council (PFAC) or other patient engagement structure. Massachusetts General Hospital initiated one of the first PFACs in 1999, and Massachusetts is the only state that mandates all hospitals (acute care, rehabilitation, and long-term acute care) to have a PFAC. This requirement became law in 2008; all hospitals had to have a council in place by October 2010 (Wachenheim, 2015). The law requires that "the council shall advise the hospital on matters including, but not limited to, patient and provider relationships, institutional review boards, quality improvement initiatives and patient education on safety and quality matters. Members of a council may act as reviewers of publicly reported quality information, members of task forces, members of awards committees for patient safety activities, members of advisory boards, participants on search committees and in the hiring of new staff, and may act as co-trainers for clinical and nonclinical staff, in-service programs, and health professional trainees or as participants in reward and recognition programs" (2015).

PFACs represent an initial step for many hospitals and healthcare organizations in starting a dialogue with the recipients of care and their families. Unlike other industries and service providers where it is assumed that dialogue with customers is a natural part of the business, healthcare struggles with professional traditions that defined relationships with patients and families and tended to reduce the ability of patients to become actively involved in the design of care in deference to the professionals. There has also been an underlying hesitancy to bring together healthcare workers and recipients of care and families. The reasons typically cited for avoiding this type of encounter is the desire to prevent patient complaints from undermining staff morale and the fear of legal liability.

Patients and family members who join PFACs typically become volunteers of the healthcare organization and with the explicit expectation of working to improve care rather than simply complaining about their individual care. They receive the same training as other volunteers but then additional orientation to the overall structure and operations of the organization. Even if the members have had problems with the organizations, their participation in the PFAC is not based on an expectation of working on their specific issue but for them to engage with the hospital to make improvements overall. Following their orientation, PFAC members participate in a variety of activities. They may serve on a quality team or a committee developing a new service. They may provide their perspectives on the development of patient materials or the renovation of patient facilities. Above all, they have the opportunity to speak to the hospital administration and clinical leadership as a patient representing the perspective of patients. This is an important step forward for American healthcare at a time when care is rapidly transitioning out of the hospital to other sites of care to reduce costs and as more care can be delivered as outpatients (Wachenheim, 2015).

Along with the development and expansion of PFACs, patient experience, in general, has become an important element in the overall quality improvement programs of healthcare organizations. PFACs create a group of patients and family members that have been oriented to the way healthcare works in a hospital and serve as a valuable resource for gaining insight into the desires and concerns of patients and family members. However, a method is required to capture the experiences of people receiving care as part of the design and improvement of healthcare services because of the number of people involved in delivering care to individuals and the complexity of the services. One approach that is getting attention is the use of design thinking with experience-based co-design to facilitate the involvement of the recipients of care in the actual work of designing healthcare processes.

Design thinking traces its roots to the industrial design of products. As defined on the Industrial Designers Society of America (ISDA) website, Industrial Design (ID) is the "professional practice of designing products, devices, objects and services…typically focus on the physical appearance, functionality and manufacturability of product…extends to the overall lasting value and experience a product or service provides for end-users" (ISDA, 2019).

Industrial design is linked to the growth of industrialization and mechanization that began with the industrial revolution in Great Britain in the mideighteenth century. Industrial manufacturing changed the way objects were made. Urbanization changed patterns of consumption. Growth of empires broadened tastes and diversified markets, and the emergence of middle class created demand for fashionable styles for a much larger and more heterogeneous population (Wikipedia, 2019).

Tim Brown describes the transition of industrial design to design thinking as "a classic path of intellectual progress" (Brown & Martin, 2008). He points to the movement of designers from designing objects such as computer hardware to designing the look and feel of the user experience with computer software and, finally, the transition to other experiences such as patient hospital visits (2008). "Design thinking is a discipline that uses the designer's sensibility and methods to match people's needs with what is technologically feasible and what a viable business strategy can convert into customer value and market opportunity" (Brown & Martin, 2008).

Jon Kolko (2015) describes the appearance of design thinking as a "shift in large organizations…that puts design much closer to the center of the enterprise" (p. 68). He believes the shift is due to complexity and the need to apply "the principles of design to the way that people work" (p. 68).

"Design thinking, first used to make physical objects, is increasingly being applied to complex intangible issues such as how a customer experiences a service" (p. 68). He specifically points to healthcare by contrasting "how much tougher it is to reinvent a healthcare delivery system than to design a shoe" (p. 68). Design thinking consists of "a set of principles" that can be applied by people other than designers, according to Kolko. These principles include "focus on users' experiences, especially emotional ones; creation of models to examine complex problems; use of prototypes to explore potential solutions; toleration for failure and an ability to exhibit restraint" (pp. 68–69).

The introduction of design thinking in the National Health Service (NHS) in the United Kingdom was undertaken beginning in the 2000s with "user-centric design" and "co-designing of user experiences" in the redesign of healthcare delivery systems. According to Paul Bate and Glenn Robert (2007), "The approach demonstrates how a combination of existing and new techniques can be used together" (p. v). The example they use is the addition to the well-established NHS practice of process mapping (analyzing the chronological steps in the patient process) of experience or emotional mapping. "Here service users and families create maps that illustrate their journey as they have felt it. They do not focus on every step but rather the critical points where they are profoundly touched by the service, leading to a positive or negative experience" (p. v). Stories and narratives with picture diaries or video film, bring to life nuances that impact massively on the service provided and received. "Project teams have been established but with equal partnership between patients and staff who have successfully developed and implemented changes to improve the delivery and experience of care" (p. v).

As a result of what they learned, they advocated that "experience-based design must become the core principle that you use when delivering health services, recognizing patients, carers and families as producers and participants rather than just receivers of healthcare services" (p. vi). They described experience-based design "isn't just a totally achievable way of engaging with patients to find out what they think about the services we provide; it is a systematic process that we can follow, it is a true combination of human resources, it's about inviting patients themselves to work alongside us to make those changes happen" (p. vi).

In comparing experience-based co-design to the traditional quality improvement work, Bate and Robert comment "By identifying the main areas (touch points) where people come into contact with the service and where their subjective experience is shaped, and therefore where the desired emotional and sensory connection needs to be established and working with the frontline people who bring alive those various touch points one can begin to design human experiences rather than just systems or processes" (p. 9). Partnering with recipients of care is an important aspect of experience-based co-design as the active participation of the patients and families becomes part of the design process.

Bate and Robert contrast "experience-based design" involving an "equal partnership and the co-design of a product or service" with the traditional view of "the user as a passive recipient of a product or service" (p. 9). They emphasize the importance of viewing the users as the co-designers of that product or service and the need for them to join and become integrally bound up in the whole improvement and innovation process. At the same time, they insist "it does not mean trying to make patients and users into healthcare or design experts but having them there because they are patients – lead users rather than leaders – with that precious and very special kind of knowledge we call the first-hand experience of a service" (p. 9). Contrasting this new approach with previous improvement efforts, they comment, "This type of approach means that designing systems, pathways, and processes – concepts which have dominated health service design and redesign work for nearly a decade and the field of total quality management (TQM) for nearly three decades – will need to move over and make some room for the experience concept" (p. 10).

With patient experience as the basis for improvement, Bate and Robert (2007) describe the struggle to truly grasp experience and to incorporate it into an organizational process of redesigning services by inviting the person experiencing it to participate in the redesign. "Placing the user of a service or a product at the very heart of the design process – what recently has been described as the "quiet revolution in design" – has become today's big idea in professions such as architecture, computer, building, product and graphic and service design" (p. 14). They encourage healthcare practitioners to consider the change to experience-based co-design as moving from "designing inanimate things like care processes to designing experiences of moving through that process" (p. 17).

This, of course, is challenging for healthcare in general as there has always been the sense of healthcare as viewing patients as the material of their clinical process and not a participant in its design. The difficulty has two parts in first for the clinician "discovering ways of seeing deeper into experience, of appreciating why it is so much more important to be designing experiences than just systems or processes" (p. 21) and secondly the challenge "to understand their experience of care at a deep level, always bearing in mind that it includes all aspects of experiencing a product or service – physical, sensual, cognitive, kinetic, aesthetic and above all emotional (the notion of the patient journey as an emotional as well as clinical experience) and to use this understanding to design a healthcare experience that will be more successful and satisfying than it has ever been before" (p. 21). Ultimately, according to Bate and Robert (2007), it is all about "the importance of being mindful of experience and to build that mindfulness into everything we do as improvement specialists" (p. 26).

A review of twenty-four studies of the use of Design Thinking in healthcare concluded that "Design Thinking is being used in varied health care settings and conditions" and "that it may result in usable, acceptable and effective interventions" (Altman, Huang & Breland, 2018). However, it qualified the findings by noting that "More research is needed, including studies to isolate critical components of Design Thinking and compare Design-Thinking-based interventions with traditionally developed interventions" (2018).

The studies that were reviewed and the analysis of the researchers identified "several challenges to consider when applying Design thinking to healthcare" (Altman et al., 2018). The first challenge involves "what users want and what providers and researchers believe to be beneficial." Whereas industry may give preference to customer preferences, the reviewers argued that healthcare must consider what is "effective and sufficiently palatable and feasible" so that providers and patients will use it (2018). The second "tension" was the lack of an adequate "needs assessment" as required by Design Thinking. The reviewers noted that "intervention developers" may rely on literature reviews or expert consultations rather than "using observation or interview strategies or to brainstorm creative solutions" (2018). The third caveat from the reviewers was to avoid "Conclusions drawn on small user samples" but to "test in broader populations their applicability" (2018). Their fourth concern about Design Thinking as exhibited in the studies they reviewed was the "inherent tension between a central philosophy of the prototyping process in Design Thinking – to rapidly move through low-fidelity then high fidelity iterations to fail early and often to more quickly reach a better design – and the risk of serious negative outcomes due to health care failures" (2018).

With the expansion of the Internet and the proliferation of smart phone, healthcare is no longer confined to the physical presence of a practitioner or to specific location such as a hospital. The information exchange can occur at anytime and anywhere that a signal can reach. The distance between the recipient of care and the people delivering care is no longer a consideration as remote monitoring and testing followed by virtual visits offer a continuous connection. Processing time between the request for information and its delivery decreases continuously. The breadth of services available for purchase through technological interface has become much greater. Within the neoliberal environment of individuals as consumers surrounded by a continuous flow of marketing and advertising by government and business, the perception of healthcare as a commodity has grown.

At the same time, social networking discussions of healthcare experiences and publicly displayed ratings offer the people receiving care greater access to quality and cost information based on the performance of organizations and people delivering care. People receiving care equate access and results for healthcare as comparable to other services with similar expectations for quality and speed. Meeting these expectations has proven challenging to the organizations and people delivering care. The new technology has radically changed the way people delivering care perform their work and communicate with each other and with the people receiving care. Expectations of people receiving care and monitoring of performance, safety, efficiency, and outcomes by regulatory agencies and payers affect payments and shape many processes and activities within healthcare organizations.

Summary of American Healthcare Epochs

American healthcare evolved in its own unique way as America developed in the nineteenth and twentieth centuries. The epochs of American healthcare described in this section offer simple metaphors to understand facets of the very complicated nature of the changes associated with each historical period of the delivery of healthcare services. Healthcare today provides services to potentially five generations of Americans who lived during the various epochs. Experiences associated with each epoch are represented in the personal and professionals lives of the people who received care and people who delivered care.

Each generational cohort brings certain life experiences to their healthcare encounter and views the results of the encounter from the context of what they have experienced in the past. People delivering care come from a variety of generations with an increasing number of the younger generations taking on important roles in organizations and in delivering care. In designing the way that healthcare is delivered, organizations also bring their own perspectives which have emerged over the years that the organization has been in operation. Epochs include influences that shape organizations perhaps even more than individuals in the ways in which they subtly continue over decades to shape work processes and resist changes from more recent events.

It is fascinating to consider the breadth of the changes that have occurred in healthcare in America in the two centuries. The Free Trade Epoch embodied the energy and dynamic of an unrestrained marketplace in which marginally helpful services associated with a diverse universe of healthcare practitioners who competed with little governmental regulation. In the Scientific Epoch, the undeniable advantages of certain services such as surgery strengthened the hand of science in the marketplace. The professional medicine establishment built upon the scientific success of surgery by establishing specific education and licensure requirements that created significant barriers to entry in favor of wealthy families who could afford to send their sons to medical schools to become physicians. Hospitals became the workshops of the physicians and the preferred place for receiving medical care for Americans who could afford the care.

The Scarcity Epoch encompassed the hardships of the Depression and the World War II in the form of empty beds due to the lack of financial resources for people who desired care and lack of hospitals and staff to meet the changing needs of the military and civilians as many practitioners went to war and the home front industrial migrations caused population shifts. Out of scarcity, however, the Prosperity Epoch roared to life in the post-war healthcare boom. The rapid expansion of specifically hospital-based healthcare was fueled by employer-sponsored healthcare insurance, the joint efforts of the federal government and state governments to construct hospitals, and passage of the Medicare and Medicaid to provide hospitals care to the elderly and the poor.

Prosperity was followed by the reality shock of the Globalization Epoch in which the forces of neoliberalism unleashed the forces of unrestrained markets and federal government support for corporations. Jobs went to lower-cost foreign countries and foreign businesses competed directly with American companies. American healthcare found itself unfavorably compared to other countries in cost and quality and sought to change using Toyota and other industrial models as the means for redesigning a Lean healthcare system. Under neoliberalism, Americans seeking care became consumers who were asked to use more of their own resources to pay for healthcare. Finally, the Sociotechnical Epoch of today brings new information and communication technology into healthcare to create very different environment. With the advent of networks of computers permeating all aspects of healthcare and society, the technical and the social aspects of healthcare are struggling to bring together organizations, people delivering care and people receiving care in a new context of meaningful experiences.

Healthcare encounters are truly microcosmic moments in which the people receiving care, the healthcare worker and the organization come together in a shared experience. Each participant in this encounter brings with them memories of epochs, generations, communities, and their own personal experiences. The epochs provide the means for rising above the individual healthcare encounter to consider how the history of the country and its people affect the way in which people deliver and receive healthcare. By keeping these epochal distinctions in mind and recognizing when they are part of the healthcare experiences can be useful in the creation of meaningful healthcare experiences.

It is important to remember that this historical information is valuable in offering the context for understanding reactions when encounters between organizations and people delivering care and people receiving care are not meaningful and the results are not satisfactory. The beliefs, values, and principles that we carry with us in life are shaped by what we have experienced and the events that have affected us in the past. People remember previous healthcare experiences and integrate these through their beliefs, values, and principles into the present experiences that use these in evaluating situations that they encounter in the future. By understanding the background from which these fundamental influences arise, organizations and workers are able to recognize in themselves their own views of what is true and valuable and important and assess how well they align with the people they serve.

Chapter 20

Ten Transitions from Twentieth-Century to Twenty-First-Century American Healthcare

Creating a perspective on healthcare as it existed in the twentieth century and imagining how it must change to meet the needs of the future represents a significant challenge. Not only is healthcare complex, but the changes that are occurring are so diverse that their implications are often difficult to discern. As difficult as this may be, the reason for undertaking it is simple. Healthcare is a vital part of the quality of life in America and we need to develop a sense of the current state and some sense of a future state to work toward improved care in the future (Figure 20.1).

My professional career has been spent working with hospitals to promote improvement in care and processes using a variety of methodologies most of which had their roots in other industries. I decided to pursue doctoral studies late in my career out of frustration with the slow progress hospitals were making in improvement and to try to understand how healthcare came to the problematic place it occupied in the early 2000s. My doctoral studies focused on a simple question: How did American healthcare become what it is today? My research focused on the development of twentieth-century American healthcare. It was not long before I found that my simple question led me into very diverse paths.

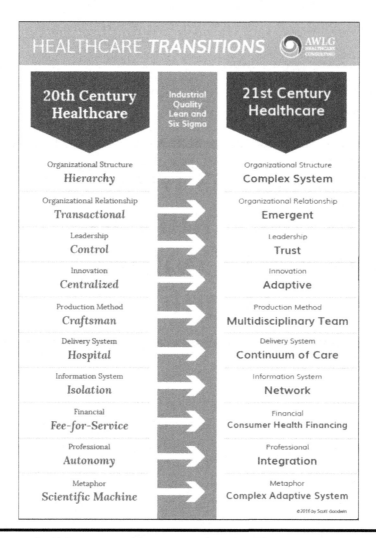

Figure 20.1 Ten healthcare transitions. American healthcare's transition from the twentieth to the twenty-first century can be understood through the metaphors describing the changes in ten areas of healthcare. On one side is a list of the twentieth-century metaphors and the other side the twenty-first-century metaphors. Between the two centuries, the industrial quality metaphors of Lean and Six Sigma are presented as the catalyst for the transitions.

As I learned in my studies, healthcare in America did not originate from a national plan or accepted body of knowledge that was utilized consistently across the country. It emerged out of the confluence of factors in the nineteenth century and took its current form in the early twentieth century. This form proved surprisingly resilient, but the twentieth-century model of healthcare was under significant pressure by the early 2000s to adapt to a very different world than the one produced it.

As I explored the early stages of American healthcare, I found that the way in which physicians worked offered valuable insights into the way healthcare developed. Physicians worked as independent craftsmen from their own offices with their own patients who paid them based on the physician's assessment of the patient's ability to pay (Rosen, 1983). Though there were competing approaches to healthcare in the late nineteenth century, scientific medicine demonstrated its ability to produce results and became dominant. Through the efforts of the American Medical Association (AMA), these "regular" physicians organized to protect their prerogatives and market positions. Through a network of state medical societies and the AMA, they promoted state licensure based on university and medical school training in scientific medicine (Starr, 1982).

To take advantage of the new developments in applied medical science such as laboratory testing, X-rays, intravenous infusion of medications, and aseptic surgery and to have access to facilities similar to those used in their training, physicians strongly encouraged community leaders to transition the community almshouses for the poor into modern hospitals with the latest equipment so that they could bring their paying patients in for treatment (Starr, 1982). America during the early twentieth century strongly supported the value of science in almost every aspect of life and efficiency as a valuable characteristic of organizations and people (Howell, 1995). People began to view physicians and hospitals as the scientific delivery system for healthcare.

A similar revolution took place in the first decades of the twenty-first century with the advent of computer technology. As computers proliferated throughout healthcare, the federal government actively promoted through financial support and regulation, the adoption by hospitals of healthcare information technology in the form of electronic health records, and the clinical support system (ARRA, 2009). In terms of direct impact, the governmentally promoted adoption of electronic medical records significantly challenged the existing workflows in almost all clinical areas and the ability of the healthcare organizations to integrate the new technology into the culture of delivering care (National Academies of Sciences, Engineering and Medicine, 2019).

The beginning of a new era in American healthcare occurred in 1965 with the Medicare/Medicaid healthcare insurance coverage for the elderly, poor and disabled, and the sudden introduction of federal and state governments into the payment of healthcare services on national scale. Initially, this proved to be a tremendous boost to American healthcare because of the cost-based reimbursement of care that was used to gain acceptance of the legislation by the hospitals and physicians (Stevens, 1999). As millions of people suddenly had access to hospital-based healthcare, the flow of resources supported the rapid expansion of facilities and services and promoted the growth of a variety of industries to provide new and better technology and services (1999). Building off the existing infrastructure, healthcare organizations got bigger and added more facilities and services over the following decades.

By the 1970s, the bill came due and the sticker shock shook the Congress and the nation. The cost of healthcare was rapidly increasing and threatened to consume larger portions of the federal budget. It was at this point that a change was introduced by the federal government that led to massive restructuring in the way healthcare operated. To control the rising costs, a prospective payment system was established for all Medicare patients receiving hospital care. The DRG or diagnosis-related groups payment system set the amount that the federal government was willing to pay for each Medicare patient based on their diagnosis (HHS Office of Inspector General, 2001).

Not only did the DRG prospective payment system create financial risk to healthcare organizations in treating Medicare patients, but it put the hospitals into a new relationship with the medical staff. Each Medicare patient that was admitted represented a payment on the day of admission. Every day after the day of admission, the patient represented a cost. With each passing day and each additional service, the amount paid to the hospitals was diminished by the costs of caring for the patient. The physician, however, received ongoing reimbursement regardless of the length of stay in the hospital. Just as cost-based reimbursement encouraged the use of services, the prospective payment encouraged healthcare organizations to find ways to reduce the use of services, particularly the length of stay. This change created a new internal environment within healthcare organizations and a new dynamic in the relationships between the administrative bureaucracy and the medical staff.

Once the payments were capped under the DRG program, the importance of operational and process efficiency inside the healthcare organization increased. Every delay in testing or procedures or treatment meant additional costs to the organization. Every delay in moving patients out of the hospital to home or skilled nursing facilities increased the cost and the likelihood that something would happen to compromise the health of the patient. Time required to deliver care suddenly became an important financial and quality measure for hospitals. In response to this new situation, hospitals created new positions and added staff to facilitate the processes of care. It was in this environment that hospitals and other healthcare organization began to seriously consider implementing industrial quality concepts to improve efficiency and reduce costs.

While trying to adapt operationally to the new technology, computer analysis of quality and cost data collected by agencies and researchers from around the world as well as in America raised serious questions about the performance of American healthcare in comparison with other highly developed countries. Americans were paying more and receiving lower quality of care based on comparative data. Significant variations in cost and quality between regions in the country also made a strong case to improve the quality of outcomes, lower the costs, and reduce adverse events in healthcare organizations (Auerbach & White, 2008).

The advancing flood of data and reports on healthcare motivated governmental agencies, commercial payers, and professional associations to begin the search for ways to make changes in healthcare. Hospitals and other healthcare organizations found change difficult due to the complexity of the structures, processes, and cultures that developed in the twentieth century and persisted into the twenty-first century. In response to the demands for improvements, healthcare looked to industry for answers as it had in the past. Scientific management and efficiency were the industrial models that were part of the development of hospitals in the nineteenth century. By the end of the twentieth century, industrial quality methods borrowed initially from American industry were promoted to healthcare organizations to improve quality and efficiency. In the early 2000s, the Toyota Production System or American "Lean" was imported from the Japanese to reduce costs associated with waste.

The Toyota Production System originated in Toyota prior to World War II but reached its modern form in the 1970s as Toyota struggled to succeed in the automotive market (Ohno, 1988). It was not the first industrial quality program to be considered by American healthcare, but it was the one program with the claim to be effective at reducing costs by eliminating waste in processes. In many respects, it was perfectly designed to address the process issues that hospitals faced in relation to prospective payment systems and other restraints on healthcare insurance payments. The part of the Toyota Production System or "Lean" that sets the stage for the appearance of adaptive innovation in American healthcare was the role of continuous improvement by the worker performing the work. This was an essential element of the success of the program for Toyota, and it was a revolutionary idea for healthcare in America (Cusumano, 1988).

The introduction of industrial quality techniques into American healthcare challenged the fundamental structures, processes, and cultures carried over the twentieth century. These had to be reconsidered if computer technology and industrial quality were to be integrated into healthcare organizations. These required significant changes in the structures, processes, and cultures of healthcare organization in order to produce the results that were desired. For many healthcare organizations, the initial approach to these industrial quality methods was to utilize them in operations that were most similar to industrial processes and to avoid their incorporation into such areas as clinical practice to prevent disruption of the professional culture and processes already in place (Berwick, Godfrey, & Roessner, 1990). It ultimately became apparent, however, that significant improvement in healthcare costs and quality required changes in the clinical areas as well as the materials and supplies.

With the adoption of industrial quality and computer-based healthcare information technology, the fundamental understanding that had defined American healthcare in the twentieth century had changed in the twenty-first century. In order to understand the past development of American healthcare and its future manifestations, a way of talking about healthcare and these changes was needed. After 4 years of doctoral study searching backwards into American healthcare's history and forward into its future, I realized there had never been a shared understanding of what American healthcare actually is and no common metaphors in healthcare.

Because healthcare is so complex, it is important to think about it in terms of metaphors. The word "metaphor" in English has its roots in the Latin "metaphora" which translates as "carrying over." George Lakoff and Mark Johnson (1980) boldly asserted that metaphors are not just embellishments of language, but "metaphor is pervasive in everyday life, not just in language but in thought and action. Our ordinary conceptual system, in terms of which we both think and act, is fundamentally metaphorical in nature" (p. 3). Lakoff and Johnson state that "the essence of metaphor is understanding and experiencing one kind of thing in terms of another" (p. 5).

Metaphors are often invisible to us. Like a light bulb above your head representing a new idea or the leg of a table, they are part of our thoughts and speech, but we fail to see how they actively shape our understanding.

Aristotle in his Poetics comments, "But the greatest thing by far is to have a command of metaphor. This alone cannot be imparted by another; it is the mark of genius for to make good metaphors implies an eye for resemblances" (Aristotle & Kaplan, 2012, 371).

Metaphors are an indispensable part of any discussion about American healthcare. It is particularly important in any discussion about the way healthcare is experienced by people receiving care and people delivering care. It is through metaphors that the complex interactions of healthcare can be described in ways that capture the nature of the moment in which the experiences occur. Keeping this in mind in considering the transitions in American healthcare helps to create an openness to new ways of thinking about healthcare organizations and experiences.

In *Images of Organizations* (2006), Gareth Morgan developed his views of applying metaphors to the "art of reading and understanding organizational life" (p. 4). He argued that all theories of organization and management are based on implicit images or metaphors that lead us to see, understand and manage organizations in distinctive ways (p. 4). Morgan pointed out that metaphors can have a generative or creative effect on organizations. Others who have written on generative metaphors are Donald Schön (1979) and Frank Barrett and David Cooperrider (1990).

Morgan (2006) developed a process for using metaphors to promote change. It began with an analysis of the current metaphor commonly used to describe an organization and followed with the development and promotion of a new generative metaphor that describes the future state of the organization. The new metaphor serves to promote a new way of thinking about the organization in order to motivate employees and to guide them in creating the future state of the organization.

It is important to realize that the motivation for initiating the ten transitions in healthcare from the twentieth to the twenty-first century is a result of the introduction of industrial quality improvement into organizations to improve quality and reduce cost due to regulatory and market forces. At the same time, healthcare organizations implementing electronic information networks hope to gain additional reimbursements and to comply with regulatory agencies. As industrial quality and the associated computer technology were introduced into healthcare organizations, the resulting conflict between the current state of the organization and the new quality improvement techniques led to the beginning of the transitions into a new state consistent with the future of the environment of the organization. In this way the implementation of industrial quality concepts and techniques became the catalyst for American healthcare to make start the transition to its future state in the ten areas.

In describing the future state that results from the implementation of industrial quality methods and the expanded use of computer technology, the language that is used is as important in many respects as the changes themselves. The reason for this comes out of the way people make sense of their reality. If we take, for example, the concept of a hierarchical bureaucratic structure, it is very hard to see such a structure with your eyes. You may see a sign for a department and meet the people in the senior management roles, but you do not actually see the bureaucracy and the hierarchical relationship because these concepts only exist in documents and in the minds of the people involved. It becomes a reality only in the way people think and act that are consistent with such as configuration. They construct this reality every day that they come to the hospital and act in accordance with its existence.

For example, if we say that the hierarchical bureaucracy of hospital administration that developed in the twentieth century is changed to a complex system in the twenty-first century, the words that are used to describe the change become very important to the realization of the new arrangement. People need to be able to imagine what this new state is like and how it works in order to understand the nature of the transition that is occurring. This is one of the principal reasons that healthcare has struggle so much with adapting to the twenty-first century environment. The images of the past are so strong that people working in healthcare and people who come to healthcare organizations for service find it difficult to imagine it working in ways different from what they have experienced in the past. This is also the reason why the use of industrial quality concepts and techniques is hard to implement but so significant when it becomes part of the way the organization does business. It is also the reason why healthcare organizations need to strive to use industrial quality techniques consistently so that the new metaphor of the future can be generated to motivate people to accept the future state and move forward.

As healthcare organizations transition into the future, they need images of the future to serve as guides for people throughout the organization. These image the "generative metaphors" because they provide a metaphor for the future that is different from the metaphor that was used to describe the twentieth-century state of healthcare. For example, the phrase "twenty-first century" serves a generative metaphor as it describes movement away from the past to a new and better future. By envisioning movement in an organization or for an individual from an older, less helpful past to a future in which individuals and organizations have more meaningful experiences is an example of the way in which a generative metaphor creates a desire or motivation for change and a sense of direction in moving into the future. As people in organizations come to use the same metaphors for the future state of the ten transitions, it provides a sense of common direction that can be understood and a goal that challenges and motivates people to achieve their future. Each of the ten transitions involves a movement from one metaphor to another that coincides with the movement from the twentieth century to the twenty-first century (Goodwin, 2016).

The metaphors for understanding the past and imagining the future of American healthcare are part of the ten transitions described in *Mapping the Path to Twenty-First Century Healthcare: The Ten Transitions Workbook* (Goodwin, 2016). American healthcare's development between its early twentieth-century origin and its future can be described using metaphors related to specific aspects of structures, processes, and cultures that occur during the periods in physicians, hospitals, and payment systems.

The structural transitions involve organizations, relationships, leadership, and innovation. The processes are production methods, delivery systems, information systems, and financial. The culture is expressed in terms of the professional status of physicians and an overall metaphor encompassing healthcare broadly. Each of the ten transitions has a category representing twentieth-century healthcare and a category representing healthcare in the twenty-first century (Goodwin, 2016).

For the twentieth-century structure group, the categories are hierarchy style organizational structure, transactional relationships with employees, leadership characterized by control, and centralized innovation. The process group in the twentieth century is characterized by a production method based on craftsman physicians, a delivery system based on hospitals, isolated and independent information systems, and a fee-for-service payment financial process. Finally, the culture group consists of autonomous professional physicians and an overall metaphor of a scientific machine (Goodwin, 2016).

For the twenty-first-century structure group, the categories are a complex system organizational structure, emergent relationships with employees, leadership characterized by trust, and adaptive innovation by healthcare workers. The process group in twenty-first-century healthcare is characterized by a production method using multidisciplinary teams, a continuum of care delivery system with multiple providers, a broadly connected network information system, and a consumer health financing financial process. Finally, the culture group for the twenty-first century consists of professional integration of physicians and an overall metaphor of a complex adaptive system (CAS) (Goodwin, 2016).

Organizational Transitions: Twentieth-Century Bureaucratic Hierarchy to Twenty-First-Century Complex System

Healthcare organizations have an inherent tendency to compartmentalize due to the categorization of the types of illnesses and conditions that they treat, and the environments and staff required for each area of care. Whether it is emergency services, medicine, surgery, obstetrics, or another specialty, specific areas are usually created to manage the care and this creates separations within the organizations. In the same way, radiology, laboratory, and other diagnostic services occupy their own unique settings and with specific staff and equipment. Finally, the areas that are not clinical such as finance, administration, materials management, information systems, and other support areas provide services to many of the clinical areas but are very different in skills and operations.

Two developments in the early twentieth century set healthcare on a track to embrace a bureaucratic or departmentalized structure and a hierarchical culture that emphasized the control of a small group in a centralized management in the administration of the hospital. The first development was the migration of healthcare from the home to the redesigned hospital to provide the environment and nursing support necessary for surgery, X-rays, laboratories, and other medical services. Facilities designed to treat the poor were reconfigured or replaced to accommodate these services and to meet the expectations of paying patients. As physicians centered their practices at the hospital, care and services to meet the needs of the physicians and the patients developed as departments.

The second development was the emergence in America of science as an approach to understanding almost every aspect of life and efficiency as a virtuous character trait and the anticipated positive outcome of scientific management (Howell, 1995). As the benefactors of the hospitals who in many cases were business people had already established their own role in managing the work of the hospitals based on their contributions in supporting it, it was not surprising that they should apply the same scientific approach to the hospital as they used in their commercial enterprises. Appointing supervisors to oversee the work and having them report to the board created the same type of structure that was so effective and efficient in business. The hospital, therefore, on the administrative side, provided an environment very conducive to the introduction of a hierarchical bureaucracy based on a scientific view of organizations in which management was centralized through the hospital administrator or supervisor reporting to the board of trustees or benefactors and providing direction to the various departments. The administrative bureaucracy and hierarchical control culture of hospitals that developed early in the twentieth century continued as the most common way to organize and operate a healthcare organization throughout the century (Howell, 1995).

Two developments in the early twenty-first century began to challenge the assumed effectiveness of the traditional hospital structure and created the need for a new vision. The first development was the introduction and expansion of computer technology as the information systems of healthcare organizations. As computers became more sophisticated and more mobile, they appeared in all areas of healthcare organizations. Through this technology, information that had previously been available to only a few individuals became accessible to large numbers of employees. In addition to the availability of information, people throughout the organization were able to communicate with each other in "real-time" and share information as changes occurred.

The second development was the movement of hospital services from inpatient to outpatient status. Initially, all the services provided by hospitals were delivered on an inpatient basis and the person receiving care would be in a bed in a room during that time and under the care of their physician. In the early twenty-first century, reduced healthcare reimbursement and concerns about infections and the deleterious effects of long periods of bed-rest encourage healthcare organizations to find ways to transition patients out of the hospital faster following an inpatient admission. With advances in technology and improved understanding of the recuperative process for procedures and illnesses, more patients were able to receive care as outpatients without long hospital stays. Improved reimbursement with lower costs for outpatient services also encouraged organizations to develop more of these services.

The cumulative effect of the expanded information access available with computer technology and the movement to expand the outpatient delivery of services led to a weakening of the departmental bureaucracy and hierarchical management that was the dominant structure in the twentieth century. These developments also placed greater emphasis on the qualitative experiences of people as they receive care as outpatients rather than the retrospective statistical quantitative measures focused on process and outcomes that predominated in the twentieth-century quality movement. In order to adapt to this environment, healthcare organizations are searching for a way to create a vision that will facilitate the development of a more effective structure.

In 1991, the World Wide Web came into existence and with it the ability for individuals to communicate via computers. The early 2000s brought increased computer mobility and companies were providing computers for many people to use in their work and individuals were using smart phones for continuous communication. At the same time, studies concerning the way in which organizations function began to identify changes associated with the use of computers and expanded access to information. As more and more people in organizations were connected via computers, they shared more information concerning their work and work situations. This sharing enabled many more individuals to collaborate in solving problems and addressing issues without using the traditional bureaucracy or centralized command structure.

As this phenomenon grew, the similarity between organizations and what were termed "complex systems" began to be recognized. As healthcare organizations evolve as complex systems, the complex system attributes appear and shape the nature of the organization. New structures, patterns, and processes within the system occur unpredictably through the interactions of the individuals connected through the system (Zimmerman, 2011). Continuous electronic communications between individuals in the organization creates the complex system and accelerates the rate that organizations react to internal and external changes due to the rapid exchange of information. Through these interconnections, the system self-organizes or creates a new order spontaneously without the intentional intervention of individuals or the central leadership and smaller systems within systems or embedded systems operate simultaneously and co-evolve over time. Design and management of the system is distributed, and simple rules serve to shape the functioning of the system (Zimmerman, 2011).

The more people who were connected and the more information that was available, the more likely they were to work together and develop responses to changes. For healthcare organizations, there is a tension between embracing the concepts of complex systems and maintaining the traditional organizational structures. The incentive for using the image of a complex system as a generative metaphor for the future lies in the reality of expanding computer technology that is part of every healthcare organizations today and the need to respond in quickly and creatively to deliver meaningful experiences to people receiving care in the outpatient environment. Via shared information people in organizations can identify changes that are needed and would respond quickly to address situations without using the bureaucratic structure.

Organizational Relationship Transition: Twentieth-Century Transactional to Twenty-First-Century Emergent

American organizations in the early twentieth century faced an interesting dilemma. As part of the industrial revolutions of the nineteenth and early twentieth centuries, inventors were connecting new sources of power to new mechanical devices to manufacture products that were good enough and inexpensive enough for many more people to purchase them. Using steam and electricity and new methods for creating metals and other materials, manufacturing became the new way to meet the needs of a growing population and offered employment beyond agriculture work. It was also a time in which immigrant were arriving in the United States from Ireland, Germany and other countries. In the South, former slaves were searching for work in the north as part of the Great Migration that began in the early 1900s.

Scientific management promoted by Frederick Taylor (Haber, 1964) and Frank Gilbreth (1914) and others in the early twentieth century believed that science offered a way to design work and the management of work to achieve greater efficiency. This meant using experts who understood these scientific concepts associated with efficiency to scientifically determine the most efficient way to perform work and to train the workers to perform the work exactly as it was designed to be performed by the experts. This meant documentation of specific tasks and the way those tasks were to be performed. Workers were hired to perform the work exactly as it was designed by the experts and were paid to perform that work. This relationship between the business and the worker can be described as a transaction or exchange in which the workers agreed to provide their labor in exchange for the wages that they were paid.

Each person in the organization has a specific role and specific work to perform and it is to be performed within the context of a hierarchy of supervisors that ensures that all the members of the bureaucracy are controlled and directed in accomplishing their work. As hospitals assumed their original form in the early 1920s, this structure offered a way to organize, train and to control the work. It complemented the existing professional arrangement between the physicians and nurses in the way that clinical care was provided. Physicians ordered the care of patients and nurses served as dependent workers in carrying out those orders. The uniforms of nurses and the hierarchy of the nursing structure supported this approach to managing work. It continues today as the dominant means for organizing work in healthcare.

The management of workers within a transactional relationship is based on clear guidelines and expectations with rewards or penalties for performance. The transactional leader reacts to penalize performance that does not meet expectations. Rewards are contingent on the performance of the worker in meeting the expectations in the way designed by the bureaucracy. Measurement and quantification set clear expectations. The personal concerns of the worker are less the concerns of leadership than that the worker fulfills the requirements established by the organization and performs in acceptable manner with either active or passive engagement by the transactional leader (MacGregor Burns, 1978).

The metaphor of a transaction in which the worker exchanges work and loyalty for rewards and to avoid penalties offers an image of the relationship between the worker and the organization that exemplified the qualities and characteristics of the work environment in the twentieth century. The job description, the organizational chart, the time clock and the many other symbols of the economic and social context of the work are ways of understanding how this transactional relationship functioned.

The metaphor of the transactional relationship began to lose it relevance as the work environment and needs of the organization required more from the worker than was encompassed in the image of rewards or penalties for completing specific tasks under the direction of a reactive bureaucracy. In the new environment in which healthcare organizations operate, the nature of the work has changed significantly. It is no longer possible to describe in simple terms the work to be performed and then quantify the exact level of fulfillment produced by the worker to determine rewards or penalties.

As workers in healthcare organizations were given computers and required to use them, they quickly realized that they could communicate with other workers throughout the organization as well with people receiving care. This connectivity created the basis for the dynamic that characterizes a complex system. This transformed organizations that had been rigidly designed around professionals and traditions into sociotechnical systems in which the technology began to shape the work and the relationships between employees and between employees and management. As a result of the complexity introduced into organizations with the new technology, employees connected with each other and to communicate and share information. As situations developed and problems required solutions, these workers would communicate with each other and collaborate to solve problems quickly and, thereby, improve the experiences of the people receiving care who needed the assistance (Mumford, 1996).

An important aspect of complex systems is the potential for the unexpected to happen. The dynamic of multiple individuals communicating with each other creates an almost infinite number of variations that can occur simply through the interactions of the people involved. This unpredictable and in many cases uncontrollable aspect of complex systems requires that people involved step outside of their assigned tasks and creatively solve the problems of people receiving care and the workers involved in delivering care. As people engaged in this type of work daily they developed a wealth of knowledge and experiences that enable them to perform work that is not part of their specific assignments nor incorporated into their evaluations for rewards or penalties and yet is essential to the job that they are performing (Goodwin, 2016).

Due to the changes associated with the transition from a bureaucratic hierarchy to a complex system, the organization's relationship to its workers transitions from a transaction in which the worker exchanges the completion of specific tasks for compensation to a relationship in which the workers understand and express the mission, vision, and values of the organization in the work. In response to the frequency in which unique problems arise that need solutions that may not be clearly identified in the training, the work emerges out of the situations as the workers respond to the needs of people around them based on their understanding of the mission, vision, and values of the organization and how it is to be operationalized.

As workers are recruited and prepared for the work, the emphasis is on their ability to understand the mission, vision, and values of the organization in the twenty-first century and to operationalize essential concepts and qualities into the various activities associated with their role. Their compensation is based on the way in which they respond to situations that they encounter each day by using these essential values in cooperation with the co-workers and people receiving care as well as by performing tasks associated with the activities required for their work. More decisions are made at the operational level as the need arises and less often within the formal structure of committees or referred upward in the hierarchy.

The transition from a transactional relationship to an emergent relationship in the way in which the worker and the organization relate to each other mirrors the transition from the bureaucratic hierarchy to the complex system. The more the people in the organization view the structure in which they work as a complex system with all the characteristics associated with this structure, the more there is a need to view their relationship to the organization as emergent and based on qualities associated with the mission, vision, and values rather than as a transaction in which compensation is based on the performance of specific tasks. The two metaphors of the complex system for the structure and emergent for the relationship are complementary.

Organizational Leadership Transition: Twentieth-Century Control to Twenty-First-Century Trust

As hospitals emerged as the centers of healthcare delivery in America in the early twentieth century, they retained their familial design from time when husbands served as superintendents or stewards and their wives as matrons. The design provided a reliable structure that permitted the full force of family control and community morality to be exerted on those who were under the care of the board of benefactor that provided the funds for this community service. For the worthy poor who were admitted to the institutions, they were expected to model themselves grateful children who were compliant with those in charge of their care (Rosenberg, 1987, pp. 42–43).

Once the curative became dominant, the parental transformed into the administrative. The superintendent or steward managed the operations of the hospital with the assistance of a matron or nurse-superintendent (Rosenberg, p. 263). The superintendent would manage the operations and staffing of the hospital and report to the board concerning the results. The board initially was typically very involved in the daily operations and often played a significant role in approving admissions and other aspects of the work of the hospital. As the organizations became more sophisticated and the services more medically focused rather than custodial, the board retreated to a role more focused on the overall governance and oversight of the superintendent.

The growth in the types of procedures and the numbers of patients increased the size of hospitals and eventually led to the bureaucracy that most people associate with hospitals. Based on the concepts of scientific management at the time, the role of the superintendent was to direct the operations through various subordinates with departmental responsibilities and to ensure accounting for the use of resources and staff. The staff were trained and directed by managers in their work. The board held the superintendent accountable for maintaining the financial viability and operational success of the organization so the superintendent's ability to exert control over all aspects of the hospital became a key qualification for the success of the superintendent and subordinates.

Within the organization, control was associated with titles and positions that had the power to direct the workers in the various departments. The superintendent had the ultimate control under the governing board. The level of control exercised by other positions was based on the title and job description and the authority allocated by the superintendent. The people performing the work in the departments were expected to respect and respond to the direction of the person who had the title and position of power for that area. Positional power associated with titles was the most common way for control over work and resources to be authorized in the hospital bureaucracy.

In addition to positional power, however, the hospital contained many people with professional power. Physicians exercised privileges granted by the medical staff and the board to control the care of their patients by issuing orders. As licensed independent practitioners, physicians practicing within their scope and privileges as defined by the medical staff controlled the work of the people in the hospital and the use of hospital resources as these related to the care of their patients. Even though physicians did not have positional power in most cases, they often exercised control outside of the strictly clinical areas due to the importance of their role in attracting paying patients to the hospital and in advising the hospital on new equipment and services.

Within the bureaucratic structure, positional power offers the means for exercising oversight and control over all aspects of the operation of the hospital. It can be effective in promoting efficiency and tracking and reporting on the use of resources. It can provide information and quantification of operation to the superintendent and the board for setting goals or planning. When adjustments are needed in resources and staff, individuals with positional power can initiate changes in the way the work is performed, the number of people doing the work and the people who are not able to perform the work and should be either trained or eliminated. The efficiency, effectiveness, and familiarity of bureaucracies using positional power made them the dominant way to exercise control in the twentieth century in large and small healthcare organizations.

But in the twenty-first century, the emergence and proliferation of computer information technology and the expansion of healthcare services beyond the hospital made the metaphor of control less helpful as a way to describe the method for guiding the work and supporting the people performing the work to increase the efficiency, effectiveness, and success of healthcare organizations. For organizations operating as complex systems with workers using computer technology to solve problems and to respond to rapidly changing work processes, individuals attempting to exercise positional or professional power to ensure that work is performed correctly are often unable to respond quickly enough to the myriad of daily events that require decisions and responses.

In *The Relational Leadership Theory: Exploring the Social Processes of Leadership and Organizing*, Uhl-Bien (2006) describes leadership relationships as occurring throughout organizations and not limited to specific roles or positions. Social order and action within twenty-first-century healthcare organizations emerge out of the interactive dynamics identified as relational leadership (p. 668). Leadership emerges in individuals as they respond to changes and function as leaders when it is needed. Uhl-Bien views the complex system as the basis for understanding relational leadership and for recognizing the socially constructed roles and relationships of leadership (p. 668). Leadership is less defined by the title and position and more by the ability and willingness of individuals to respond to changes and exercise leadership at the moment it is needed and where it is needed (Goodwin, 2016).

In an environment that is changing rapidly, it is often impossible for those with authority who are outside of the immediate situation to offer meaningful assistance or guidance in the timeframe required. In such cases, the people performing the work need to have confidence that they have the support and trust of those in authority in order to exercise leadership and to collaborate with other workers as well as people receiving care to ensure that the issues are resolved and the process is able to proceed.

In complex systems, the metaphor of control loses its relevance as the metaphor of trust takes precedence. Trust rather than control forms the basis for the way in which the person in positional power or professional power conveys to the person performing the work their confidence that the work will be done in a manner that is consistent with the mission, vision, and values of the organization and with the intention providing the care or services that are needed. As part of this trust, the person performing the work understands that leadership is not limited to certain positions or certain work but is inherent in being in relationship with others in the organization. Anyone who identifies an opportunity for providing leadership to address an issue is expected to exercise leadership with the confidence that it will be supported by those who have positional or professional power over the area.

The metaphor of trust rather than control requires a significant reorientation for those in authority. How is someone responsible for the work to fulfill that responsibility if they are trusting others to perform the work with less oversight? The number of situations that may require problem-solving and the limited response time available to resolve issues creates a very difficult situation for someone with even a small area of responsibility. For many people in healthcare organizations in senior-level positions, their areas of responsibility are quite large. Often they spend their time in the meetings with little time remaining for responding to issues that occur at the operational level. This makes it imperative that the role of people with responsibility for large sections of the organization embrace the concept of trust as exemplifying their relationship with the people performing the work.

For people in authority to actively demonstrate trust as the basis for the exercise of leadership throughout the organization, there needs to be an understanding of what that trust entails. Does it mean that the person doing the work will always be right if they take a leadership role to respond to a situation? That would be unrealistic. Does it mean that the person in authority will not engage in situations and make changes if that is necessary? Again, if something requires that higher authority, it would be expected that an intervention would occur. The way that trust is demonstrated, and leadership is exercised is based on a common perspective of how work is performed and how people behave in the organization that is shared by everyone in the organization. The trust between the people is based on the shared commitment by everyone to make all decisions and to always act consistently with the mission, vision, and values of the organization. Rather than control by one person as the basis for ensuring decisions and actions are acceptable, trust operates on the idea the everyone has been trained and understands the operational implications of the mission, vision, and values of the organization and how they are to be expressed in the work and whenever leadership is provided regardless of who is doing it (Goodwin, 2016).

By creating a new vision of leadership as a response to a situation or issue that anyone in the organization can provide and to base the exercise of leadership on trust that everyone will act on the basis of a common commitment to a shared mission, vision, and values broadens the capacity of the organization to respond effectively whenever it is necessary. For this approach to work, it is imperative that one of the key roles of those in authority is to provide training to everyone in the operationalization of the mission, vision, and values. At the same time, those in authority will be the models that everyone watches to understand how it works to lead and to make decision based on these organizational values.

It will also be important for those in authority to recognize and acknowledge when someone performing the work exercises leadership in a manner that meets the expectations of the organization. Since one of the most treasured prerogatives of those in authority is to the allocation of resources, it is important that those who are performing the work understand how they can access resources to respond to situations that require them. Developing a way for operational people to access resources to resolve issues is an important statement of trust by those in authority and represents a significant step forward in developing the meaning of the metaphor of trust as defining leadership in the organization.

Organizational Innovation Transition: Twentieth-Century Centralized to Twenty-First-Century Adaptive

Innovation was first used as a term for something new in the 1540s where it meant "a novel change, experimental variation, new thing introduced in an established arrangement" (Etymonline). Though more recent uses of the term are often associated with the introduction of a new product or service into a market, it is the older definition that is most appropriate for understanding the nature of innovation in healthcare as presented in this transition. The organizational transition of innovation from centralized to adaptive focuses on the way in which healthcare organizations respond to changes in the environment and the way innovation originates and is promoted.

As American healthcare developed in the early twentieth century, the AMA promoted scientific medicine as the standard and training in medical schools associated with universities and hospitals as the appropriate venue for the education of physicians (Starr, 1982). In establishing this standard, the practice of medicine and the latest developments were learned in academic medical centers. These were the centers of innovation for American medicine and the places where the standards of care were set. Once they were educated in an academic medical center, physicians practiced what they were taught. Innovations in care were processed through the medical centers and then shared with physicians in other settings. Nurses were taught nursing standards of care in nursing schools. In practice, they followed these standards under the direction of nursing superintendents and followed the orders of the physicians in delivering care to their patients.

Within the hospital administrative structure, the bureaucratic hierarchy emphasized control and the performance of work based on specific jobs with specific tasks. Each person working in the hospital was hired to perform tasks and was rewarded or penalized on how well they followed the directions and performed the work. The people in positions of authority with oversight for the operation of the hospital obtained information as it was channeled through the hierarchy from the departments. Based on this information and their own knowledge and observations, people in authority would initiate changes.

From the perspective of the bureaucracy and the medical staff, innovation represented a threat to the control and stability of the organization and required careful management. It was assumed that those people performing the work would not initiate changes on their own as their responsibility was to follow instructions (Taylor, 1911). For those who had management responsibilities and authority to initiate changes, it was assumed that any innovations would be carefully vetted with the superintendent or administrator and with others in management positions in order to avoid any disruption to the work or in the relationships with the medical staff and the community. The centralized innovation metaphor conveys an image of all potential changes that arise in the operations of the hospital being drawn into the center of the organization's bureaucratic hierarchy for processing. The goal is as much to limit the spread of innovation as it is to capture ideas that might be used to improve operations.

Improvements would typically originate in the central bureaucracy from the people with authority over the operation of hospital. Changes in regulations and changes in the environment around the hospital might necessitate changing the way work is performed. This, however, would be something that would not be expected every day. Healthcare for much of the twentieth century got bigger as time went on and as more people gained insurance or other means of affording care, but the way the hospital worked remained and did not change rapidly or dramatically. When new medical technology or new specialties appeared, the hospital incorporated these additional services into the existing structure with a minimum of disruption to the basic infrastructure of the bureaucracy or the medical staff.

As healthcare organizations in the twenty-first century begin to view themselves as complex systems and as the people who have positional power recognize the ability of workers to use the mission, vision, and values of the organization to guide them in their work, the people performing the work began to feel trusted to assume the role of leaders in promoting solutions to problems and the metaphor of adaptive innovation helps to guide the overall vision of the organization.

Adaptive innovation places emphasis on the interface between the organization and its environment. Innovation within complex systems arises out of the need for the organization to change in response to changes in the environment. These changes occur at the point of contact between the organization and the community and the people the organization is serving. The people performing the work at the point of contact have existing knowledge and experience with the way the organization has related to its environment successfully in the past. They recognize or sense when the current way work is performed is no longer successful or when the people being served react negatively to the services they receive. At this point, there is motivation for the people performing the work to respond with innovations or new ways of performing the work that are more effective.

If innovation is viewed as acceptable only when it comes from people with positional authority, this limits the sources of innovation to the ideas of people who are not performing the work or actively engaged at the point of contact with the community. It also slows the process of adaptive innovation by limiting it to people who do not experience the need for change every day and may not have the same motivation to do the extra work of developing and implementing innovations. It also diminishes the ability of the people who know how the work is performed and how the environment has changed of sharing their insights on ways to adapt the work through innovation to the new environment.

Innovation becomes a daily event as information flows more rapidly throughout the organization and adapting to change becomes a routine part of the work. Individuals respond to changes that require innovation by using their tacit knowledge or knowledge based on their experience and the practice of their work and their understanding of the mission and values of the organization to recreate the work in response to the new situation they perceive (Nonaka & Hirotaka, 1995; Goodwin, 2016). Once they conceive of the innovation or idea for recreating the work in a new way, they make this idea explicit as they share it with others who are able to recognize and respond to it (Nonaka & Hirotaka, 1995; Goodwin, 2016).

As the work is performed each day, individuals develop their knowledge and experience about the work, the organization and the people that receive services. As the people performing the work recognize opportunities for making improvements through small incremental innovations as modeled by the Toyota Production System, they can become the source of adaptive innovation at the interface between the organization and its environment. In identifying innovations that solve problems or improve services, they can make changes and learn from them. They are then able to share their innovations with co-workers and to promote innovation at the point where the work is accomplished. This improves the organization but also expands the sources for innovation.

Adaptive innovation is a powerful metaphor that enables organizations to seek the sources of innovation in the people performing the work and empowering them to rapidly respond to changes in the environment that will permit the organization to be successful. As people in the organization learn to operationalize the mission, vision, and values, they can recognize when these important aspects are not effectively expressed in the work and proactively develop adaptive innovations to address this lack of alignment. This will inspire others to view adaptive innovation as part of their work and encourage people to share their ideas about improvements to make the organization more successful.

Process Transition: Production Method – Twentieth-Century Craftsman to Twenty-First-Century Multidisciplinary Team

In the early twentieth century, American healthcare was rapidly migrating from the home to the hospital and physicians were establishing themselves as a "sovereign profession" through the efforts of the AMA operating on the national and state levels (Starr, 1982). The AMA established educational standards based on training at medical schools associated with hospitals and universities and state medical societies established licensure requirements that included membership in the AMA and completion of AMA-recommended training. The hospitals followed the minimum standards established by the American College of Surgeons that required an organized medical staff in which "membership upon the staff be restricted to physicians and surgeons who are (a) full graduates of medicine in good standing and legally licensed to practice in their respective states or provinces" (Wright, 2017, p. 708). In addition to state licensure, professional associations developed for the various medical specialties and established standards that physicians were required to achieve to become board certified by these associations.

Through these various efforts, physicians achieved professional preeminence in medicine. Freidson (1988) argued that "…the most strategic distinction lies in legitimate, organized autonomy – that a profession is distinct from other occupations in that it has been given the right to control its own work" (p. 71). Once the medical staff and the board at the local hospital accepted a licensed physician's application and granted that physician privileges to practice a given medical specialty and to perform procedures associated with that specialty, the physician exercised those privileges without supervision by anyone else. The physician was able to admit patients, write orders concerning their care, prescribe medications, and order their administration. All aspects of the care of their patients were essentially under the control of the attending physician.

This professional autonomy finds its true expression in the relationship of the physician with the hospital in accessing resources. The fuel of the hospital is the physician's order and nothing beyond the most rudimentary services can be provided until a physician has ordered it. Once the physician has ordered it, however, it is very possible that the hospital and its clinical and non-clinical staff may expend hundreds of thousands of dollars in resources and staff time caring for a patient who may not be able to pay for the services. In most cases, the care ordered by a physician is not reviewed by anyone else as the physician holds the position of being an independent practitioner.

In the Hippocratic Oath, the physician refers to "techné" which can be translated as "art or craft" as what is received and what is to be passed on (Hippocrates, 2002). The art of medicine and the practice of medicine are common ways of expressing the work physicians perform. It is reasonable, then, to place them into the context of artists or craftsmen in considering the way they work. An important aspect of both the description of the work from antiquity and the modern understanding of a profession is the singularity of the person and their autonomy in the work. It is this aspect of the work of physicians that has shaped the operation of hospitals during the modern period (Freidson, 1988).

If we consider the role of the physicians as those of craftsmen, how does this help to understand the way in which twentieth healthcare is delivered? The organization requires orders from the physicians to initiate all the activities associated with the care of the patient. Regardless of whether the physician is in a solo practice or a group practice or has numerous assistants, the license is issued to the individual physician. There is no one else who can order these activities. From the admission of the patient to discharge and beyond, the orders of the physician shape all the work and are the basis for the compensation that the hospital and the physician receive. The physician is the one who defines the illness and the treatment and evaluates the outcome care. Though many people may be involved in carrying out the physician's orders and even delivering care, the physician and the physician's orders are the key elements to the delivery of care in America.

An important turning point in the way healthcare evaluated and the autonomy of the craftsman physician occurred with the Medicare and Medicaid program prospective payment system in the 1980s. This system established the federal government's payment to the hospital for care delivered to Medicare patients. The physician's payment was not included in the DRG. However, though the physician's payment was unaffected, the hospital suddenly had a strong motivation to encourage physicians to facilitate the discharge of patients as soon as possible.

Under the craftsman production model, the determination of when the patient should be discharged rests solely with the physician. With prospective payment, the physician continued to retain the responsibilities for ordering the care of patients as before, but the hospital began to build support services around the physician to promote awareness of costs and to identify physicians who had a history of longer lengths of stay for their patients or higher costs.

An important result of the implementation of the prospective payment system and managed care for both the physicians and healthcare organizations was the realization that in the future the cost of healthcare as well as the quality would be concerns of more than just the individual physician and the individual patient. The physician would no longer be able to practice with the level of autonomy that had been achieved in the early twentieth century. Instead, the physician would be viewed within the context of the processes of the healthcare organization and the payment procedures of the government and commercial insurers. Within this context, the physician represented an important decision maker but also a potential threat simply in the way the physician practiced medicine. To mitigate this threat by facilitating the decision making of the physician, healthcare organizations and insurers developed groups of people to support physicians and to monitor and evaluate the cost and quality of care.

In the twenty-first-century healthcare, the complexity of healthcare processes was finally recognized and the ability of individual physicians to function as craftsmen and individually manage all aspects of care was viewed as inefficient if not impossible. This realization appeared first in the growth in staff to manage the requirements of federal and commercial insurance companies. The demand for information about the care of patients and the demand for responses from physicians to questions about their orders for care increase significantly. As the cost to process information required by insurers increased, many physicians gave up private practice and joined groups or sought employment with healthcare organizations and hospitals.

With ever-increasing computing power and the ability to use codes and claims for data, the care delivered to patients and the costs associated with the care were mined to determine opportunities for recommending improvements to hospitals and physicians. Lengths of stay, complication rates, readmissions, infections, and other aspects of the quality of the care of patients became visible through the analysis of the data. Patterns of care and comparisons between practitioners and organizations became the focus of federal and commercial insurers and agencies interested in the quality and costs of healthcare.

As physicians experienced the increasing visibility of their decisions and the results of their orders for their patients, they found their work as craftsmen and the care of their patients was constantly monitored and reviewed by non-physicians interested in reducing cost or improving outcomes of care. During hospital stays, case management and utilization review nurses would review the status and care of patients to identify delays that prolonged length of stays. Infection control nurses would monitor infections and infection prevention strategies to ensure they are meeting the standards. Quality nurses reviewed outcomes and complications and initiated teams to collect data, design improvements in care, and implement and monitor the improvements. Much of this work began to appear in public reporting on healthcare organizations as a means for encouraging healthcare consumers to make better decisions on where to receive care.

In the twenty-first century, the multidisciplinary team approach to healthcare has supplanted the craftsman model in practice if not wholly acknowledged by the practitioners. Team-based care is defined by the National Academy of Medicine (formerly known as the Institute of Medicine) as "... the provision of health services to individuals, families, and/or their communities by at least two health providers who work collaboratively with patients and their caregivers – to the extent preferred by each patient – to accomplish shared goals within and across settings to achieve coordinated, high-quality care" (Schottenfeld et al., 2016).

Wen and Schulman (2014) note that team-based care has been offered as an improvement in care delivery, especially for the treatment of patients with complicated medical conditions. When properly implemented, team-based approaches have been shown to improve clinical decision making. In practice, team-based care takes many forms, such as inpatient care management teams or multidisciplinary disease-oriented care programs. Teams may be large or small and are found in a variety of practice settings, from private clinics to academic medical centers (2014).

Primary contributors to the team approach to care have been the implementation of electronic medical records and the ability for computers to mine information from the medical record. With the electronic medical record, large numbers of people in many disciplines can access information and learn the status of the person receiving care and to contribute their own perspective to the conversation. Physician notes, test results, care coordination notes, vital signs, and much more are readily available to nurses, therapists, social workers, financial analysts, infection control nurses, quality directors, and others. All these disciplines can read and comment and engage in conversations about the patient's care while the patient is still in the hospital. Through these conversations, the physicians receive valuable insights into the patient's condition and recommendations on the next steps in the care process. At the same time, everyone involved in the patient's care can contribute to the ongoing conversation, and this creates the identity of the team that is providing care to the patient. It also helps to clarify the goals of treatment as individual members record their interactions with the patient and their understanding of the patient's goals and their own plans for treatment.

Equally important in terms of continuously improving the processes of care are the patterns and trends that become visible through the data mined in the electronic medical records. Healthcare as a craftsman production system was focused on the activities of the individual physician and the condition of the individual patient. As healthcare moves to a multidisciplinary team environment with everyone documenting in a common electronic record, different aspects of the work become more visible. Nursing care, physical therapy treatments, medication administration, and other parts of the care of the patient can be identified and evaluated. All of this information along with the results of care and the financial data come together in the record and the data to provide a more complete view of the care delivered to the patient by the team along with the physician and results of their work.

Ultimate responsibility for the care of the patient remains with the physician of record and decisions made in the care of patients rely on the licensed independent practitioners as was the case in the twentieth century, but the craftsman's model of care in which the lone practitioner oversees all aspects of care has changed. Healthcare is becoming more of a multidisciplinary team production method in which specialists in a variety of fields are engaged with physicians in designing and delivering care. Though the biggest push for such a team arose out of the financial side of healthcare, the results for the twenty-first century are improved care overall and a greater emphasis on the patient's goals and experiences.

Process Transition: Delivery System – Twentieth-Century Hospital to Twenty-First-Century Continuum of Care

Hospitals emerged as the center of American healthcare in the early twentieth century for the simple reason that the benefits of surgery were becoming apparent to potential patients and surgeons needed operating rooms to properly care for their patients. As Joel Howell (1995) points out, operations had been performed in homes in the past, but with the advent of electrical lighting, surgeons and their patients benefitted from reliable electrical lights. In addition to the lighting, surgeons needed surgical instruments that were properly sterilized to prevent infections. And, finally, as Howell notes, the hospital's ability to manage the flow of patients into and out of the operating room and was as important as the operating room itself. There was a dramatic increase in the number of surgical patients beginning in the first two decades of the twentieth century that made the movement and coordination of patients in and out of surgery an important part of performing surgery in the hospital (p. 59).

Surgery was the premier service provided by hospitals, but the physicians also depended on additional medical technology that was available only in the hospital. X-rays and laboratories were also part of the support services that physicians relied on in the early twentieth-century hospital. For their paying patients who needed treatment, the hospital developed rooms and suites suitable to the position on the society of the patients. The wealthy could have rooms for servants and private duty nurses and décor like their home environment. For middle-class patients, semi-private rooms were available to provide a measure of privacy compared with the wards that were the remnant of the almshouse for the poor who required care. Howell (1995) indicates that hospitals adopted accounting techniques and technology early in the twentieth century (p. 34).

During the Civil War, Confederate and Union soldiers were treated in field hospitals that began poorly but improved during the war. This was the first time that many men had experienced healthcare as an organized process delivered to large numbers of people through an institution (Rosenberg, 98). In World War I, according to Rosemary Stevens (1999), the "efficiency of specialized medicine and the importance of hospitals" (p. 105) were demonstrated. She points out that by the 1920s, "hospitalization had become an accepted consumption good" and the hospital as a new "middle class institution" was viewed as the place to go for "obstetrical deliveries, appendectomies, and tonsillectomies and adenoidectomies" (p. 105). Depending on the size of the community, hospitals ranged in size from a converted house to large institution. Stevens describes hospitals as "offering their services to an increasingly receptive consumer-oriented population" and the hospitals were perceived as the "stations for the diffusion of medical technique" (p. 105).

The problem for many smaller communities was the lack of hospitals or very poorly equipped facilities. As training for physicians became more standardized in universities with medical schools and hospitals, it was logical that they would want to practice near a hospital that offered the services and support staff that they required to diagnose and treat illnesses and injuries. The Hill-Burton Act of 1946 promoted joint federal and state efforts to expand the availability of hospital services into areas that did not have hospitals in support of the concept of "hospital medicine as science" and the value of the expansion of inpatient hospital services as "an unambiguous social good" (Stevens, p. 220).

As hospitals were constructed in the years following World War II, they became not the most visible part of the delivery of healthcare in the community but also served as the hub for healthcare activity. For many communities, hospitals became leading employers and recruiting physicians, nurses, and other healthcare professionals to the hospitals brought well-educated people into the community. Hospitals also served as sources of healthcare information and education for patients and families and as educational resources for local area schools and workplaces. In smaller communities, hospitals offered facilities for meetings and administrative and technical expertise to assist community efforts to improve health and quality of life. In many ways, hospitals symbolized the aspirations of the community and reflected its values in providing care for the ill and injured. For residents, the community hospital serves as the setting for the births and deaths and for emergency care of family and friends.

The hospital served as the metaphor for the delivery of healthcare services through most of the twentieth century, but that began to change by the end of the century. Hospitals retained their architectural presence in communities, and they continued to provide emergency and acute care services, but the relationship with the community changed as costs, quality, and convenience became important considerations for the hospitals and their patients.

After decades of full employer-based insurance, employees of businesses were asked to assume a larger share of the costs of insurance premiums and deductibles for hospitalizations as their companies tried to reduce costs. Medicare patients were admitted under the prospective payment program which encouraged hospitals and physicians to reduce costs by shortening lengths of stay. During the same period, new healthcare service businesses began to complete with hospitals by offering outpatient laboratory testing, outpatient imaging, and outpatient surgery services for lower costs.

Retail pharmacies began to add clinics to provide routine healthcare services and skilled nursing facilities and home healthcare services took care of higher acuity patients following shorter hospital stays. Urgent care and freestanding emergency departments competed with hospital emergency services based on price and convenience. As technology expanded into home computers and smartphones, individuals were able to have virtual physician visits from their homes or offices. These provided more convenient and less expensive care. Insurers promoted the use of virtual services and outpatient facilities rather than hospitals as a way for patients to save money and time.

With the growing number of service providers available to twenty-first-century patients, the image of healthcare needed to change from the iconic hospital as the single source for healthcare services to a continuum of care more like a circle containing a number of organizations and services to meet a variety of healthcare needs. Hospitals play an integral role in the circle of care and may continue to be a central component in terms of integration of services. For many people, however, the trip to the hospital has become more of once a decade event while more frequent contact occurs with a variety of community healthcare services. For example, cardiac surgery may take place at a hospital, but routine care may be provided at a clinic in local pharmacy by a nurse practitioner. Virtual visits online with physicians may take the place of scheduling and driving to a physician's office for a visit.

An important element of the continuum of care circle is the electronic record that documents all healthcare information and is readily available to the healthcare practitioner at whatever site the patient my choose for care. It is this aspect that may become the most important for the image of the future of healthcare. With a variety of organizations capable of providing services depending on the seriousness of the healthcare concern, access to the information in the electronic medical record will play an important role in the delivery of care.

Process Transition: Information System – Twentieth-Century Isolation to Twenty-First-Century Network

From Imhotep's surgical notes recorded in hieroglyphics around 3000 BCE in Egypt and preserved today in the Edwin-Smith Papyrus to the Code of Hammurabi recorded in Babylon in Mesopotamia in the 1700s BCE to the Oath of Hippocrates in Greece in 500 BCE to the present, there are records describing the relationship between people who are sick or injured and the people who are trying to help them. In the same way, physicians in the twentieth century kept notes concerning their patients. In most cases, the notations were for the personal use of the physician without any real concern that someone else should be able to decipher them. This was the beginning of what would become the hospital medical record and using the metaphor of isolation to describe these private notes offers a useful starting point for considering what transpires later.

As physicians took care of their patients and made notes and reminders, they developed their own sense of how to record encounters and charges and treatments. They would have some degree of training from their teachers on what had proved useful to note and how to organize an office in order to be able to recall the care of a patient in the past when the patient returned. In the early twentieth century, however, changes began to take place in the way information was collected and used. Howell (1995) describes an example of a patient's record from 1902 that was one page of handwritten notes that covers a 3-month hospital stay (p. 43). In evaluating the length of records and comparing it to the length of hospital stays, Howell found that in two large hospitals, the average length of stay declined from 1900 to 1925, but the median length of the record more grew from two to six pages in one hospital and from five to eleven pages in another (p. 44). During the same period the "length of the patient record produced per day of admission" increased by three times at one hospital and five times at another (p. 44).

Howell (1995) attributes the increase in the size of the patient record to a variety of factors that reflect the changes occurring in the hospitals during the early years of the twentieth century. He notes that the "records became longer in part because more and more people were becoming involved in patient care and leaving a written record to their presence" (p. 44). At the same time, "patient records also reflected the creation of new administrative units" (p. 45). As these new units, such as radiology or social work, appeared in the hospital and began to be involved in the care of patients, they documented in the patient record. Initially, as Howell points out, the documentation was a simple note, but over time standardized forms were developed by the units. He notes that "Each form also served to isolate some aspect of the person lying in the bed. The narrative of a single patient, the smooth flow of a story about a human being's travail was starting to become fragmented, discontinuous" (p. 45). Based on reviews of records in two large hospitals, Howell determined that "people who worked in the early twentieth-century hospital between 1900 and 1925 saw a 438-fold increase in the use of forms" (p. 48). He also indicates that the graphical presentation of information began to proliferate during this same period. "Between 1900 and 1920, hospital charts started to be filled with graphs for all manner of information" (p. 52). These ranged from routine observations such as temperature to specialized tracking such as vital signs on anesthesia forms (p. 52).

Howell (1995) uses the changes in the "overall appearance of patient records" to describe changes occurring in the large hospitals as they adopted business processes and sought to enhance efficiency. There was a transition from the individualistic documentation of physicians and others to more standardized forms and the use of "visual devices" to convey information (p. 56). He notes that "the standard forms allow whoever designs the forms to determine precisely how information is presented" (p. 56). In evaluating the nature of documentation as it developed in early twentieth-century hospitals, Howell concludes that the changes in documentation were "important parts of how the ideology of the efficiency movement was operationalized in the hospital setting" (p. 56).

Howell's analysis of the patient record captures an important aspect of the way that business efficiency models entered the operation of hospitals. Individual units in hospitals standardized the capture of information in forms they developed. Describing the effects as part of the "balkanization" of the hospital into its various parts, there was another aspect that was retained from the beginning and exemplifies the culture of the twentieth-century hospitals and its operational implications. Handwritten medical notes or physician progress notes remained a part of all patient records throughout the twentieth century and into the twenty-first century as articles on patient safety bemoaned the ongoing prevalence of illegible handwriting well into the 2000s.

The culture of healthcare organizations perpetuated the isolation of information in the individual units or departments and within the hardcopy patient medical record throughout the twentieth century. Each area retained its own section of the record and its own forms. Just as the departments used their own forms, the implementation of new electronic technology for analysis was also departmental. One of the earliest was in the laboratory. The "Robot Chemist" appeared for clinical laboratory use in 1959. The results were printed or typed into standardized forms and delivered to the patient care areas for inclusion in the medical record.

In the 1970s, large hospitals began work on electronic medical records. By the 1980s, portable computers made it possible for more people in hospitals to have access to information in electronic forms. However, it was in 2001 that the Institute of Medicine in its report, "Crossing the Quality Chasm: A new Health System for the Twenty-First Century," strongly encouraged healthcare organizations to recognize the potential for improving care through expanded use of computerized healthcare information technology and improving access to information in the medical record.

It was not until 2009, however, that health information technology on a national level received an important boost through the American Reinvestment & Recovery Act (ARRA) which included the "Health Information Technology for Economic and Clinical Health (HITECH) Act." The HITECH Act included a proposal for the development of meaningful use of electronic health records throughout the United States healthcare delivery system as a critical national goal with an investment of $25.8 billion for health information technology.

The introduction of computer information technology into healthcare represented a cultural as well as a technical challenge. The hardcopy patient medical records shaped the workflows of nearly every clinical process in the hospital. The collection, documentation, and storage of clinical information were all tied into the paper record. The attempt to convert this document into a virtual record and to adapt all the workflows associated with this conversion would represent one of the most difficult technical problems to confront twenty-first-century American healthcare. The goal was to move from the isolation of the departments and the paper record into an electronic record that would be accessible by anyone authorized to view the record with appropriate computer access wherever they were and whenever they needed to review the record.

Network is the metaphor for the twenty-first-century information system because it places the emphasis on overcoming the fragmentation inherent in healthcare organizations and in healthcare in general. The term "network" is a compound word that in the sixteenth century referred to "anything made of threads or wires in the pattern of intersecting lines or meshes like a net." It has been used historically to designate "modes of human connection." In the 1940s, it came to mean a group of individuals with common interests, and in the 1960s, it was first used to denote "a system of interconnected computers" (https://www.dictionary.com/browse/network).

In applying the metaphor of network to twenty-first-century healthcare, the intention is to create a motivating vision of people and technology connected to promote the delivery of high-quality healthcare. It is also important to recognize that the transition of healthcare organizations to complex systems is a result of the effectiveness of the interconnectivity that people in the organization share through information technology.

Process Transition: Financial – Twentieth-Century Fee-For-Service to Twenty-First-Century Consumer Health Financing

A truly unique aspect of American healthcare throughout the twentieth century as compared with other developed countries was the way in which physicians, insurance companies, and the government struggled with healthcare payments. It is appropriate to think of twentieth-century American healthcare financially as the century of "fee-for-service." Defined as payment for individual services, fee-for-service was originally an itemized list of what services were provided and what the charge was for the service. However, over the course of the twentieth century, the view of this method of paying for healthcare grew darker as its potential for promoting overutilization of healthcare services became clearer. When the physician is compensated for each service, then the more services provided the larger the compensation. Though physicians as members of the AMA are ethically charged to provide only the services the patient requires, the professional judgment of the physician determines what is to be done.

As George Rosen (1983) describes the situation in 1934, the AMA had established a position that it was to maintain in the future. The crucial points were specifically, "All aspects of medical service had to remain under the control of the medical profession and no third party could be permitted to intervene between patient and physician" (p. 114). According to Rosen, the AMA "mobilized all the resources" to defend the autonomy of physicians with the major objective "to prevent or restrain expansion of governmental involvement in health affairs" (p. 115).

Even as the AMA succumbed to the pressures of the marketplace and agreed to healthcare insurance in 1938, the association attached four stipulations to protect physicians. Among these was the requirement for fee-for-service reimbursements (Chapin, 2015, p. 27). Chapin argues that under fee-for-service physicians had "incentive to cater to patient requests for unnecessary services" and this would lead to service overutilization (p. 28). She also noted that fee-for-service discouraged physicians from improving their own productivity and so work to create higher healthcare costs (p. 28).

It is interesting to note that physicians and hospitals were able to maintain their reimbursement strategies through most of the century. However, rapidly rising healthcare costs for governmental and commercial insurers in the 1970s finally pushed the payers to take action to address the issues. For Medicare, the response was DRGs prospective payment for Medicare hospital admissions to limit payments and to encourage hospitals and physicians to address the issue of rising costs. At the same time, commercial insurers facing questions from employers who paid premiums for employee health insurance migrated to a managed care arrangement. The insurers would negotiate with physicians to set up physician networks that provided market share to the physicians in exchange for more rigorous utilization review, reduced or capitated fees, cost containment provisions that included treatment guidelines and physician gatekeepers and regulation of access to specialist (Chapin, p. 242).

Though managed care eventually faded due to particularly poor public relations and because Americans as patients were not willing to accept restrictions on access to care, Medicare continued to work to reduce costs through a variety of initiatives to promote cost reduction and by reducing the rate of reimbursement to hospitals. In 2010, the passage of the Patient Protection and Affordable Care Account (PPACA) provided a broad range of initiatives for expanding coverage while reducing costs. It significantly increased the number of people with access to health insurance and promoted a variety of ways for people to prevent illness, improve health, and better manage their insurance coverage.

In the twenty-first century, the emphasis has shifted from the professional dominance of the physician to an environment where health and healthcare are viewed much more broadly than simply the cure of illness. The means for financing healthcare services requires the metaphor of consumer health financing due acknowledge the breadth of services and financial arrangements available in the twenty-first century. Patients and their families are assuming a greater role in making decisions about their health and they have many more options and they are looking for ways to manage their healthcare payments using a combination of insurance and personal financing.

Employer-based insurance and commercial insurance purchased by individuals are available with a range of services and prices. Employers are looking for their insured workers to assume a greater share of the burden of their insurance costs by including higher deductions and copays. In exchange, the workers are offered more flexibility in where they obtain healthcare and are encouraged to compare pricing when there are options available. Insurers, for example, are offering virtual physician visit online for reduced cost to address routine health issues at less cost and with great convenience for the patient. Insurance websites offer guidance on types of services that should be selected to address healthcare conditions in order to aid patients in saving money by choosing the least expensive service that meets their needs. A retail pharmacy-based clinic with a nurse practitioner may be all that is needed rather than a trip to urgent care of the emergency department of a hospital.

In the healthcare environment of the twenty-first century, individuals and families are encouraged to take responsibility for preventing illness and for managing chronic conditions. The Internet has made it possible for insurers, healthcare agencies, and others to make more information available and to promote self-help opportunities for individuals who are interested in losing weight or stopping smoking or learning more about managing a chronic condition such as asthma and pulmonary disease. Fitness centers offer exercise and wellness program that encourage individuals to develop more active and healthier lifestyle and working out financing for these through employers and insurance companies can be useful.

America continues to struggle with conflicting image of healthcare. One image envisions each person and family assuming full responsibility for their healthcare and healthcare costs with the government having little involvement besides promoting good health. In this image, there is little help for people who are unable to afford healthcare or are unable to understand what they need for healthcare. The other image involves a more active role for government and the society in which the welfare of the people in the country is considered to be in the national interest and resources and guidance are available to ensure that everyone has access to care and the support to understand the care that they need.

Consumer health financing offers a metaphor that engages both images by recognizing that each person has a responsibility for managing their health and the related costs and the country has a responsibility for helping when it is needed. The conflicts of the past in defining professions and creating the means for delivering the healthcare that is needed has started on a path in which the connectivity of a healthcare network and a broad spectrum of services offers the potential for most people to be able to access care and to live healthier lives.

Cultural Transition: Professional – Twentieth-Century Autonomy to Twenty-First-Century Integration

An editorial in the New York Times on September 12, 2019, by Sandeep Jauhar, cardiologist, reported that in 2020 Medicare would "require doctors to use a computer algorithm to vet imaging tests to determine 'appropriateness'" (Jauhar, 2019). Based on the regulation, if the CT scans or MRIs do not meet "appropriateness criteria," Medicare may not reimburse the cost (2019).

With increasing frequency, the use of clinical decision-making support computer systems is becoming a part of every healthcare professionals' daily work routine. From medication systems embedded in hospital electronic medical records that raise red flags when orders are different from standardized guidelines to algorithms that provide guidance on treatments for specific illnesses to numerous alerts and reminders, the physician today is bombarded by electronic signage that demands attention and guides care decisions. As the Medicare program requirement for the vetting of imaging orders through a computer program illustrates, the world of medicine has changed significantly in the past 100 years.

During the heyday of free enterprise medicine in the early nineteenth century, the general assumption was that dealing with minor aches, pains, injuries, and illness was something that anyone could do with just a little instruction. Healthcare was viewed as just another part of living the way cooking, cleaning, and other activities contributed to daily life. If you were a reasonable person, you should be able to manage most of the problems related to your physical health with common sense and locally available remedies. For the major events such as births or serious illnesses and injuries, you ask experienced neighbors to help or manage the best that you could. If a physician or midwife were nearby and you could afford it, you would seek their assistance only when necessary. Dispensaries in larger towns and cities offered help to the poor.

According to Paul Starr (1982), all of this changed at the end of the nineteenth century with the professionalization of nursing, the rise in the importance of hospitals for surgery and acute illness and the bond between the physicians and hospitals that developed at the end of the nineteenth century. By the 1920s, physicians with medical degrees and hospitals with operating rooms had become the sources of medical care for the wealthy and the poor and for middle-class people who could afford it. Through most of the twentieth century, physicians reigned supreme as a unique profession that grew out of the "elaborate system of specialized knowledge, technical procedures and rules of behavior" associated with modern medicine (p. 3). Starr notes that its success as a profession has been based on its success in reducing the burden of disease that had afflicted people (1982).

Starr goes further, however, in describing physicians as a "sovereign profession" (p. 5) and views its preeminence as a result of more than its medical expertise. He states that "In the distribution of rewards from medicine, the medical profession, as the highest-paid occupation in our society, receives a radically disproportionate share" (p. 5). He states that the profession has been able to turn its authority into social privilege, economic privilege and political influence (p. 5). "At all these levels, from individual relations to the state, the pattern has been one of professional sovereignty" (p. 5).

In assessing the rise of "medicine into an authoritative profession" (p. 18), Starr (1982) points to several factors. The "cohesiveness" of the profession increased due to the need for referrals associated with specialization and access to hospitals (p. 18). The urbanization of society broke down the previously prevailing reliance on family and communities and increased willingness to rely on the "specialized skills of strangers" (p. 18). From the 1890s to the 1920s, the rise in Progressivism with its emphasis on science gave rise to experts or professionals with specialized knowledge and organizational hierarchies (p. 19). The institutionalization of physician status through the system of medical education and licensure increased public confidence in physicians (p. 19). The growing importance of hospitals contributed to the view of physicians as having authority and strengthened the dependence of the physicians on each other (p. 21). All these influences translated into economic benefit as physicians successfully prevented state or organizational intrusion into their patient relationships and maintained their institutionalized autonomy (p. 25).

Charles Perrow (1963), sociologist, offers interesting insights into the way in which professional authority and autonomy of physicians worked to their benefit in hospital environment during the mid-twentieth century. He studied a 300-bed voluntary, general hospital from 1957 to 1958 and the development of its power structures. He concluded that it passed through three eras that were shaped by what he describes as the "dominant task areas" (p. 114) and considered this to be the usual evolution for hospitals. "The dominant task areas in voluntary general hospitals are asserted to change over time in a sequence that is believed to be typical and to reflect changes in technology and the needs of the community" (p. 114).

Perrow (1963) summarized his findings for this hospital as eras of trustee control, doctor control and a final era that was trending toward administrative domination (p. 114). Trustees dominated the organization during a time between 1885 and 1929 in which capital investment and community acceptance were emphasized (p. 114). Doctors emerged as dominant in the following era from 1929 to 1942. During this period, Perrow points out, there was a shift from free care to service for paying patients; technical facilities were expanded; quality of care improved; and, finally, the hospital emphasized research as a way to gain recognition which was supported by the medical staff (p. 118). In the final era that Perrow included in his study, the new administrator of the hospital during a 10-year period emphasized "the increased importance of internal administration, rationalized the procedures, improved business practices, placed the medical staff on a constitutional basis that defined their official powers and even raised medical standards" (p. 124).

It's clear from Starr (1982) that physicians achieved a high level of autonomy and professional prestige during the early twentieth century and in concert with the development of hospitals and this continued throughout the century. By the middle of the century based on Perrow's study, however, physicians were beginning to negotiate more with the administrative side of the organization in the exercise of their prerogatives due to the increasingly complex operations of the hospital. Physician reliance on hospitals for facilities, equipment, and trained support staff as well as the administrative support provided ensure compliance with regulations and billing, increased the value of administrators to the physicians and strengthened the administrator role in the operation and management of the hospitals. This reduced the ability of physicians to exert their claims to autonomy.

By the end of the twentieth century, physician autonomy continued to be expressed in several ways in organizations and in relationships with other people engaged in delivering healthcare. The fundamental basis for the sense of autonomy described by Starr (1982) was slow being chipped away by increasing disruption from a variety of sources. The relationship between physicians and administrators became contentious as the federal government began to take an active role in reducing the payments to hospitals for care delivered to Medicare patients. With the implementation of DRG prospective payments in the 1980s, administrators were forced to engage with physicians in the actual processes of care in order to prevent the costs of care from exceeding the reimbursement provided by the government. The increase in the pool of paying patients through the government programs increased the volume of patients coming to hospitals which reduced the ability of any one physician to control admissions. However, the prospective payment method of reimbursement increased the financial risk and the need for efficient hospital operations. This strengthened the administrative efforts in working with physicians on improving care.

Even as physicians were being encouraged by administrators to change their processes in the hospital to facilitate discharge, the commercial insurers in the 1980s were creating managed care networks of preferred physician providers (Chapin, 2015, p. 242). Though these networks offered physician access to patients, they came with greater involvement by the insurers in the way the physicians managed care (p. 242). These networks used a variety of techniques to reduce utilization of specialists and expensive services to reduce costs which further reduced physician autonomy due to utilization review processes and gatekeeper physicians reviewing requests for services (p. 242). Insurers also developed sophisticated claims monitoring software programs to identify physicians with higher costs or higher complication rates.

The AMA had been a strong advocate of physician autonomy throughout the twentieth century, but after the passage of Medicare, which it opposed strenuously, the AMA was unable to maintain its dominant position as in the past. "The membership in the AMA fell from 75% of US doctors in the 1950s to approximately 15% of doctors in 2011" (Collier, 2011, p. 713). The reasons for the decline in membership were identified as the rise of specialty medical organizations that offered continuing medical education and certifications and a shift in the desire and need of physicians to belong to large groups such as the AMA (p. 713).

Where physician autonomy was taught and promoted by the AMA and academic medical centers as a defining aspect of the medical profession in the twentieth century, a new metaphor is needed for the future to define what it means to be a professional. Surprisingly, a defining aspect of physician professionalism in the future will be its integration into the team of professionals that will manage healthcare of each patient. Physicians will continue to be unique in their status as licensed and privileged practitioners within healthcare organizations, but their ability to integrate their knowledge and practices into the overall process of care through engagement with other professionals will be the means for transitioning to the future.

Specialization in American healthcare was promoted by increased financial rewards and higher prestige for physicians who attained specialized skills beyond those of the general practitioner. In recent years, there has been a continuing tendency to define all types of physician practice as a specialty in order to preserve a measure of respect and to promote higher compensation. It has become difficult to find a general practitioner due to continuous refining of turfs and territories.

With the multiple subdivisions within medicine and surgery, the need for integration becomes even more acute as a patient may have multiple specialists attempting to provide care simultaneously. The Lucian Leape Institute at the National Patient Safety Foundation issued a report, *Order from Chaos: Accelerating Care Integration*, in 2012. Integration is defined by the Institute in the broad sense as "the process and activities through which healthcare organizations and systems achieve integrated care at the level of the individual patient" (p. 8). Within this context, the Institute identified several critical components including handovers, sequencing, interdependency, and storage and retrieval. The one that is important for the purposes of this book is the "interdependency of members of a multidisciplinary team" (p. 8).

One of the barriers to integration cited in the report is physician autonomy. This autonomy has its source in the way physicians are trained.

"Deeply ingrained in the profession of medicine is the teaching that a physician has an individual and personal responsibility for his or her patient..." (Lucian Leape Institute, 2012, p. 11). This concept is also included in the understanding of what it means to be a professional and serves as a foundational principle in the code of ethics of the medical profession (p. 11). Information asymmetry that increased the patient's dependence on the physician played a significant role in promoting the autonomy of physicians as did public stereotypes of the profession (p. 11).

In addition to what has already been described as creating a fragmented environment in healthcare between various medical and surgical disciplines, a much more disruptive transition is taking place that will further amplify the importance of integration. Even as the number of primary care physicians has declined, the number of advance practice nurses or nurse practitioners has increased to begin to fill the gap in primary care services in a number of specialty areas. The growth in the number of nurse practitioners as an important professional group in the delivery of primary care will be needed to meet the demand for care due to the shortage of primary care physicians (AAMC, 2019). Other professions increasing educational requirements to keep pace with new developments are pharmacists and physical therapists who are now required to have doctoral or professional degrees, according to the Bureau of Labor Statistics (Pharmacist, 2019; Physical Therapist, 2019).

The Institute (2012) acknowledges that the traditional image of the autonomous physician made sense in the past with the solo practitioner managing all aspects of care, but today, the complexity of medical science and technology requires multiple professionals in various sites managing the care of patient simultaneously. This environment requires a very high level of communication and integration that begins with a genuine sense of interdependency rather than the silos inherent in autonomy (2012). It is, therefore, appropriate that the metaphor for professions is integration rather than autonomy for the future.

Cultural Transition: Metaphor – Twentieth-Century Scientific Machine to Twenty-First-Century Complex Adaptive System

In a sense, the cultural metaphor is a "metaphor of metaphors." Each of the transitions has a twentieth-century metaphor of the past and a twenty-first-century metaphor of the future, but what would be the metaphor to include them all. In a sense, the second culture transition, metaphor serves the purpose of forming a context for all the others. The twentieth-century culture metaphor of the scientific machine and the twenty-first-century metaphor of the CAS encompass the other metaphors that were associated with the two centuries. These metaphors serve a valuable purpose of enabling conversations about the two periods in American healthcare to reflect unified perspectives and to contrast the differences as expressed in these two metaphors (Goodwin, 2016).

The scientific machine metaphor for the twentieth century draws its inspiration from the progressive movement perspective that the world around us operates in particular ways and we can learn how it operates and work to make it better through scientific methods. Like the machines that were revolutionizing manufacturing, transportation and power generation, organizations such as businesses and hospitals could be viewed as operating like machines. Frederick Taylor and others sought to apply the concepts of scientific management to manufacturing and businesses and hospitals and even to surgery to find new ways to make them more efficient and, therefore, better (Howell, 1995).

Frank Gilbreth (1914), an associate of Frederick Taylor for a time and a strong proponent of the application of science to work, took a particular interest in hospitals and surgeons and the need to apply scientific management to these organizations to achieve efficiency in the people and in the hospitals. He describes the urgent need in a paper he read at a meeting of the American Hospital Association in St. Paul Minnesota in the summer of 1914 titled "Scientific Management in the Hospital." This paper later appeared in *The Modern Hospital*, a publication of the time. This was a time when hospitals and physicians were rapidly becoming the foundation of American healthcare and an increasingly important symbol of science in communities across the country.

Gilbreth (1914) developed and promoted the use of motion studies to improve efficiency. He advised the gathered hospital superintendents and administrators that scientific management was "better defined as Measured Functional Management" (p. 1). "It rests on the principle of applying accurate measurement to present practice, deriving from the results of this measurement and the observation made while taking it, the standard practice, and so dividing the work to be done that the standard practice may be carried out by those best fitted to do each part of the work" (p. 1). Gilbreth then challenged the hospital leaders by remarking, "These being the underlying principles of the scientific of management, it is obvious that they are applicable to all fields of activity, and our investigations prove conclusively that the hospital can avail itself of this science with greater results than have been obtained in the industries where the science was first discovered and applied" (p. 1).

Having anticipated some resistance, Gilbreth assured his audience that "...we are able to tell you with authority not only that the same laws which govern efficient shop practice also govern efficient practice in the hospital, but also that many of the problems involved are only similar but identical, and that many of the solutions which we have found to those problems in the shop can be carried over bodily into the field of hospital management" (p. 2). Gilbreth identified several concessions required of his audience: accurate measurement applied to your present methods and practices; non-hospital experts to apply the measurement and determine standards; recognition of the standard; and dividing or functionalizing the work assigning individuals who are trained to perform it... (p. 3). He then describes the steps to take to move forward as "taking a survey of the present practice and members of your organization; reduce your present practice to writing and identify what kinds of work each member of the organization performs; study the members of the present organization as related to one another in your organization chart (p. 5)."

In conclusion, Gilbreth (1914) offers the good that can be achieved by following his advice and his dark assessment of the current state of management in hospitals. "When your management becomes a science, there will result greater efficiency in you as individuals and in the great work of the hospitals to which you devote your lives" (p. 10). He solemnly intones at the end, however, that despite his being invited to talk at the AHA conference, he states "we have not been able to obtain any action to amount to anything; because of the fact that the entire structure upon which hospital management is built is wrong. As the incentive, so will the result be, sooner or later. The incentive necessary to adopt the best from the industries does not exist at present" (p. 10).

Gilbreth did not confine himself to the administrative offices of hospitals to promote scientific management but plunged boldly into the bowels of the hospital in his later paper, "Motion Study in Surgery" which was printed in *The Canadian Journal of Medicine and Surgery* in 1916. He describes the special investigation that led to the paper as the result of a lecture by Frederick Taylor in which he stated "that the surgeon was the best mechanic and the best teacher of the learners of anyone in any craft..." (p. 1). Gilbreth had wide experience with surgeons including observing at over two hundred surgeries and working with surgeons in building hospitals and his recollections did not correspond to those of Taylor (p. 1). Gilbreth initiated studies in a number of hospitals using "motion studies and intensive methods for obtaining efficiency in teaching and practicing surgery and in changing management so that the methods of the best may be recognized, standardized and available to all" (p. 2). Based on this, he argues through the remainder of the paper for the use of motion studies to standardize work by the surgeon, the surgical clinic and in the hospital (1916). He summarized his experiences gloomily by stating, "in studying these many hospitals, we find the conditions, as a rule, much worse from a managerial standpoint than in the average factory, and some hospitals are so bad that they should be actually closed immediately" (p. 2).

Gilbreth (1915) authored an article, "Hospital efficiency from the standpoint of the efficiency expert," in which he explained his own occupation but also defined hospital efficiency and waste. In his mind, the expert brings the skill of measurement and the perspective of objectivity to the hospital its application to hospitals. Gilbreth relates these qualities to the scientific nature medicine and the hospitals. Concerning the hospital, he states, "In considering hospital efficiency, there are two questions which must be asked: '(1) What does this factory, called a hospital, manufacture; what is the hospital's aim; and how it is attempting to attain this aim?' (2) Are we getting the product as cheaply, as quickly, and in as large quantities as is possible? (1915)."

Technology such as radiology, microscopes, and sterilizers and administrative technology such as typewriters, calculators, and cost accounting were all viewed as contributing to the improved healthcare for patients and improved efficiency for the hospital. Physicians and nurses were trained in medical schools and nursing schools in the latest techniques for improving the care of patients. The hospital was organized in departments and staffed appropriately trained people and supplied with the materials that were needed for physicians and nurses to deliver care. The professionals would deliver the care to the patients using the skills they had learned, and patient would recover and return to their homes. The hospital represented the best expression in many communities of an organization designed to provide modern care with scientific medicine and scientific management.

Contributing to the image of the scientific machine of modern hospitals was the organization chart that described the various departments in the hospital, their functions, and their reporting relationships to the central authority of the superintendent and the board. The superintendent served as the central authority of the hospital ensured that the organization was operating properly by receiving regular reports from the departments and sending information out of changes that were to be made to address any issues that should be identified. Each department had job descriptions defining the tasks to be performed and supervisors to monitor the performance of the workers. If serious concerns were raised by a department or physician, the superintendent could take the matter to the board and resolve it.

An important part of the scientific machine metaphor is the sense that the world and the hospital within the world can be understood by the people charged with its operation. This understanding is based on experience and training and the belief that through proper planning and execution the predicted outcome of the organization can be achieved. The issues that come up can be anticipated and timely responses can be prepared to ensure that work is completed, and the hospital fulfills its purpose to the community. This predictability is inherent in the sense of the hospital and world operating in a mechanical manner appropriate to a scientific machine.

Through most of the twentieth century, the basic concepts of hospitals as organizations consisting of bureaucracies that are designed operate with machine-like efficiency if they are properly constructed was used to preserve the image of this most scientific of organizations. The community hospital was designed to function in a way that reassured the community that all was well, and they could depend on it if they should suddenly become ill. This was particularly important in the era of the world wars and economic depression. Rather than being a frightening concept, the scientific machine was viewed as the pinnacle of human reason and society's best response to problems.

The recognition of the need for new twenty-first-century metaphor for healthcare emerged from new thinking about organizations that was exemplified by Wheatley (1992) in *Leadership and the New Science: Learning about Organizations from An Orderly Universe.* She commented that "In the history of human thought, a new way of understanding or a new frame for seeing the world often appears seemingly spontaneously in widely separated places or from several disciplines at once" (Wheatley, 1992, p 139). After describing ways in the past that ideas appeared simultaneous in art and science and in different places, she noted that it was happening again in the late twentieth century. She commented that "in the past few years, a new way of thinking about organizations has been emerging. Whether they be large corporations, microbes, or seemingly inert chemical structures, we are now interested in learning about any organization's 'self-renewing' properties" (p. 140).

Wheatley was referring to the emerging field of complexity science that seeks to understand why "Systems as apparently diverse as stock markets, human bodies, forest ecosystems, manufacturing businesses, immune systems, termite colonies and hospitals seem to share some pattern of behavior" (Zimmerman, Lindberg & Plsek, 2001, p. 3). Zimmerman, et al found in surveys that leaders in healthcare organizations "no longer trusted many of the methods of management they had been taught and practiced" (p. 3). They indicated that the new way of thinking from complexity science more closely resembled what they were already trying to do but which was different from the way they were taught to think about organizations (p. 4).

Complexity science, according to Zimmerman et al., "is not a single theory" but "the study of complex adaptive systems – patterns of relationships within them, how they are sustained, how they self-organize and how outcomes emerge. Within this science there are many theories and concepts" (p. 5). Perhaps most central to understanding complexity science and the use of CASs as a metaphor for twenty-first-century healthcare lies in contrast with what came before.

According to Zimmerman et al., the models of economics, management, and physics that prevailed in the twentieth century were based on Newtonian scientific principles (p. 4). "The dominant metaphor in Newtonian science is the machine. The universe and all its subsystems are seen as giant clocks or inanimate machines" (p. 4). The best way to understand machines, as any child with a screwdriver knows, is to take it apart and look at its pieces and how they come together. With simple mechanical devices, the parts working together produce the outcome and this fits the older model.

However, complex systems such as life forms, ecosystems and human organizations such as hospitals have emergent characteristics and qualities that exceed the sum of their parts and the older model is no longer helpful in understanding these systems. "Living organizations, living computer systems, living communities and living healthcare systems are important because of our interest in sustainability and adaptability" (p. 6). Complexity science brings a new way of thinking to healthcare from the physical, natural, and social sciences. It also "creates a bridge or a merger of quantitative and qualitative explanations of life" (p. 7).

CAS is a metaphor that brings together key aspects of complexity science. "Complex implies diversity – a great number of connections between a wide variety of elements. Adaptive suggests the capacity to alter or change – the ability to learn from experience. A system is a set of connected and inter-dependent things that are connected by a shared purpose. The things in a CAS are independent agents. An agent may be a person, molecule, a species or an organization, among many others. These agents act based on local knowledge and conditions" (p. 8). A CAS can be described as a system that consists of multiple independent agents that are connected through a network and able to communicate with each other and able to individually adapt to changes in their environment (p. 9).

In the Institute of Medicine report, *Crossing the Quality Chasm: A New Health System for the Twenty-First Century*, the authors identified ways that healthcare resembles a CAS. It is adaptive rather than rigid and mechanical; composed of individuals including patients and clinicians who change in response to their experiences; actions by individuals in healthcare are not predictable and vary according to local and larger environments and huge variation exists as a result of unpredictability of behavior (p. 64). In light of the ways healthcare exhibits characteristics of CASs, the report encourages recognition that situations require different approaches such that minimizing variation may be appropriate in situations where there is a high level of certainty while remaining flexible in other situations where variation occurs is appropriate.

A key finding in the view of healthcare as a CAS is the recognition that simple rules can lead to "complex, innovative system behavior" (p. 64). Based on studies of biological systems involving birds and fish and computer studies, a few simple rules enable complex adaptive systems to move toward a goal (p. 64). In a CAS, a group of independent agents with a common purpose and motivation and whose actions affect each other can move toward a goal by following simple rules that guide individual behavior (p. 64). It was out of this conclusion that the report identified ten simple rules for the creation of a twenty-first-century healthcare system.

Paul Plsek (2001), an early proponent of CAS thinking in healthcare, expands on the ways that this metaphor helps to describe twenty-first-century healthcare in Appendix B of the IOM report. He points out that it is important to recognize the difference between complex mechanical systems and CASs. Complex mechanical system "rarely exhibit surprising or emergent behavior" because the parts are well known, and their responses are predictable. "In complex adaptive systems, on the other hand, the parts (in the case of the US healthcare system, this includes human beings) have the freedom and ability to respond to stimuli in many different and fundamentally unpredictable ways. For this reason, emergent, surprising, creative behavior is a real possibility" (p. 310).

Plsek (2001) points out that the Renaissance thinking of Newton and others led to a view of all aspects of the universe as a complex mechanical system in which it made sense to study the parts of the system to understand it (p. 311). He contends that Frederick Taylor and the scientific management perspective applied to organizations in the early twentieth century was based on this view and the idea of "one best way" continues to be applied today. This approach does work in many situations and has "led to great progress in the past century" (p. 311). In healthcare, for example, routine surgical procedures are designed as complex mechanical systems to ensure predictable outcomes (p. 311).

It has been challenging for organizations to move from the view of control of parts inherent in the concept of complex mechanical systems and to embrace the concept of simple rules that encourages self-organizing innovation in CASs. "Because the parts of a CAS are adaptable and embedded within a unique context, every change within a CAS can stimulate other changes that we could not expect. This approach to a system design can never provide the assurance that is possible in mechanical system. This is the nature of a CAS" (p. 317).

CASs represent a new metaphor for twenty-first-century healthcare. This metaphor embraces the various transitions that preceded it. Healthcare is a CAS made of many people in multidisciplinary teams of professionals in a continuum of care that shares information through a network. Individuals working in healthcare discover much of their work as it emerges in doing it through the application of the simple rules inherent in the mission, vision, and values. Leadership emerges in relationships between many people as situations require it throughout the organizations. The application of the simple rules leads to adaptive innovation that enables individuals and the organization to move toward the goals of the CAS.

Summary

America's healthcare journey from the twentieth to the twenty-first century represents America's journey as a country in many respects. Healthcare in the form of physicians, hospitals and payment systems defined the way

Americans in their towns and cities came to understand the application of scientific medicine to improve the quality of life in local communities through the relief of pain and suffering, the provision of care during illness and injury, and to attend to the needs of people at the beginning and end of life. By the beginning of the twenty-first century, the rate of change accelerated and the nature of the changes became much more disruptive of the traditional way in which healthcare was delivered. The sociotechnical epoch of healthcare provoked the transitions described above and compelled the use of metaphors to find some means of identifying what happened. Understanding the transitions and the influences that produced them can help to provide a clearer vision of the way in which meaningful healthcare experiences are designed and created in healthcare organizations.

REFLECTIONS ON AMERICAN HEALTHCARE

5

Chapter 21

The World's Greatest Creation – An Allegory

A voice whispered "I have a story to tell that involves you and me and the World's Greatest Creation. Do you have a few minutes?"

This is a story about a curious being, like a person in many respects but different in other respects, who enjoyed observing others like himself who lived in the same area where he lived. This Observer, probably as good a name as any, enjoyed watching how individuals in his world moved about and how they interacted with each other, but most of all he enjoyed watching them change color.

The most common color was a lovely shade of green. Not too dark or light but just a pleasant green color that felt normal to him. When he saw someone green, they looked like they should look. But not everyone stayed this normal, natural green color. Many were green one day and then became blue or red or yellow. Some were a dark, intense color, and the others were lighter shades.

There were times when the Observer changed colors. He had never changed into a dark color, but he remembered being a light blue for several days and felt terrible. He also remembered once when he was hurt and he changed to a very ugly pink color that lasted as long as the pain lasted. Each time, however, he returned to the normal green color, when he felt better. He associated changing colors with suffering. When someone changed color, he thought of them as a Sufferer.

The Observer watched everyone around him each day and began to write down in a record he kept a symbol and their color for each day and whether their color was dark or light. Over time, he noticed patterns in the colors and patterns in the way they acted and it reminded him of his own experiences in changing colors and how it affected the way he felt. He began to talk to Sufferers, individuals whose color had changed, and documented what they told him. They asked if he knew what it meant when their colors changed. He began to tell them what he had seen and heard from others whose color changed. After a while, Sufferers began to come to the Observer when their color began to change to find out what it was and what would happen. He developed names for the colors and for the shades of colors and he would name them for the Sufferers who came to him. He could even tell them, depending on the shade of the color, what would happen to their color.

One day, he met someone who was holding a tube up to his ear and pressing the other end against someone else. This looked interesting so he asked her why she did this. "I can hear the sounds inside them through the tube," the Listener responded. "The sounds change when their color changes. Based on the sound, I can tell them what is going to happen to their color." As he told her about his study of colors and patterns of colors, she found it very interesting and they decided to work together to develop their observations of colors and sounds.

Another day, he and the Listener were talking with others who came to them to ask about their colors and their sounds and they saw someone they did not recognize walking around with a strange rock in his hand. He would walk up to individuals he met who were not green and he would hold the rock up to them. He would then talk to them for a few minutes and the individual would leave and he would repeat the process with someone else. The Observer and Listener went to him and asked what he was doing with the rock. "I can see changes inside them," he commented. "When their color changes, I can see the changes in them and let them know what is happening inside." The Observer and Listener talked with the Seer and invited him to join with them. He did and they began to meet each day together with people who changed color and told them what their change meant.

Another day, he and the Listener were talking with others who came to them to ask about their colors and their sounds and were told that there was a new individual in the area who could help people change their colors by giving them something to eat. This was a very interesting development so they went to see for themselves. They found the individual and he was sitting with several buckets of berries. As they watched, someone who was a red color came up to him and he took some berries from a bucket and gave it to them and they went away. Someone else who was a blue color came up to him and gave him some money and he gave the blue individual some blueberries from the bucket. He ate the berries and walked away. This process was repeated a number of times. The next day, they saw the individual who had been blue the day before and he was now a normal green color. So, the Observer and the Listener and the Seer talked with Changer and invited him to join them. And he did.

Another day, the Associates were walking in a different area and they found a neat building with people waiting in line to go in. The Sufferers were all the same color, but it was not the normal green. It was a strange dark shade of orange which they had seen but not often. They walked into the building and saw a very unique sight. Orange Sufferers were reclining in chairs around the room. Each one was approached by someone carrying a small bag with a tube attached to it. They would take the tube in their mouth and suck on the tube. Their eye would close and they looked asleep. The individual with the tube moved to another chair and repeated the process. Following the Sleepmaker, an individual came with small sharp looking knife. Carefully, the Cutter made a very small cut in a particular place on the sleeping Orange individual and took a small grasp and removed a tiny orange seed. A couple of stitches were used to close the small cut. In a little while, the Orange individual woke up and left the building. This went on over and over again. The Observer and Listener and Seer left talking among themselves about this strange process.

The next day they returned to the area and saw several of the Sufferers who had the procedure the day before. They were no longer Orange but were now a normal green color. The group returned to the building and talked with the Sleepmaker and Cutter. They learned that their process changed the color of Sufferers who had a particular orange color and made them feel better. They asked if they would like to join with them. As they talked, they realized that with some adjustments the building they were using could be made to provide rooms for each of them to provide their special service. They decided to work together and made plans to shape the building to accommodate all of them.

They also gave up their other jobs to focus their time on their new profession. As Sufferers of different colors came to the building each day, they would consult with the Observer and the Listener and the others. As they were leaving they would place some money in a box by the door. At the end of the day, the money in the box was divided between the associates in the group in the building.

As the group met each day at the building, they waited for Sufferers of different colors to come. As they arrived, they went to the Observer and he would refer them to the Listener and the Seer who would analyze their color. They would tell them what to expect from their change in color. Depending on their color, they would go to the Changer who provided the right berries and they would leave. Or, if they were orange, the Observer referred them to the Sleepmaker and Cutter and they would go to a different room with reclining chairs. Over time, more and more individuals came to the building and the group was able to make a lot of money.

One day, the Observer noticed that there were others in the area doing things similar to him and the others in the building. He pointed this out to the Listener and Seer, and they decided to talk to the new individuals in the area to see who they were and what they did. They found some who were like the associates in the building and these wanted to join with them. There were others who were different. These did not want to join the associates.

Back in the building, the new group made of all the ones who were Observers, Listeners, Seers, Changers, Sleepmakers, and Cutters like the original group discussed the differences between them and the others who did not join the associates. They decided that they needed a name that would show people they were different from others. They thought about a name for a long time and finally decided on a name that they felt would work. They called themselves the Amazing Magical Association or AMA since people often said that what they did seemed like magic. They began to train others to do what they did and to join with the AMA.

The AMA group decided that those who observed, and listened and saw differently from themselves were not only different but wrong. They called them the Others. They needed to stop or to leave the area. They developed a plan. They appointed a group to watch for the Others outside the AMA. When they saw them, they should go as a group and drive them away and tell people that only the AMA could help them. The plan worked. More and more Sufferers came to the AMA. As the number of Observers, Listeners, Seers, and Cutters outside of the AMA decreased, the AMA increased the price Sufferers paid to enter the AMA.

Over time, newcomers appeared at the AMA building and brought new devices for listening, seeing, and cutting. These devices improved care but were expensive and bigger. Some took up lots of space and required special rooms to work correctly. With these devices, the Listeners heard more. The Seers saw more. The Cutters cut better. The Changers acquired more ingredients to help change colors.

As the AMA members acquired new devices, they realized that the AMA building no longer had enough space and new types of rooms were needed. They redesigned the building and expanded it to accommodate the new equipment and new members. The cost of the expansion and equipment grew. The training to use the new equipment and the Helpers to support the use of the equipment increased expenses.

As the AMA grew and expanded, the members realized that they needed to increase their prices to pay for the equipment and materials. They had found people who they trained to be Helpers. How would they persuade individuals with color changes to pay the prices? They needed a way to make their service more valuable. They held a planning retreat and came up with many ideas but nothing they all supported. Finally, the founding member, the original Observer, offered his idea. It was simple but powerful. "We should create a building that has two parts. The first part welcomes the Sufferer and the Observers evaluate them. The second part of the building has a grand entrance with a sign that reads, The World's Greatest Creation, and this leads to the rooms with the Listeners, Seers, Changers, and Cutters." The AMA members embraced the idea.

The new building design and image brought more Sufferers to the AMA to gain access to the World's Greatest Creation. As the numbers increased, Sufferers traveling long distances asked if a new building could be created near their homes for the Sufferers in their area. The associates discussed the idea. They decided that expansion was a good idea. The original AMA would oversee the new branches of the AMA and the new buildings would follow the design and practices of the original World's Greatest Creation. The AMA expanded to new areas and built new buildings designed like the original AMA and World's Greatest Creation and following the same practices. The AMA and its many branches provided services to many more Sufferers throughout the land.

After a while, hard times came to the area. Sufferers would come to the AMA and enter the World's Greatest Creation, but when it was time to leave, they said they did not have anything to pay for the service. After a while, the associates realized they were not making as much money as before because fewer Sufferers were putting money in the box and their costs were going up. It was getting to be a serious problem. The head of the Helpers came to the Observer and said that he and the other Helpers in the World's Greatest Creation were concerned they might lose their jobs and they were concerned that the AMA might not survive. They decided that in addition to the Observer at the entrance, there would be a Payment

Helper. The Payment Helper would have the money box and talk to each Sufferer to make sure they had enough money to put in the box at the end of their visit. Due to the hard times, the Payment Helper told many Sufferers they could not come into the World's Greatest Creation because they did not have enough money.

One day, an individual who was a natural color green came to the AMA. He knew a local business that wanted their workers to be able to come to the AMA and have access to the World's Greatest Creation when their colors changed, but they could not afford to pay for the services. He had an idea. His employees would pay a little bit each month to the company and the company would give it to the Observer. When they became Sufferers, they would come to the AMA and not have to pay because they paid each month. The AMA associates discussed the idea, but they were not sure if they wanted it. The Helpers, who were afraid the AMA would lose business, encouraged the associates, and they finally agreed. They called the idea "Sufferer Care." Sufferer Care members came to the World's Greatest Creation more and more. Sufferers who did not have Sufferer Care came less and less. Over time, more and more businesses decided they needed Sufferer Care to attract good employees. Employees at the businesses felt that Sufferer Care helped them to access the World's Greatest Creation.

Sufferers who worked at businesses were offered Sufferer Care, but the old and the young Sufferers did not have enough money to pay to enter the World's Greatest Creation. Leaders in the towns and communities gathered together and came to the AMA. They wanted to provide Sufferer Care for the old and the young. The associates in the AMA did not like the idea. If the leaders of the towns and communities have Sufferer Care, they will want to manage the World's Greatest Creation. The Helpers in the World's Greatest Creation liked the idea. They talked to the associates in the AMA. Let's accept the offer from the towns and communities to pay for the Government Sufferer Care for the old and the young. This will make the AMA very successful. The associates agreed to the idea and the leaders of the towns and communities began to pay for Government Sufferer Care for the old and the young.

With workers having Sufferer Care and the young and the old having Government Sufferer Care, and both paying more than it cost the World's Greatest Creation, an amazing thing occurred. The World's Greatest Creation had so much money that they began to expand. Each day, individuals who were not Sufferers came to the AMA and offered new ways of listening, seeing, changing, and cutting. The Helpers in the World's Greatest Creation built bigger and bigger buildings to accommodate all the amazing new devices developed to take care of the Sufferers. These buildings grew to contain many rooms with many Listeners, Seers, Changers, and Cutters.

As the number of new ways to listen, see, change, and cut increased, an amazing thing happened. There were so many new ways of listening, seeing, changing, and cutting that the associates formed groups that wanted to do only one type of listening, seeing, changing, or cutting. One group used one type of tube for listening. Another group used a different tube for listening. Each group formed its own rules, practices, and requirements. Only Listeners trained in their way of listening could be a member of their group. Each group of Listeners determined what they would accept as payment and the Sufferer Care paid the fees charged by each of the groups. The Seers, Changers, and Cutters did the same. The AMA and the World's Greatest Creation buildings across the land grew bigger and bigger and added more and more rooms for all the different groups of Listeners, Seers, Changers, and Cutters. Sufferer Care paid whatever costs the AMA and the Helpers in the World's Greatest Creation requested.

One day, a group of leaders from the towns and communities arrived at the original building of the AMA and the World's Greatest Creation and asked for a meeting. The group of the senior Associates and Helpers met with the leaders. The leaders explained that Government Sufferer Care costs had grown so much and took so much money out of their towns and communities that they had little left for schools and roads and other important services. What could be done to make sure that the Government Sufferer Care only paid for care that Sufferers really needed and did not pay for mistakes or poor care? The Associates angrily responded to the leaders that all the care they delivered was care that Sufferers needed and the care was good. The Helpers protested that they needed all the rooms that they built to deliver the care. At the end of the talks, the leaders explained that it would be helpful to manage the costs of Sufferer Care if they could pay a set amount for the care of each Government Sufferer required when they came to the World's Greatest Creation. They also told the Associates and Helpers that they would only pay for the care the patient needed and not poor care or mistakes in care. The Associates agreed to changes in their payments for their services in the World's Greatest Creation could be set, but the fees of the Listeners, Seers, Changers, and Cutters could not be set. The leaders of the towns and communities agreed and presented a list of colors and payments for light colors and dark colors to the Payment Helper.

Each year after that initial meeting, the leaders of the towns and communities returned to the AMA and presented to the Payment Helpers the list of colors and the payments for light and dark colors. Each year, these payments grew less and less. Even the payments to the Observers, Listeners, Changers, and Cutter fell after several years. The Helpers gathered together inside the World's Greatest Creation. They looked at the list of colors and the declining payments from the towns and communities. The Payment Helpers worried that soon they would not have enough money to run the World's Greatest Creation. Companies selling new listening tubes, new seer stones, new changing ingredients, and new cutting tools raised their prices all the time. Adding new rooms to the World's Greatest Creation cost more and more as the associates asked for different types of rooms. The Helpers needed a plan or they would soon not be able to meet the requests of the associates and they would lose their jobs.

One day, a Helper in the World's Greatest Creation visited a business down the road. He talked to the owner of the business about the changes made by the leaders in the towns and communities. The Business Owner said he understood that situation. His company had customers every day asking for lower prices. The Helper asked him what he did to keep from going out of business. The Business Owner said his workers were taught to get rid of everything that increases costs and keep only the things that customers will pay for. This kept his costs low and he could still make enough money from what his customers wanted to pay him. The Helper asked him how his workers found costs to cut. The Business Owner said there were lots of things. Each day his workers found more and more things like products that did not work or broken pieces or wasted time because of misplaced materials that added costs but did not help his customer. He called all of these costs "waste" and his workers were constantly looking for more of them. The Helper decided that the World's Greatest Creation should operate like a business and get rid of waste. He hurried back to meet with fellow Helpers. They talked about removing waste like a business. They decided that they needed to be more like a business or maybe even a factory. They could remove waste and save money. This would mean the World's Greatest Creation could survive. Business owners were invited in to the World's Greatest Creation to teach them the principles of they used to remove waste and to be efficient. They taught them to standardize processes and to measure inputs and outputs and flow. The World's Greatest Creation industrialized.

After a while, the business owners found that Sufferer Care costs consumed more and more of their revenue. Their employees really liked it.

They depended on it for care when their color changed and they became Sufferers. The costs to the businesses, however, reduced their profits more and more each year. After trying many ways to reduce the costs of Sufferer Care, the business owners made a subtle change to save money. They increased the amount the workers paid for the care they received. They told the workers these changes would give them the power to make healthcare decisions and they would be in control of the money they spent. They could choose the care they needed and wanted. The costs for Sufferer Care would go down to leave more money in the business for worker raises. The workers did not understand all these changes, but they felt they needed to accept them to keep Sufferer Care.

Sufferer Care costs rose more slowly and the Helpers industrialized the World's Greatest Creation care processes like a factory to improve production and remove waste. The business owners and leaders of towns and cities thought they had solved the problem of costs. But, over time, the costs to change colors continued to increase faster than the costs of other things. New listening tubes, seer stones, and changer berries continued to go up. AMA associates wanted the best available tools for the World's Greatest Creation which grew ever larger. The Associates developed their specialties to the point that certain Listeners only listened to patients who were a particular shade of a color. They could not help others who were different shades or colors. As they specialized in their specific shades and colors, they increased their fees as specialists.

Businesses quietly moved more of the costs to their employees and the leaders of towns and cities quietly reduced the payments they made to the World's Greatest Creation by raising the requirements for quality of care and outcomes in order to receive payment.

One day, a Sufferer who had been to the AMA and entered the World's Greatest Creation with a dark color and his color was still not quite a normal green sat on a hill side and looked down on the landscape around him. He worked in a local business and had Sufferer Care. He was able to go to the AMA and the World's Greatest Creation, but his part of the payment put him in debt and took part of his children's college fund. Most of his raises had been erased by payments for Sufferer Care.

As he sat on the hill, he thought about friends and neighbors he knew who did not have Sufferer Care and who could not go to the World's Greatest Creation. When their colors changed they asked their neighbors if any knew what could be done without going to the AMA and World's Greatest Creation. As he thought about it, he realized that was happening at work too. He, himself, actually had thought about becoming an Observer when he was younger, but it did not work out. However, when he noticed someone at work whose color was not quite the normal green, he would offer suggestions on what it meant. People had begun to ask him about their color. They did not want to go to the AMA or the World's Greatest Creation because it would cost too much. He had even recommended people with certain shades of color to talk to certain co-workers who had been a similar shade and had gotten better. There were even groups in his neighborhood and at work of Sufferers who had similar color shades and who shared what they were doing and how it was working. The ones he talked to said this was helpful. The ideas they shared with each other were reasonable and much cheaper than the AMA and World's Greatest Creation. For people who were a dark color, he always recommended that should go to the AMA and World's Greatest Creation, but for others they seemed to do fine with the help of co-workers and neighbors.

As time went by, the Helpers noticed that fewer and fewer people were coming to the World's Greatest Creation unless they were a very dark color. The associates noticed that fewer and fewer people were coming to the AMA for the Observers to direct them to care in the World's Greatest Creation and those who did come often just said "no thank you" and left when the Observer recommended that they go the World's Greatest Creation for the Listeners, Seers, Changers, and Cutters to help them. They just said they could not afford it and would ask their neighbors and co-workers for help.

One day, the original Observer was walking through town and a shop had opened on Main Street. It was a simple shop, smaller than most, and there was a sign. He walked up to the sign and it read "Server." Server, the Observer thought. What is Server? He had always been a curious person, so he walked in. There were two chairs facing a table and an individual seated on the other side of the table facing the door. She looked up and smiled welcomingly. "Are you interested in a connection?", she asked. The Observer sat down in the chair and looked at her. "What is a connection?"

She patiently explained that she provided a service that connected individuals to groups that shared similar interests. Anyone who was interested in connecting with a group was given a special stone that enabled them to talk to others in the group and to hear them just by holding the stone. She said that business had been very good since she set up her shop. She asked if he would like a stone to connect with a group. He asked about the most popular groups. She said that the groups tended to be individuals who were changing colors. They wanted to talk to others who were changing to similar colors. The Observer left without getting a stone.

Over time, Sufferers who were specific colors that were hard to change used stones to connect others like themselves. They researched the latest information and on their colors and shared what they learned with each other through their stones. They would also meet to talk and they found that the meetings actually helped them to understand their color better and to take better care of themselves. Particular sufferers became very knowledgeable over a period of time and often acted as Observers in the groups. Others had tried various ingredients for changing their colors and could tell others what worked for them like a Changer. Sufferers actually enjoyed talking with each other about their color and sharing their experiences.

As more time passed, the AMA associates noticed that fewer and fewer Sufferers were coming to the World's Greatest Creation. Some of them began to go to the meetings of Sufferers with colors that were their specialty. They offered their services to the groups and helped them. Others left the AMA and began to provide help to Sufferers in other ways. And others left the AMA and started new careers. Smaller groups of associates formed to develop ways to help their particular Sufferers.

A few of the associates remained at the World's Greatest Creation and worked with the Sufferers with the darkest colors. The Helpers soon found that they could not afford the World's Greatest Creation because it did not serve enough Sufferers. They sold the buildings to factories and retail outlets and moved the World's Greatest Creation into much smaller buildings that only took care of Sufferers with very dark colors. When their colors lightened, they went to other buildings or back to their homes to recover.

In the end, the World's Greatest Creation became the experiences of Sufferers helping each other.

Chapter 22

Reflecting on the Beautiful Death and Implications for Healthcare

What if dying were perceived as a meaningful experience that was inte-grated into our relationships with the people in our lives? How would this affect our views of healthcare?

Based on death certificates, the Beautiful Death first began to appear in the mid-2000s in countries around the world. Initially, there was no sense that something unusual was happening. Older people who seemed to be fine and healthy when they went to bed did not wake up. They seemed to die peacefully in their sleep at some point in the night. The reason that people began to take notice was that autopsies that were performed could find no evidence of disease or any other obvious reason for the death. The deceased did not show any signs of distress. Their faces in almost all cases were peaceful.

In terms of the broader society, the peaceful deaths of the elderly were less concerning than another phenomenon that began to occur around the same time. Many people younger than those who were dying in their sleep appeared to be sleeping more. It wasn't that they were ill or incapacitated in any way. Medical examinations could identify no maladies. They simply started going to bed earlier and sleeping longer. The people experiencing the sleep said that it was the best sleep they had ever experienced. Going to sleep began to be the most exciting prospect of the day for them. They also reported dreams that were beautiful and gave them a sense of well-being when they woke up. Over time as they slept more each day, they too began to die in their sleep. What made this so noticeable is that it was happening to a large segment of older people in increasing numbers.

As the older people who slept and woke up shared their dreams with families and friends, the sense of well-being that the dreamers experienced was in some way communicated to the people they were talking to. The younger people experienced a renewal of their own sense of well-being. Even more interesting, they developed an intense desire to take care of the dreamers in their families. It wasn't that the younger adults stopped working or radically changed their lives, but they wanted to spend time with the older people and to ensure their comfort.

After a number of years, patterns began to develop in the populations around the world that were pleasantly puzzling. In addition to what was being called the "Beautiful Death" phenomenon, two other patterns developed. The incidence of disease and illness declined in the populations in general. Gradually, over a number of years, routine and chronic illnesses disappeared. People were surprisingly healthy in both their lifestyles and in their physical conditions. On their own, people began to eat and sleep and exercise in ways that led to better overall health. And, people who ordinarily would develop chronic conditions due to aging remained in good health as they entered the sleeping pattern of aging with a final culmination in the Beautiful Death.

In addition to better health overall for people, their desires and interests seemed to converge with a deep concern for the people in their lives. From infancy to maturity, people exhibited all the normal aspects of growing up but with a surprising twist. As people grew up, they became more and more interested in the welfare of others. Initially, the focus was on their family. As they aged, however, their desire to find ways to be helpful and supportive to others expanded to classmates in school and people in their community. Parents were devoted to the welfare of their children and attentive to the needs of their own parents. And people of all ages spent time listening and talking with the dreamers in their lives because it made them feel so good to spend time with them.

As people aged and spent more time sleeping, their dreams gradually became more focused and clearer. They seemed to want to talk about their dreams and their family and friends all felt good as they listened to their dreams. The dreams seemed to involve another place that none of them had ever been. The increasing clarity of their dreams made it seem to them that they were in a sense traveling toward the place and getting closer as they slept longer. There was an anticipation that they would eventually arrive at the place when they finally entered their Beautiful Death. The thought of reaching this new place was exciting and they wanted to share what they saw. As their dreams grew more detailed, they remembered more and more about the place and the people they met there and the conversations they had with them. They would often share thoughts or ideas from those conversations that were meaningful to the younger people. It was as if they were gaining wisdom as they slept and sharing it with the younger people. For the younger people, it was as though they were learning new things about themselves and their world as they listened to the dreams of their elders.

Though many things remained the same for people after the appearance of the Beautiful Death and the sleep patterns of aging and the dreamers with their stories of a different world, many things also changed. The aging process became something that people anticipated as much as they had previously anticipated their maturing into adults. The fears of pain and suffering and approaching death were gone and the interest in becoming a dreamer and sharing new information with younger people made it seem to be a very meaningful time in life. As they watched their elders spend more time in dream-filled sleep and share with them what they saw and heard, those who listened were inspired and motivated to use the new information in their own work and relationships.

For people of all ages, the desire to be helpful and supportive of others became a major motivating force in their lives. This desire seemed to flow from the dreamers to the parents to the children as part of their heritage from the dreamers. As people performed their work or other activities, they found a heightened sense of satisfaction when they felt they had helped someone. This became the most important motivation as a goal for whatever they were doing. In their work, they sought to find ways for their work to help others whether they were farmers or manufacturers or sales people. Though this pursuit of the feelings associated with helping others was powerful, there were still times when people felt sad or disappointed. But these periods did not last and they found that reflecting back on things they heard from the dreamers or others renewed their sense of meaning and purpose in their lives and the joy they felt whenever they could help someone.

As dreamers dreamed dreams and shared their wisdom and as the old slipped into the Beautiful Death in a peaceful sleep, society as a whole began to change. The balance of work and family seemed to occur naturally as individuals at all ages sought to do what was most needed and helpful at any particular time. Thoughts and feelings about possessions shifted from accruing more to producing more with the goal of providing for family and others. The profit motive for businesses was important to sustain the business, but it was not so important that it replaced the well-being of people. As people worked to make a living the desire to work for the good of others found expression in the workplace and in the production of goods and services.

Perhaps the most noticeable change in terms of services involved healthcare. Healthcare was still needed as people were injured in accidents and babies were born the old fashioned way, but the ability of individuals to heal from minor injuries and to maintain their health reduced the need for healthcare services significantly. Since most of healthcare focused on illnesses and end of life care, these resources were no longer required as the dreamers gently slipped into the Beautiful Death while being attended to by their families and friends. As the years passed, hospitals grew smaller and more specialized to treat accidents and injuries rather than illness and disease. Nursing homes declined as families were able to care for their dreamers. People who were seriously injured and unable to recover or suffered intractable pain moved to the dreamer stage and quickly into their final sleep.

This new place was the source of wisdom that the dreamers passed on to their descendants. Not only were the dreamers passing on wisdom, but they were also sharing a vision of the future for those who would follow them and in sharing this vision the lives of their descendants were renewed as well. The end of life had become a time in which the dreamers lived purposefully in sharing wisdom. Their families derived inspiration and wisdom from them and cared for the dreamers as a source of meaning in their lives. As the dreamers grew closer to their death, the place in their dreams became clearer until their passing was really like stepping into a world that was already home to them.

Author's Note: In imagining the Beautiful Death and the dreamers, I was interested in how it could help me to understand healthcare. If we were to suddenly find that the end of life began with sleeping a little longer each day and ended with a peaceful passage into a place familiar to us, how would that change our views of healthcare? What if the end of lives were a time in which we felt a renewed sense of meaning and purpose in sharing our visions of life and death with the people around us to bring them comfort and joy and to contribute to meaning in life for them? Does that help us to think about providing care for each other in a different way?

References

AAMC. (2017, December 18). More Women than Men Enrolled in U.S. Medical Schools. Retrieved December 24, 2019, from: https://www.aamc.org/news-insights/press-releases/more-women-men-enrolled-us-medical-schools-2017.

AAMC. (2019, April 23). New Findings Confirm Predictions on Physician Shortages. Retrieved December 24, 2019, from Association of American Medical Colleges: https://www.aamc.org/news-insights/press-releases/new-findings-confirm-predictions-physician-shortage.

Akl, E. A., Mustafa, R., Bdair, F., & Schünemann, H. J. (2007). The United States physician workforce and international medical graduates: Trends and characteristics. *Journal of General Internal Medicine, 22*(2), pp. 264–268. doi:10.1007/s11606-006-0022-2.

Altman, M., Huang, T. T., & Breland, J. Y. (2018). Design thinking in health care. *Preventing Chronic Disease: Public Health Research, Practice, and Policy*, pp. 1–13. doi:10.5888/pcd15.180128.

American Immigration Council. (2018, January 17). Special Report: Foreign-Trained Doctors are Critical to Serving Many U.S. Communities. Washington, DC: American Immigration Council. Retrieved December 24, 2019, from: https://www.americanimmigrationcouncil.org/research/foreign-trained-doctors-are-critical-serving-many-us-communities.

American Recovery and Reinvestment Act (ARRA). (2009, January 6). Retrieved December 30, 2019, from: https://www.govinfo.gov/content/pkg/BILLS-111hr1enr/pdf/BILLS-111hr1enr.pdf.

Aristotle & Kaplan, J. (2012). *Pocket Aristotle*. New York: Simon and Shuster. Retrieved December 23, 2019, from: https://www.azquotes.com/author/524-Aristotle/tag/metaphor.

Auerbach, D., & White, C. (2008). Regional Variation in Health Care Costs. Washington, DC: Congressional Budget Office. Retrieved January 2, 2020, from: https://www.cbo.gov/publication/24753.

Aulisio, M. P. (2016, May). History of medicine: Why did hospital ethics committees emerge in the USA? *AMA Journal of Ethics, 5*(18), pp. 546–553.

Barrett, F. J., & Cooperrider, D. L. (1990). Generative metaphor intervention: A new approach for working with systems divided by conflict and caught in defensive perception. *The Journal of Applied Behavioral Science, 26*(2), pp. 219–239.

Bate, P., & Robert, G. (2007). *Bringing User Experience to Healthcare Improvement.* New York: Radcliffe Publishing.

Bellavite, P., Conforti, A., Piasere, V., & Ortolani, R. (2005). Immunology and homeopathy. 1. Historical background. *Evidence-Based Complementary and Alternative Medicine, 2*(4), pp. 441–445. doi: 10.1093/ecam/neh141.

Berger, P. L., & Luckmann, T. (1966). *The Social Construction of Reality: A Treatise in the Sociology of Knowledge.* New York: Penguin Books, Inc.

Berlinger, N. (2016). *Are Workarounds Ethical? Managing Moral Problems in Health Care Systems.* New York: Oxford University Press.

Berwick, D., Godfrey, A. B., & Roessner, J. (1990). *Curing Healthcare: New Strategies for Quality Improvement.* San Francisco, CA: Jossey-Bass.

Bologna, C. (2019, November 8). What's the Deal with Generation Alpha. Retrieved January 2, 2020, from: https://www.huffpost.com/entry/generation-alpha-after-gen-z_l_5d420ef4e4b0aca341181574.

Brown, T. (2008, June). Design thinking. *Harvard Business Review, 86*(6), pp. 84–92. Retrieved November 12, 2015.

Brown, T., & Martin, R. (2008, September). Design for action. *Harvard Business Review, 93*(9), pp. 56–64. Retrieved November 15, 2015.

Bunn, L. (2018, December 27). What Percentage of Physical Therapists Are Women? Retrieved December 24, 2019, from: https://careertrend.com/about-5568437-percentage-physical-therapists-women.html.

Burns, J. M. (1978). *Leadership.* New York: Harper Perennial Political Classics.

Chapin, C. F. (2015). *Ensuring America's Health: The Public Creation of the Corporate Health Care System.* New York: Cambridge University Press.

Cherns, A. (1976, August 1). The principles of sociotechnical design. *Human Relations, 29*, pp. 783–792.

Collier, R. (2011, August 8). American Medical Association membership woes continue. *Canadian Medical Association Journal, 183*(11), pp. E713–E714. Retrieved September 12, 2019, from https://www.cmaj.ca/content/cmaj/183/11/E713.full.pdf.

Corwin, E. H. (1946). *The American Hospital.* New York: The Commonwealth Fund.

Costin, V., & Vignoles, V. L. (2020, April). Meaning is about mattering: Evaluating coherence, purpose, and existential mattering as precursors of meaning in life judgments. *Journal of Personality and Social Psychology*, 118(4), pp. 864–884. doi:10.1037/pspp0000225

Cunningham III, R., & Cunningham Jr., R. M. (1997). *The Blues: A History of the Blue Cross and Blue Shield System.* Dekalb: Northern Illinois Press.

Customer. (2019, December 14). Retrieved December 24, 2019, from: https://www.merriam-webster.com/dictionary/customer.

Cusumano, M. A. (1988, October 15). Manufacturing innovation: Lessons from the Japanese Auto Industry. *MIT Sloan Management Review, 30*(1). Retrieved April 4, 2015, from https://sloanreview.mit.edu/article/manufacturing-innovation-lessons-from-the-japanese-auto-industry/.

DATAUSA: Pharmacists. (2017). Retrieved December 24, 2019, from: https://datausa.io/profile/soc/291051/#about.

Edwards, B. (2011, October 23). The IPod: How Apple's Legendary Portable Music Player Came to Be. Retrieved December 31, 2019, from: https://www.macworld.com/article/1163181/the-birth-of-the-ipod.html?page=2.

Epstein, E.G., Delgado, S. (2010, September 30). Understanding and addressing moral distress. The Online Journal of Issues in Nursing, 15(3), Manuscript 1. doi:10.3912/OJIN.Vol15No03Man01.

Flannery, M. A. (2002). The early botanical medical movement as a reflection of life, liberty and literacy in Jacksonian America. *Journal of the Medical Library Association, 90*(4), pp. 442–454.

Foucault, M. (1994). *The Birth of the Clinic: An Archaeology of Medical Perception.* New York: Vintage Books.

Foucault, M. (1995). Strategies of power. In W. T. Anderson (Ed.), *The Truth about Truth: De-Confusing and Re-Constructing the Postmodern World* (pp. 40–45). New York: A Jeremy P. Tarcher/Putnam Book.

Frankl, V. E. (2006). *Man's Search for Meaning.* Boston, MA: Beacon Press.

Freidson, E. (1988). *Profession of Medicine: A Study of the Sociology of Applied Knowledge.* Chicago, IL: The University of Chicago Press.

Frijda, N. H., Manstead, A. S., & Bem, S. (2000). The influence of emotions on beliefs. In N. H. Frijda, A. S. Manstead, & S. Bem (Eds.), *Emotions and Beliefs: How Feelings Influence Thoughts* (pp. 1–9). Cambridge, UK: Cambridge University Press.

Gable, S., & Haidt, J. (2005). What (and why) is positive psychology? *Review of General Psychology, 9*(2), pp. 103–110. doi:10.1037/1089-2680.9.2.103.

George, L., & Park, C. L. (2016a, September 1). Meaning in life as comprehension, purpose and mattering: Toward integration and new research questions. *Review of General Psychology, 20*(3), pp. 205–220. doi:10.1037/gpr0000077.

George, L., & Park, C. L. (2016b). The multidimensional existential meaning scale: A tripartite approach to measuring meaning in life. *The Journal of Positive Psychology,* 12(6) pp. 1–15. doi:10.1080/17439760.2016.1209546.

Ghaffarian, V. (2011). The new stream of socio-technical approach and main stream information systems research. *Procedia Computer Science,* pp. 1499–1511. doi:10.1016/j.procs.2011.01.039.

Gilbreth, F. (1915, May 27). Hospital efficiency from the standpoint of the efficiency expert. *Boston Medical and Surgical Journal, 172,* pp. 774–775.

Gilbreth, F. (1916, July). Motion study in surgery. *The Canadian Journal of Medicine and Surgery, 40,* pp. 22–31.

Gilbreth, F. B. (1914). *Scientific Management in the Hospital.* St. Paul, MN: American Hospital Association.

Glasgow, J. M., Scott-Caziewell, J. R., & Kaboli, P. J. (2010, December). Guiding inpatient quality improvement: A systematic review of lean and Six Sigma. *The Joint Commission Journal on Quality and Patient Safety, 36*(12), pp. 533–540. doi:10.1016/S1553-7250(10)36081-8.

Goodwin, S. (2016). *Mapping the Path to 21st Century Healthcare: The Ten Transitions Workbook*. Boca Raton, FL: CRC Press.

Haber, S. (1964). *Efficiency and Uplift: Scientific Management in the Progressive Era, 1890–1920*. Chicago, IL: University of Chicago Press.

Hall, E. T. (1966). *The Hidden Dimension*. New York: Anchor Books Doubleday.

Harvey, D. (2005). *A Brief History of Neoliberalism*. New York: Oxford University Press.

HCAHPS. (2019, October 15). Patients' Perspectives of Care Survey. Retrieved December 31, 2019, from: https://www.cms.gov/Medicare/Quality-Initiatives-Patient-Assessment-Instruments/HospitalQualityInits/HospitalHCAHPS.

HHS Office of Inspector General. (2001). Medicare Hospital Prospective Payment System How DRG Rates Are Calculated and Updated. Office of Inspector General. Washington, DC: HHS Office of Inspector General. Retrieved April 4, 2019, from https://www.oig.hhs.gov/oei/reports/oei-09-00-00200.pdf.

Hippocrates. (2002, September 16). Hippocratic Oath. Retrieved January 2, 2020, from: https://www.nlm.nih.gov/hmd/greek/greek_oath.html.

Howe, N., & Strauss, W. (2007, July–August). The next 20 years: How customer and workforce attitudes will evove. *Harvard Business Review, 85*, pp. 41–52.

Howell, J. D. (1995). *Technology in the Hospital: Transforming Patient Care in the Early Twentieth Century*. Baltimore, MD: Johns Hopkins University Press.

Industrial Designers Society of America. (2019). Retrieved December 3, 2019 from https://www.idsa.org/what-industrial-design

Institute of Medicine. (1999). *To Err Is Human: Building a Safer Health System*. Washington, DC: The National Academies Press.

Institute of Medicine. (2001). *Crossing the Quality Chasm: A New Health System for the 21st Century*. Washington, DC: The National Academies Press.

Jameton, A. (1984). *Nursing Practice: The Ethical Issues*. Englewood Cliffs, NJ: Prentice Hall.

Jauhar, S. (2019, September 12). Physician, Regulate Yourself. Retrieved September 12, 2019, from: https://www.nytimes.com/2019/09/11/opinion/health-care-regulation.html.

Jha, A. (2005, June 30). Where Belief Is Born. *The Guardian*. Retrieved December 16, 2019, from: https://www.theguardian.com/science/2005/jun/30/psychology.neuroscience.

Jove Science Education Database. (2019). Peripheral Intravenous Catheter Insertion. Nursing Skills. Cambridge, MA, Retrieved December 16, 2019, from: https://www.jove.com/science-education/10264/peripheral-intravenous-catheter-insertion.

Kenney, C. (2008). *The Best Practice: How the New Quality Movement Is Transforming Medicine*. New York: Public Affairs.

Kohn, L. T., Corrigan, J. M., & Donaldson, M. S. (Eds.). (2000). *To Err Is Human*. Washington, DC: National Academy of Sciences.

Kolko, J. (2015, September). Design thinking comes of age. *Harvard Business Review*, *93*, pp. 66–71.

Lakoff, G., & Johnson, M. (1980). *Metaphors We Live By*. Chicago, IL: University of Chicago.

Lamia, M. C. (2012, October 31). Feeling Is Believing. Retrieved December 26, 2019, from: https://www.psychologytoday.com/us/blog/intense-emotions-and-strong-feelings/201210/feeling-is-believing.

Lawson, C. (2002, January 1). The Connections between Emotions and Learning. Center for Development and Learning Blog. Metairie, LA, Retrieved December 16, 2019, from https://www.cdl.org/articles/the-connections-between-emotions-and-learning/.

Lucian Leape Institute. (2012). *Order from Chaos: Accelerating Care Integration*. Boston, MA: National Patient Safety Foundation. Retrieved January 3, 2020.

Magids, S., Zorfas, A., & Leemon, D. (2015a, November). The new science of customer emotions. Harvard Business Review. Reprint R1511C, pp. 1–11.

Magids, S., Zorfas, A., & Leemon, D. (2015b, December). What separates the best customers from the merely satisfied. *Harvard Business Review*. Reprint H02IC9, pp. 1–5.

MacEachern, M. T. (1957). *Hospital Organization and Management*. Chicago, IL: Physicians' Record Company.

Mannheim, K. (1972). The problem of generations. In P. Kecskemeti (Ed.), *Karl Mannheim: Essays* (pp. 276–322, 22–24 (introduction)). Abingdon-on-Thames, UK: Routledge Publishers.

Martela, F., & Pessi, A. B. (2018). Significant work is about self-realization and broader purpose: Defining the key dimensions of meaningful work. *Frontiers in Psychology*, *9*, p. 363. doi:10.3389/fpsyg.2018.00363.

Martela, F., & Steger, M. F. (2016, January). The three meanings of meaning in life: Distinguishing coherence, purpose and significance. *The Journal of Positive Psychology, 11*(5), pp. 531–545. doi:10.1080/17439760.2015.1137623.

Mclaughlin, H. (2009). What's in a name: 'Client', 'patient', 'customer', 'consumer', 'expert by experience', 'service user', – what's next? *British Journal of Social Work, 39*, pp. 1107–1117. doi:10.1093/bjsw/bcm155.

Member and Fellows Profile. (2019, January 1). Retrieved from American College of Healthcare Executives: www.ache.org/learning-center/research/members-and-fellows-profile.

Morgan, G. (2006). *Images of Organizations*. Thousand Oaks, CA: Sage Publishers.

Mullan, F. (2001, January–February). Interview: A founder of quality assessment encounters a troubled system firsthand. *Health Affairs, 20*(1), pp. 137–141. Retrieved December 17, 2019, from: https://www.healthaffairs.org/doi/pdf/10.1377/hlthaff.20.1.137.

Mumford, E. (1996). *Systems Design: Ethical Tools for Ethical Change*. London: MacMillan.

Mumford, E. (2006). The story of socio-technical design: Reflections on its successes, failures and potential. *Information Systems Journal, 16*, pp. 317–342.

National Academies of Sciences, Engineering and Medicine. (2019). *Taking Action against Clinician Burnout: A Systems Approach to Professional Well-Being.* Washington, DC: The National Academies Press. doi:10.17226/25521.

National Council on Disability. (2019.). Appendix B. A Brief History of Managed Care. Retrieved from: https://www.ncd.gov/policy/appendix-b-brief-history-managed-care.

Nonaka, I., & Hirotaka, T. (1995). *The Knowledge Creating Company: How Japanese Companies Create the Dynamics of Innovation.* New York: Oxford University Press.

NP Facts. (2019). Retrieved December 24, 2019, from: https://www.aanp.org/about/all-about-nps/np-fact-sheet.

O'Grady, A. (2015, June 9). Magic and Meaning: Stop Sprinkling Emotion and Start Creating Magic and Meaning. Retrieved December 24, 2019, from: https://uxmag.com/articles/stop-sprinkling-emotion-start-creating-magic-and-meaning.

Ohno, T. (1988). *Toyota Production System: Beyond Large Scale Production.* Portland, OR: Productivity Press.

Papanicolas, I., Woskie, L. R., & Jha, A. K. (2018, March 13). Health care spending in the United States and other high-income countries. *Journal of the American Medical Association, 319*(10), pp. 1024–1039. doi:10.1001/jama2018.1150.

Parsons, L. H. (2009). *The Birth of Modern Politics: Andrew Jackson, John Quincy Adams and the Election of 1828.* New York: Oxford University Press.

Patient. (n.d.). Retrieved December 24, 2019, from: https://www.etymonline.com/word/patient.

Patients' Bill of Rights Title XI Chapter 151 Section 151:21. (2019, October). Retrieved from: http://www.gencourt.state.nh.us/rsa/html/XI/151/151-21.htm.

Pencak, W. (2012, January). Free health care for the poor: The Philadelphia dispensary. *Pennsylvania Magazine of History and Biography,* CXXXVI(1), pp. 25–52.

Perrow, C. (1963). Goals and power structures: A historical case study. In E. Freidson (Ed.), *The Hospital in Modern Society* (pp. 112–146). New York: The Free Press Glencoe.

Pew Research Center. (2015). The Whys and Hows of Generations Research.

Pharmacists (2019). *Occupational Handbook Outlook: Pharmacists.* U.S. Bureau of Labor Statistics U.S. Department of Labor. Washington DC: US Department of Labor. Retrieved January 3, 2020, from https://www.bls.gov/ooh/healthcare/pharmacists.htm.

Physical Therapists (2019). Occupational Outlook Handbook, Physical Therapists, Bureau of Labor Statistics, U.S. Department of Labor. Internet at https://www.bls.gov/ooh/healthcare/physical-therapists.htm

Physician Assistants (2019). Occupational Outlook Handbook: Physician Assistants. Washington, DC: U.S. Bureau of Labor Statistics. U.S. Department of Labor. Retrieved November 6, 2019, from US Department of Labor Bureau of Labor Statistics: https://www.bls.gov/ooh/healthcare/physician-assistants.htm

Pierce, D., & Goode, L. (2018, December 7). The Wired Guide to the iPhone. Retrieved December 31, 2019, from: https://www.wired.com/story/guide-iphone/.

Pilcher, J. (1994, September). Mannheim's sociology of generations: An undervalued legacy. *The British Journal of Sociology, 45*(3), pp. 481–495. doi:10.2307/591659.

Plsek, P. (2001). Appendix B: Redesigning health care with insights from the science of complex adaptive systems. In *Crossing the Quality Chasm: A New Health System for the 21st Century.* Committee on Quality of Health Care in America, Institute of Medicine (pp. 309–317). Washington, DC: National Academy Press.

Quinn, J. B. (1992). *Intelligent Enterprise: A Knowledge and Service-Based Paradigm for Industry.* New York: The Free Press.

Reker, G. T., & Wong, P. T. (1988). Aging as an individual process: Toward a theory of personal meaning. In J. E. Birren, & V. L. Bengston (Eds.), *Emergent Theories of Aging* (pp. 214–246). New York: Springer.

Rosen, G. (1963). The hospital: Historical sociology of a community institution. In E. Freidson (Ed.), *The Hospital in Modern Society* (pp. 1–36). New York: The Free Press of Glencoe.

Rosen, G. (1983). *The Structure of American Medical Practice.* Philadelphia, PA: University of Pennsylvania Press.

Rosenberg, C. E. (1974, January). Social class and medical care in nineteenth-century America: The rise and fall of the dispensary. *Journal of the History of Medicine and Allied Sciences, 29*(1), pp. 32–54.

Rosenberg, C. E. (1983). Prologue: The shape of traditional practice 1800–1875. In G. Rosen, & C. E. Rosenberg (Eds.), *The Structure of American Medical Practice* (pp. 1–12). Philadelphia, PA: University of Pennsylvania Press.

Rosenberg, C. E. (1987). *The Care of Strangers: The Rise of America's Hospital System.* New York: Basic Books, Inc.

Schon, D. A. (1979). Generative metaphor: A perspective on problem-setting in social policy. In A. Ortony (Ed.), *Metaphor and Thought* (pp. 254–283). New York: Cambridge University Press.

Schottenfeld, L., Petersen, D., Peikes, D., Ricciardi, R., Burak, H., McNellis, R., & Genevro, J. (2016). *Creating Patient-Centered Team Based Primary Care.* Rockville, MD: Agency for Healthcare Research and Quality. Retrieved January 3, 2020, from: https://pcmh.ahrq.gov/sites/default/files/attachments/creating-patient-centered-team-based-primary-care-white-paper.pdf.

Schumann, J. H. (2016). *A Bygone Era: When Bipartisanship Led to Health Care Transformation.* Tulsa, OK: National Public Radio. Retrieved November 11, 2019, from: https://www.npr.org/sections/health-shots/2016/10/02/495775518/a-bygone-era-when-bipartisanship-led-to-health-care-transformation.

Schwab, K. (2016, January 14). The Fourth Industrial Revolution: What It Means, How to Respond. Retrieved December 30, 2019, from: https://www.weforum.org/agenda/2016/01/the-fourth-industrial-revolution-what-it-means-and-how-to-respond/.

Seligman, M. E. (1999, August). The president's address. *American Psychologist*, pp. 559–562. Retrieved August 13, 2019, from: https://positivepsychologynews.com/ppnd_wp/wp-content/uploads/2018/04/APA-President-Address-1998.pdf.

Seligmann, M. E., & Csikszentmihalyi, M. (2000, January). Positive psychology: An introduction. *American Psychologist*, *55*(1), pp. 5–14. doi:10.1037/0003-066X.55.1.5.

Sittig, D. F., & Singh, H. (2010, October). A new socio-technical model for studying health information technology in complex adaptive healthcare systems. *BMJ Quality and Safety*, *19*, pp. i68–i74. doi:10.1136/qshc.2010.042085.

Starr, P. (1982). *The Social Transformation of American Medicine: The Rise of a Sovereign Profession and the Making of a Vast Industry*. New York: Basic Books, Inc.

Steger, M. F. (2009). Meaning in life. In C. R. Snyder, & S. J. Lopez (Eds.), *Oxford Handbook of Positive Psychology* (2nd ed.) (pp. 679–689). New York: Oxford University Press.

Steger, M. F. (2010). The Meaning in Life Questionnaire. Retrieved December 19, 2019, from: http://www.michaelfsteger.com/?page_id=13.

Steger, M. F., Frazier, P., Oishi, S., & Kaler, M. (2006). The meaning in life questionnaire: Assessing the presence and search for meaning in life. *Journal of Counseling Psychology*, *53*(1), pp. 80–93. doi:10.1037/0022-0167.53.1.80.

Stevens, R. (1999). *In Sickness and in Wealth: American Hospitals in the Twentieth Century*. Baltimore, MD: The Johns Hopkins University Press.

Taylor, F. W. (1911). *The Principles of Scientific Management*. Public Domain Books, Kindle Edition. Seattle, WA: Amazon Digital Services, Inc.

The Joint Commission. (2019.). Sentinel Event Policy and Procedures. Retrieved December 31, 2019, from: https://www.jointcommission.org/resources/patient-safety-topics/sentinel-event/sentinel-event-policy-and-procedures/.

Thomas, K. K. (2006, November). The hill-burton act and civil rights: Expanding Hospital Care for Black Southerners 1939–1960. *The Journal of Southern History*, *72*(4), pp. 823–870. Retrieved December 3, 2019.

Thomasson, M. (2003, April 17). Health insurance in the United States. In R. Whaples (Ed.), EH.Net Encyclopedia. Retrieved September 7, 2015, from: http://eh.net/encyclopedia/health-insurance-in-the-united-states/.

Tomes, N. (2016). *Remaking the American Patient: How Madison Avenue and Modern Medicine Turned Patients into Consumers*. Chapel Hill, NC: University of North Carolina Press.

Trist, E. L. (1981). The Social Engagement of Social Science Volume II: The Socio-Technical Systems Perspective Introduction. Retrieved December 31, 2019, from: http://moderntimesworkplace.com/archives/ericsess/sessvol2/SESS_Volume_2_Contents_Intro/sess_volume_2_contents_intro.htm.

Twenge, J. M. (2014). *Generation Me: Revised and Updated: Why Today's Young Americans Are More Confident, Assertive, Entitled – and More Miserable than Ever Before*. New York: Simon & Shuster.

Twenge, J. M. (2017a). *iGen: Why Today's Super-Connected Kids Are Growing Up Less Rebellious, More Tolerant, Less Happy – and Completely Unprepared for Adulthood – and What that Means for the Rest of Us.* New York: Atria Books.

Twenge, J. M. (2017b, September). Have Smartphones Destroyed a Generation. Retrieved January 28, 2019, from: https://www.theatlantic.com/magazine/archive/2017/09/has-the-smartphone-destroyed-a-generation/534198/.

Uhl-Bien, M. (2006, November 16). Relational leadership theory: Exploring the social processes of leadership and organizing. *The Leadership Quarterly*, pp. 654–676. doi:10.1016/j.leaqua.2006.10.007.

VBP. (2019, November 19). Hospital Value Based Purchasing (VBP) Program. Retrieved December 31, 2019, from: https://www.cms.gov/Medicare/Quality-Initiatives-Patient-Assessment-Instruments/Value-Based-Programs/HVBP/Hospital-Value-Based-Purchasing.

Wachenheim, D. (2015, December 8). Patient and Family Advisory Councils: The Massachusetts Experience. Retrieved December 31, 2019, from: https://www.psqh.com/analysis/patient-and-family-advisory-councils/.

Walker, A. (2017, July 10). First Opinion: More Female Leadership: A Different Kind of Healthcare Reform. Retrieved from: https://www.statnews.com/2017/07/10/female-leadership-health-care-reform/.

Walmart – Our Story. (2019). Retrieved December 27, 2019, from: http://coporate.walmart.com/our-story.

Wen, J., & Schulman, K. A. (2014, July 11). Can Team-Based Care Improve Patient Satisfaction? A Systematic Review of Randomized Controlled Trials. doi:10.1371/journal.pone.0100603.

Wheatley, M. (1992). *Leadership and the New Science: Learning about Organizations from an Orderly Universe.* San Francisco, CA: Berrett-Koehler Publishers.

Wikipedia. (2019, December 11). Industrial Design. Retrieved January 1, 2020, from: https://en.wikipedia.org/w/index.php?title=Industrial_design&oldid=930234996.

Wong, P. T., & Fry, P. S. (1998). Implicit theories of meaningful life and the development of the Personal Meaning Profile. In P. T. Wong, & P. S. Fry (Eds.), *The Human Quest for Meaning: A Handbook of Psychological Research and Clinical Applications* (pp. 111–140). New York: Routledge.

Wright, J. R. (2017, May). The American College of Surgeons, Minimum Standards for Hospitals, and the Provision of High Quality Laboratory Services. *Archives of Pathology and Laboratory Medicine, 141*, pp. 704–717. doi:10.5858/arpa.2016-0348-HP.

Your Medicare Rights. (2019.). Retrieved December 14, 2019 from:https://www.medicare.gov/claims-appeals/your-medicare-rights.

Zimmerman, B. (2011). How complexity science is transforming healthcare. In P. Allen, S. Maguire, & B. McKelvey (Eds.), *Sage Handbook of Complexity Management* (pp. 617–635). Thousand Oakes, CA: Sage Publications.

Zimmerman, B., Lindberg, C., & Plsek, P. (2001). *Edgeware: Lessons from Complexity Science for Healthcare Leaders.* Irving, TX: VHA, Inc.

Index

Printed in the United States
By Bookmasters